Roadways To Success

FOURTH EDITION

James C. Williamson

NORTHEASTERN TECHNICAL COLLEGE

Debra A. McCandrew

FLORENCE-DARLINGTON TECHNICAL COLLEGE

Charles T. Muse, Sr.

FLORENCE-DARLINGTON TECHNICAL COLLEGE

PEARSON

Prentice
Hall

Upper Saddle River, New Jersey
Columbus, Ohio

Library of Congress Cataloging-in-Publication Data

Williamson, James C.
   Roadways to success / James C. Williamson, Debra A. McCandrew, Charles
T. Muse, Sr. — 4th ed.
      p.   cm.
   Includes bibliographical references and index
   ISBN 0-13-171210-1
1. Success—Psychological aspects.   I. McCandrew, Debra A.   II. Muse,
Charles T.   III. Title.
   BF637.S8W5216 2007
   378.1 ' 70281—dc22   2005037485

Vice President and Publisher: Jeffery W. Johnston
Executive Editor: Sande Johnson
Editorial Assistant: Susan Kauffman
Developmental Editor: Jennifer Gessner
Production Editor: Alexandrina Benedicto Wolf
Production Coordination: Holcomb Hathaway
Design Coordinator: Diane C. Lorenzo
Cover Designer: Jeff Vanik
Cover Image: Corbis
Production Manager: Pamela D. Bennett
Director of Marketing: Ann Castel Davis
Marketing Manager: Amy Judd

This book was set in Sabon by Integra. It was printed and bound by Courier Kendallville, Inc. The cover was
printed by Phoenix Color Corp.

Pearson Education Ltd.   Pearson Education Australia Pty. Limited
Pearson Education Singapore Pte. Ltd.   Pearson Education North Asia Ltd.
Pearson Education Canada, Ltd.   Pearson Educación de Mexico, S.A. de C.V.
Pearson Education–Japan   Pearson Education Malaysia Pte. Ltd.

10 9 8 7 6 5 4 3 2 1
ISBN 0-13-171210-1

CONTENTS

1 *Stopping To Ask for Directions*   1

CONNECTING WITH YOUR CAMPUS RESOURCES

Planning To Reach Your Destination on Time   27

TIME MANAGEMENT

Sights, Sounds, and Sensations   105

INFORMATION PROCESSING AND LEARNING STYLES

Scanning the Radio   125

COMMUNICATIONS

Charting Your Journey   **151**

THE PROCESS OF NOTE TAKING

Driver Training   **171**

LEARNING HOW TO STUDY

11 Reaching Your Destination   237

CAREER PLANNING

Financing Your Roadtrip   259

MONEY MANAGEMENT

The People You Meet Along the Way   281

DIVERSITY

Note: Every effort has been made to provide accurate and current Internet information in this book. However, the Internet and information posted on it are constantly changing, so it is inevitable that some of the Internet addresses listed in this textbook will change.

PREFACE

*A*n open letter to the students who will benefit from this book: You have no doubt begun a journey of education that will take you far. The roadway you have chosen will not always be clear, for there are bumps, twists, and turns that no one can anticipate. Maybe you have started this journey before, or maybe this is your first venture into higher education. Whatever your destination and regardless of your starting point, hope abounds.

This book is intended to assist you in your journey by providing some practical, tried, and proven techniques that will make you a better student. It will challenge you and ask you to examine your assumptions about studying and your ability to study. Although it is intended to be a guide, it will *not* answer all of your questions. Much of what you will learn will be through self-discovery and self-analysis. It is our hope that you will be better able to manage your time and your life after reading this text. Throughout this edition, we have used the case study method to assist you in understanding how the ideas in this book can be applied to real life. Read the case study at the beginning of the book carefully—you will refer back to it after you have read each chapter. Additionally, this book will help you maneuver through a technologically challenging landscape.

Good habits take time to develop and you will no doubt become discouraged somewhere along the way. Stay the course, stay on track, and make your dreams and goals your reality. We wish you well on your journey and trust that you will receive practical information here that will ultimately help all of your "roadways" lead to success!

ACKNOWLEDGMENTS

*T*he authors wish to thank and acknowledge the work and contributions of each of the following:

Dr. Robert M. Sherfield, friend and colleague. Dr. Sherfield is currently a faculty member at the Community College of Southern Nevada and is an internationally known speaker and lecturer. He is the author of five texts that deal with the struggles of the first-year college experience. This book is a product of Robb's constant encouragement and his creativity and thinking. Robb, we appreciate your support and guidance over the years. Thanks for being our friend.

Sande Johnson, Executive Editor, Prentice Hall. Thanks for all of your guidance and suggestions to make this edition even more useable and topical than previous editions. Your insight has been valuable and we appreciate your friendship.

David P. Eldridge is employed by Blue Cross–Blue Shield of South Carolina. David is an adjunct instructor at Florence-Darlington Technical College and teaches history. Much of the technology embedded in this text has passed through the capable and expert eyes of David. David's current writing, for completion of a Ph.D. at Mississippi State University, focuses on the U.S. Navy's role in the capture of Vicksburg, Mississippi. We sincerely appreciate your contributions to the unique feature of this text, our technology component.

In addition, we would like to thank the following individuals who reviewed our text and offered invaluable assistance in the development and completion of this and previous editions: Gary Kay, Broward Community College; Deborah Kimbrough-Lowe, Nassau Community College; Martha Madigan, Lansing Community College; Diana L. Ciesko, Valencia Community College; Margaret Kennedy, Lansing Community College; Ronald Nichols, Alfred State College; and Cathy Pearson, Kent State University.

THE PRENTICE HALL COMPANION WEBSITE: A VIRTUAL LEARNING ENVIRONMENT

Technology is a constantly growing and changing aspect of our field that is creating a need for content and resources. To address this emerging need, Prentice Hall has developed an online learning environment for students and professors alike—Companion Websites—to support our textbooks.

In creating a Companion Website, our goal is to build on and enhance what the textbook already offers. For this reason, the content for each user-friendly website is organized by chapter and provides the professor and student with a variety of meaningful resources.

COMPANION WEBSITE RESOURCES

- Chapter objectives provide an overview of the main concepts to be explored.
- Interactive self-quizzes provide students an opportunity to practice test taking and check their comprehension of the concepts presented. The online study guide includes multiple choice, true/false, and fill-in-the-blank questions.
- Links to outside Web destinations, which are new to this edition, offer resources and additional information to expand the content. Instructors will also find a link to PowerPoint slides to support classroom presentations.

The companion website can be found at **www.prenhall.com/williamson** or accessed through our supersite (**www.prenhall.com/success**), which offers a wide array of resources to support students and instructors.

CASE STUDY

INTRODUCTION TO THE CASE STUDY

Throughout this edition of *Roadways to Success*, you will be asked to refer to the Case Study found on the following page. This is a story of a typical community college student (we've named her Gwen) who faces obstacles and challenges as she tries to make a better life for herself and her family by continuing her education. You may be able to identify with Gwen in some ways. Be sure to read and understand this story fully—you'll be asked to refer back to it at the conclusion of each chapter. You will be given an opportunity to examine what you have learned in each chapter and apply those principles to Gwen's life. (Hint: you may want to "tab" or "dog ear" the next page so that it will be easy to find when you are asked to refer back.)

We hope that you will see the practical applications to the theories and principles in each chapter. Once you can distinguish how these principles apply to Gwen's situation, you should be able to apply those principles to your life as well.

THE CASE STUDY

Gwen is a 28-year-old single parent of two beautiful children. Her oldest daughter, Kristin, is 7 years old and in the first grade. Her youngest child, Randy, is 4. Randy has special needs and attends a special school. He requires a lot of Gwen's time. Gwen lives with her mother, who helps with the children.

Gwen has been working minimum-wage jobs since she dropped out of high school at 16 with a 10th-grade education. She works at a local restaurant during the day as a cook and for a cleaning company on the weekend. Her mother and children depend solely on Gwen's income.

A few years ago Gwen realized that the only way she could make a better life for her family was by getting an education. Although she had never been crazy about school, she enrolled in an adult education program and earned her GED. While she earned her GED, the counselors at adult education worked with Gwen to help her decide on a career. She knew that she wanted to work in the medical field and, after a lot of research, decided on a career in radiology.

After making an appointment with the admissions office at the local community college, Gwen began the process of being accepted to college. She completed the online application (her computer skills were limited), filed for financial aid, and took the college placement test. Everything was going well until she heard the results from the placement test. She had not passed the math portion of the test. The admissions office counselor shared with Gwen that she would be allowed to begin her curriculum classes but would also have to take a prerequisite math class (Algebra I).

That fall semester Gwen registered for four classes: Psychology 201, English 101, Music 105, and Math 101. The semester seemed to be off to a good start, but it quickly turned into more of a challenge for Gwen. She took her first exam in English 101 and failed. Gwen did not understand what had happened on the test—she had tried to study, as best as she knew how. After the next class, she asked the instructor for assistance and was referred to the Success Center, where she could practice her writing and English skills with the help of a peer tutor. Her grades gradually improved and she ended the term with a C in each of the classes.

The semester also seemed to be challenging from other perspectives, which Gwen had not expected. Suddenly, the little free time she had when not working and caring for her children was spent studying. She did not have the blocks of time available to her for her family or her friends. Also, she encountered some professors who came from backgrounds different from hers. To Gwen, they talked funny and had different ideas. Financially speaking, things could not have been worse. Her hours at work had to be reduced. As a consequence, her take-home pay was also reduced. Everything seemed to be stacking up against Gwen as she tried to make a better life for herself and her family, but she was determined NOT TO QUIT this time!

Stopping To Ask for Directions

1

1

*E*mil's high school experiences had never taken him from his home campus to the local community college campus. As a result, when he arrived for orientation he was overwhelmed, not only by the various departments, but also by the sheer number of buildings on campus! How would he ever find his way around, much less navigate a sea of people and key places? Emil soon realized that much of what he needed could be found in the materials that were given to him when he applied: the college catalog, handbook, and brochure. Emil enrolled in a course designed to help him maneuver his way through the college experience and soon was able to use the library, the computer lab, the financial aid office, and the career services office to his advantage.

Emil was also unfamiliar with the concept of "professor" rather than teacher. The new class enabled him to understand the differences and engage the instructors on a more sophisticated level. Emil liked his new environment, and by using the campus resources that were available to him, he was soon a proficient student.

THE IMPORTANCE OF RESOURCES

*T*his chapter is designed to help you understand what resources are typically available on a college campus. Colleges vary in the types of resources and services they offer to students based on where they are located, the kind of student that they serve, and the proportion of commuter to residential students. In addition, this chapter is devoted to helping you understand your professor and to make some sense of this new world you have entered. At the end of this chapter, you should be able to:

- Identify tangible and intangible resources
- Understand what resources are typically available on college campuses
- Discuss campus resources such as the library, computer labs, and special-needs labs (writing, math, reading, etc.)
- Use resources available on your campus
- Understand more about the role of a professor
- Understand the concept of academic freedom

"The real object of education is to give students resources that will endure as long as life endures; habits that time will not destroy; occupations that will render sickness tolerable, solitude pleasant, life more dignified and useful, and death less terrible."

SIDNEY SMITH

- Understand what makes a good student
- Understand basic classroom etiquette

Before you begin this chapter, take a few moments to complete the Milestones checklist. The statements are designed to determine what you already know about the resources and people available to you at your college.

If you want to turn more of your "No" and "Sometimes" answers into "Yes" answers, you may want to consider the following activities. First, learn what is available to you by reading all of the printed material that you are given by the college. Next, locate and visit each of the campus services offices. Finally, locate and record your professors' office locations and office hours. If most of your responses were "No," don't despair. This chapter is designed to help you get familiar with the road so that your journey will be easier and more worthwhile.

TANGIBLE VS. INTANGIBLE RESOURCES

Before a discussion of resources, some discussion about "tangible" resources vs. "intangible" resources is necessary. Tangible resources are things you can see, feel, taste, hear, or smell. Tangible resources are things such as money for college, books with which to learn, computers to use for producing papers, etc. Intangible resources, on the other hand, cannot necessarily be touched or seen. In a college setting, intangible resources are resources that are in place to support your overall education. These resources take the shape of "services" and include such things as tutoring, counseling, help with academic subjects, and advice from your professors. All resources, both tangible and intangible, are important and all play a major role in helping you become a successful student.

In the space below, list some tangible and intangible resources that you are aware of on your campus.

TANGIBLE RESOURCES

INTANGIBLE RESOURCES

MILESTONES

WHERE ARE YOU NOW?

Answer each statement by checking "Y" for Yes, "N" for No, or "S" for Sometimes.

1. I know how to use the college catalog. Ⓨ Ⓝ Ⓢ

2. I know how to find services that I need. Ⓨ Ⓝ Ⓢ

3. I am aware of the computer options available to me on the campus. Ⓨ Ⓝ Ⓢ

4. I know where to find my academic advisor. Ⓨ Ⓝ Ⓢ

5. I know where to go to get help with my classes. Ⓨ Ⓝ Ⓢ

6. I am aware of campus organizations and clubs. Ⓨ Ⓝ Ⓢ

7. I understand academic freedom. Ⓨ Ⓝ Ⓢ

8. I know how to find my professors' offices. Ⓨ Ⓝ Ⓢ

9. I know how to approach my professors in their offices. Ⓨ Ⓝ Ⓢ

10. I know all of my professors' office hours. Ⓨ Ⓝ Ⓢ

What sort of "Tangible Resources" did you list? Did you include computers? The library? Maybe even the college catalog? Maybe the health center? Under "Intangible Resources," were you able to mention advisors, counselors, and student organizations? All of these resources form a network of services on your campus. This chapter is designed to explain in further detail some of these resources and direct you to others on your campus.

THE OWNER'S MANUAL: YOUR COLLEGE CATALOG

When you buy a new car, you usually can depend on having an owner's manual included with the purchase. The owner's manual helps you understand every aspect of your new car—from how to check the oil to how to dim the lights. ALL aspects of owning your new car are covered in this one little book. Just as you receive an owner's manual when you purchase a new car, you will have (should have!) received a college catalog when you were accepted to your institution.

Some colleges will provide you with a college catalog before you register for courses, but all colleges are obligated to provide you with a catalog once you enroll. This college catalog is an "owner's manual" for your time in college—hang on to this catalog and consult it often. It is important that you keep this document as you move through your educational experience. Many requirements may change during your enrollment; colleges will typically "grandfather" the old rules so that they still apply to students already enrolled. That is to say, if requirements change, you will not typically be required to meet the new requirements; rather, you will be bound by the requirements that were in effect at the time you matriculated.

Your college catalog should offer answers to questions such as "What are the graduation requirements for this institution?" "What grades do I have to make to be able to be on the Dean's List?" and "What are the courses required in my major in order for me to graduate?"

A catalog is one tangible resource that you should use often. Refer to the catalog to see what is required and what you have left to do in order to graduate. For this next exercise, find your major in your college catalog. Below, write the name of your major, the degree you will receive, as well as the page number on which the course requirements are listed. For example:

Major: Machine Tool Technology

Degree: Associate of Applied Science

Page: 43

Major: _____

Degree: _____

Page: _____

Also, to complete this exercise, and to record this work for the future, you may wish to prepare a "Graduation Checklist."

Review the courses required for you to graduate in your major. How many hours (semester or quarter) will be required for you to graduate?

(Hint: some colleges divide the courses into suggested schedules for each term you are enrolled; often, the hours represented by the courses are added for you.)

List the number of hours required to graduate from your program:

_____

Doing some simple division, estimate the number of semesters or quarters that will be required for you to complete your degree. For example: 60 semester hours required to complete, 15 hours each semester, 4 semesters or 2 years.

_____

_____

This is your "projected completion time"—the time after which you will reasonably expect to graduate. Of course, if you are able to take fewer hours per semester or quarter, or more hours, this schedule will differ. Students with families and/or full-time jobs may limit themselves to 9 hours per semester, for example.

Determining your projected completion date will help you put your studies in perspective. Just as you use milestones as you are traveling, knowing where you are throughout your educational journey will help you keep your final destination (graduation) in focus and help you see the progress that you are making.

Now, take a look at the courses that are required for your particular major; check the catalog to see if these courses have prerequisites. Prerequisites are courses, or requirements, that must be satisfied before you can take a specific course. Do any of your courses have prerequisites? What are some of the prerequisites?

List some of the courses with prerequisites and write out what the prerequisites are:

_____

_____

_____

_____

_____

College catalogs are wonderful resources for many other questions that may arise. For example, if you want to know the policy on repeating courses, just turn to the catalog's index and it will refer you to the page for the answer. Often, college catalogs list professors' complete names and the schools from which they earned their degrees—if nothing else, it is interesting to see where your professors studied. In addition, the college catalog can explain how to become involved in student activities or list the hours of operation for the student bookstore, student union, etc., to name a few.

CATALOG SCAVENGER HUNT

1. My college was founded in   .

2. My college president is   .

3. My college offers   degrees.

4. My Department Chair is   .

5. The college Mission Statement is on page   .

6. Information about student records is found on page   .

7. A map of the campus is on page   .

8. My college has   campuses.

9. College fees are listed on page   .

10. The withdrawal/expulsion policy is on page   .

11. I will be put on academic probation if my GPA falls below   .

12. The policy for plagiarism is found on page   .

13. My campus' mailing and Internet addresses are

In short, the college catalog should be your best friend as you go through the process of earning your degree. *Keep the catalog and refer to it often!*

Now take a moment to discover more about your college through your college catalog. Complete the "Catalog Scavenger Hunt" above.

Knowing where to find particular items in the catalog is important—the catalog is a "road map of your educational journey," and being able to read a map is important (especially if you get lost). Spend some time getting to know your catalog—you'll be glad that you did when you need to find important information in a hurry. Equally as important is knowing how to access your campus website. Generally, information listed in the catalog is also listed on the website, and any changes, additions, or deletions may be reflected there in a more timely manner.

THE LIBRARY

f the classroom is the "heart" of the college, the library is the "brain." The library is a wonderful resource that will enable you to get the most out of your educational journey. The library is one place on campus that houses numerous resources, usually under one roof. In the library, you will find books, magazines or journals (referred to collectively as *periodicals*), tapes (audio and video), maps, government documents, microfilm, microfiche, DVDs, CDs, and computers that will link you to the information superhighway—more about that later.

LIBRARY SCAVENGER HUNT

1. Who wrote *Gone with the Wind?*

2. Find an article on computers

3. Locate a book dealing with human behavior

4. For how long can you check out a book?

5. The overdue fee is

6. The head librarian's name is

7. The first line of Shakespeare's *Hamlet* is

8. The call number for the *Dictionary of Occupational Titles* is

9. Carl Sandburg won a Pulitzer Prize for

10. What was the lead story in a newspaper published the day you were born?

The library is best used as a daily tool—whether as a quiet place to study or as a place in which to "get directions" and find out more about "points of interest" throughout your journey. The library can make you feel uncomfortable too—that is, until you learn to use it properly.

Most libraries have some sort of "tour" that will help you become acquainted with what is available. Take the time to take the library tour. It's likely you will be glad you did. If you are still unclear about where a particular item is located, or how to use a special piece of equipment, ASK! Librarians earn their living by giving out information—most are *happy* to help you at any time. Librarians won't do your work for you, however. The librarian is also a resource. Use the librarian's knowledge and time wisely. The library tour will also help you to determine which cataloging system the library is using, Dewey Decimal (DD) or Library of Congress (LC). A cataloging system is simply a way in which libraries group similar books together. Don't let this make you feel uncomfortable. The system is easily learned and again, if you get "stuck," a librarian is always ready to help.

COMPUTER RESOURCES: A TRIP ALONG THE INFORMATION SUPERHIGHWAY

early all colleges and universities today are required to include computer literacy as part of the program of study they offer students. You will likely be required to take a course that deals with either computer concepts or computer applications. The definition of a well-rounded student today includes computer literacy. Computers are such a way of life today that many of the services you will need to access while you are in college are delivered through some form of computer application. Most colleges and universities offer Internet services to their students; take advantage of this service if it is offered to you.

Computers can also help you to be a better student. Today, there are software packages that will help you with your math, your writing, and your grammar. Check with your library or tutoring center to see what software packages are available to help you with various subjects. Your academic advisor can also direct you to resources on campus that are related to learning while using computers.

ALTERNATIVE ROUTES: DISTANCE EDUCATION AND OTHER NONTRADITIONAL FORMATS

A number of colleges are now utilizing nontraditional formats for course delivery, such as the Internet, videotaped courses, and interactive video courses. Course content can vary for each of these formats, and students are expected to be motivated and able to work independently. These courses can be exciting and challenging but also overwhelming for students who are having academic difficulty. Before you register for a course such as this, consult your academic advisor.

MAKING A PIT STOP: LEARNING RESOURCE CENTERS

Occasionally, your academic journey can be a little "bumpy." Maybe you turned in a paper and did not receive the grade that you had expected. Maybe you took a math test and didn't do as well as you had hoped. Don't despair! On most campuses, help is available in learning centers, often referred to as "The Math Center," "The Reading Center," or "The Writing Center." If these services are available on your campus, take advantage of the help they offer.

These centers employ students and professional tutors who can help you through your academic problems. Often, these centers also have video- or audiotapes, DVDs, or CDs that can help with specific problems. Help is available in one form or another. For instance, if you are having a problem with fractions, someone from the math center can show you how to add, subtract, multiply, or divide fractions. Maybe he can go through your homework or your class assignments and then show you a videotape or DVD that covers fractions. The same would be true if you were having problems with adverbs; help would be available in the writing center. Often, these centers can give you practice work and let you work on specific academic problems you may be having while you are in the center. Use these centers to your advantage and benefit. You can only be a better student in the long run by utilizing these services.

On your campus, what is the name of your tutoring center?

Where is it located?

What is the phone number?

What are the hours of operation?

TRAVELING COMPANIONS: YOUR FRIENDS

A discussion about resources is not complete without mentioning one of the most valuable resources: your friends. Friends can make your journey easier, help you understand difficult material, and even "quiz" you before an exam. Friends can help you through the "rocky roads" you may encounter along the way and make your journey more enjoyable. A supportive friend can keep you going when you feel like giving up and can help you understand your options.

Friends are valuable resources, but they can also be your biggest problem. When choosing friends, choose carefully. If a friend is causing you to get behind in your school-work because you are constantly being encouraged to do other things and be involved with activities that keep you from studying, think about whether or not you want to be a friend with that particular person. Don't let someone else rob you of your chance to be a more educated person.

COUNSELING SERVICES

There are times in almost everyone's life when they might need a little help dealing with a variety of problems. Sometimes, we just need to talk to someone who can look at our situation with an open mind and help us work toward solutions. On the college campus, these services can take the form of emotional counseling services or career counseling services. Usually, your college will have trained professionals in each area to help you make healthy decisions regarding your problems. One of the most important things to remember is that if you are in need of career, academic, or emotional counseling, the best

Learn about and take advantage of the services offered on your campus, including counseling, financial aid, learning centers, and others.

advice is to seek out someone on campus with whom you feel comfortable and talk with him or her. It probably isn't a wise decision to let the situation fester. These services are free to you and may make your days as a freshman easier. Some students feel embarrassed or ashamed to have to seek counseling, but the fact of the matter is that many students need and seek advice on everything from money problems to relationship breakups every day. Asking for advice and help is a wise decision for many students.

FINANCIAL AID SERVICES

Even the best-laid plans are sometimes disrupted by financial problems. Many students wait until it is too late to seek financial counseling and apply for financial aid. It may be that you see that your funds are running low and you may have to temporarily withdraw for a year or a semester. Wait! Before you make that decision, talk to a financial aid counselor. They are trained in the art of helping students find scholarships; federal, state, and local aid; and jobs. You may not need to interrupt your studies after all.

The most obvious type of financial assistance is federal and state financial aid. These programs have been in place for many years and they are the staple of many college students. The types of aid available from the federal government are:

- Federal Pell Grants
- Federal Direct Loans

STUDENT ELIGIBILITY FOR FEDERAL FINANCIAL AID

To receive aid from the major student aid programs, you must:

- Have financial need, except in some special instances.
- Have a high school diploma or GED or pass an independently administered test approved by the U. S. Department of Education, or meet the standards established by your state.
- Be enrolled as a regular student working toward a degree or certificate in an eligible program. You may not receive aid for correspondence or telecommunications courses unless they are a part of an associate, bachelor, or graduate degree program.
- Be a U. S. citizen.
- Have a valid Social Security number.
- Make satisfactory academic progress.
- Sign a statement of educational purpose.
- Sign a statement of updated information.
- Register with the Selective Service, if required.

Source: Student Guide, U.S. Department of Education.

- Federal Family Education Loans (FFEL)
- Federal Supplemental Educational Opportunity Grants (FSEOG)
- Federal Work Study (FWS)
- Federal Perkins Loans

Not every school takes part in every federal assistance program. To determine which type of aid is available at your school, you should contact the financial aid office.

Some students may be confused about the difference among loans, grants, and work-study. According to *The Student Guide* published by the Department of Education, each is defined as:

- **Loans.** Borrowed money that you must repay with interest.
- **Grants.** Monies that you don't have to repay.
- **Work-Study.** Money earned for work that you do at the college. These earnings belong to you and need not be repaid.

As an undergraduate, you may receive all three types of assistance.

One of the biggest mistakes students make when thinking about financial aid is forgetting about scholarships from private industry and social/civic organizations. Each year, millions of dollars go unclaimed, apparently because students simply did not know about the scholarship or where to find information about it. Below, you will find several resources that are worth researching and applying to. To find out more about all types of financial aid, examine the following publications:

Free Dollars from the Federal Government (Prentice Hall)

Winning Scholarships for College (Henry Holt and Company)

How to Obtain Maximum Financial Aid (Login Publications Consortium)

Peterson's 4-Year Colleges (Peterson's)

Free Money for College (Facts on File)

Paying for College (Villard Books)

Financial Aid for College (Peterson's)

Paying Less for College (Peterson's)

College Costs and Financial Aid Handbook (The College Board)

Winning Money for College (Peterson's)

Free Money for Athletic Scholarships (Henry Holt and Company)

Don't Miss Out (Octameron Press)

You will also want to research the following:

Your college catalog (for scholarships at the college)

Your place of employment

Your parents' or spouse's place of employment

Social and civic groups within your community or hometown

The Internet

- Do not miss a *deadline.* There are no exceptions for making up deadlines for federal financial aid!

- Read all *instructions* before beginning the process.

- Always fill out the application *completely* and have someone proofread your work.

- If documentation is required, submit it according to the instructions. Do *all* that the application asks you to do.

- *Never lie* about your financial *status.* This could cost you dearly in the long run.

- Begin the application process as soon as possible. *Do not wait* until the last moment. Some aid is given on a first come, first served basis. Income tax preparation time is usually financial aid application time.

- *Talk* to the financial aid officer at the institution you will attend. Person-to-person contact is always best. Never assume anything until you get it in writing.

- Take copies of flyers and *brochures* that are available in the financial aid office. Many times, private companies and civic groups will notify the financial aid office if they have funds available.

- If you are running late with the application, call and *ask* if there are ways to apply electronically.

- Always keep a signed *copy* of your tax returns for *each* year!

- In order to *receive* almost *any* money, including some scholarships, you *must* fill out the Free Application for Federal Student Aid form.

- Apply for *everything* possible. After all, you will get nothing if you do not apply.

HEALTH SERVICES

Most college campuses across the nation have some type of health or physical services. It is important to know where these facilities are located and what services are available to you. Some colleges include the cost of minor medical care with tuition. Other colleges offer students a health insurance policy for a very nominal fee. The health services on campuses vary drastically. One college may have a person who only can assist you in finding outside help, while other colleges retain doctors and nurses for your medical needs. In the space provided below, determine what types of health services are available to you on your campus.

The health service office is located at

_____

The phone number is _____

What type of insurance plan does your college offer? _____

_____

What is the price of this insurance? _____

THE LIFE OF A PROFESSOR

Although it may seem that your professor's life is one of leisure with lots of free time, the opposite is true. For professors to keep up with what is happening in their field, they must *constantly* read, study, and learn about the latest developments. A professor spends a great deal of time reading. Committed and dedicated professors are not always satisfied with teaching a course the same way time after time. Great professors are always trying to improve what they bring to the student. Because of this, professors spend a great deal of time doing research for courses and for publishing articles and books. Publishing is extremely important to most professors, and they are very proud of the works they have published. In addition, professors are asked to present their research at conferences and to give workshops and seminars.

> *"To teach is to learn twice."*
>
> JOSEPH JOUBERT

In addition to teaching classes, doing research, writing articles and books, and presenting at conferences, a professor's time is also taken up by students. More than likely, you have a professor as your academic advisor. The academic advisor provides assistance to you semester after semester. Most advisors have a large number of students they must meet each semester.

Ranking, or seniority, is very important to a professor. Because this is so vital, the professor will spend many hours trying to become a better teacher or researcher in order to be "ranked" at a higher level. Generally, ranking follows the order listed below:

- Instructors are often "beginning" professors
- Instructors then become Assistant Professors
- Assistant Professors become Associate Professors
- Associate Professors become Professors (this step is sometimes referred to as "full" professor)

Although it is not extremely important to know what rank your professor is, this explanation should help you understand what is important to your professor. This discussion should also help you understand the words you may hear the professor use when he or she talks about "rank."

ACADEMIC FREEDOM AND WHAT IT MEANS TO YOU

The "right" of the professor to teach controversial subject matter or subject matter that might be viewed as "different" or uncommon is known as academic freedom. As long as the basic ideas of a course are taught, colleges and universities usually leave the method of instruction to the professor. The professor decides when exams are given and their format. Professors also decide if they want to lecture most of the time, use classroom exercises to show a point, or have students complete outside assignments. Basically, academic freedom allows professors the freedom to approach the subject matter in whatever manner they choose. For the student, it gives the opportunity to experience many different approaches to learning. The student may be asked to write a paper in one class, put together a group presentation in another class, and recite a reading in yet another class.

Another benefit for the student is that the teacher has chosen the approach with which he or she is most comfortable. Controversial subject matter can be discussed within the framework of academic freedom, and so the subject matter can be quite different from that you encountered in high school. Subjects that might be viewed as "taboo" in high schools can be discussed, debated, and deliberated upon in college, all because of academic freedom.

Academic freedom makes the American system of higher education unique; as such, it allows students to experience a wide variety of approaches and can make the collegiate experience richer and more rewarding.

Briefly list several different assignments or projects you have had to do this semester:

1. _____
2. _____
3. _____
4. _____

Which assignment did you enjoy the most?

_____

Why do you think you enjoyed this particular assignment?

_____

_____

_____

_____

Which assignment did you enjoy the least?

_____

Why do you think you did not enjoy this particular assignment?

_____

_____

_____

_____

Examine the teaching style of your favorite professor. What is his or her dominant style? Is it the "lecture method"? Do you like this style? Many teachers use both a so-called left- and right-brain approach to teaching. This type of teaching is appropriate for all types of learners. Some instructors will present information using only an analytical, or "left-brain" approach. Their instruction usually includes a lot of teacher explanation and visual aids with specific, detailed directions and lots of tests. Teachers who use a global, or "right-brain," approach might introduce a lesson with a joke or short story. This kind of instructor would encourage students to think for themselves and would probably use group learning or discovery as an important part of teaching. The professor who uses this kind of approach may test using presentations, charts, games, etc. As a student, it is very important that you be able to recognize these differences in certain professors and be able to learn from either of these or possibly other techniques. Just as you have preferences in the way you like to learn, professors have preferences in the way they like to teach. Being a successful student means being able to identify the professor's method or style and then changing your study habits to adapt to that particular method.

Examine the teaching style of one of your current professors. Describe it:

_____

_____

_____

_____

Do you like this particular style? Why or why not?

_____

_____

_____

_____

UNDERSTANDING WHAT THE PROFESSOR WANTS

Your professor will give you a syllabus on the first day of class. The syllabus outlines specifically what he or she expects from you during the course. A syllabus is a contract that assures you that course requirements cannot be changed in the middle of the term. On the syllabus, you may be able to find out when tests are to be given, what other work will be required for the course (papers, book reviews, etc.), and how much each will count toward your final grade. You will probably also see the attendance policy for the course. Some professors also include important dates during the semester, such as the last day to withdraw, last day to add, and so on. As is discussed in Chapter 2, a syllabus is very helpful for planning your semester. Important dates and events listed in the syllabus should be recorded in a calendar or planner. (Figures 2.2 and 2.3 show sample pages from a planner.) You may also record important information about each course on a "Course Syllabus" form.

What you might not find out by reading the syllabus is what the professor "really" expects of you. Does he expect you to "skim" chapters and be familiar with ideas, or does he expect you to be specific in your reading? One of the best ways to find out what your professor expects is to ask! Ask her how you should prepare for class each day. The professor will be impressed that you care enough to find out what is expected of you, and you will begin to understand more about what the professor expects. Another helpful hint is to ask other students who had the professor during a previous term what the professor was like. Find out what the professor expects and how you can adapt your study habits to be successful in the class.

QUESTIONS TO ASK OTHER STUDENTS ABOUT PROFESSORS

1. How much outside reading does the professor require?
2. Are the tests multiple choice, true–false, or essay?
3. How closely does the professor follow the grading scale?
4. What grade did you receive? Why do you feel that you were awarded this grade?
5. What would you change if you had to take the course again?
6. Would you take another course with the professor?
7. Did you learn a lot?

Above all else—*ask, ask, ask!* If you do not ask the instructor or some of your peers, you are dealing with an unknown. This "unknown" could cost you a grade during the first part of the term, and it may be impossible for you to get caught up later.

WHAT MAKES A GOOD STUDENT?

A survey of professors around the nation was taken that asked what makes a good student. They were invited to comment on the biggest differences that they had noticed in students of today from students of the past. Additionally, they were asked what they liked most about today's students and what they liked least about them. The following answers were given:

- "The biggest difference in students of today has to do with the fact that students of today are more opinionated and more verbal."
- "Students of today are better prepared academically."
- "Students of today face a limited job market and so they are more focused; they 'know' why they are in school. I also like the diversity that I see today."

Another question was asked: "Beyond the information that you give daily, what is the most important message that you want to leave with your students?" One of the best answers is quoted below:

- "I hope that I can instill in my students the ability to look *beyond* and not simply accept that a problem will automatically have an answer that is black or white, right or wrong, good or bad. To see shades of differences and to have empathy is important. I also want my students to be able to deal with change and to *like learning!*"

Finally, professors were asked what they thought made a "good" student. The responses are very interesting and you may want to take a few minutes to read them.

- "A 'good' student is . . . one who is self-motivated and who wants to do more than just memorize. One who really *wants* to understand and apply concepts."
- "A 'good' student is . . . a student who has a genuine desire to learn and takes the *time* to learn new information."
- "A 'good' student is . . . one who wants to learn, explores the boundaries of information, is not passive but rather active in pursuing knowledge."
- "A 'good' student accepts academic responsibility."

To summarize, professors seem to like students who (1) want to learn, (2) are self-motivated, (3) question what they are learning and try to relate it to "real" issues, and (4) have a sense of why they are in school.

WHAT MAKES A GOOD PROFESSOR?

Just like professors, students were also given a survey and asked to respond to questions. The first question was, "What is the biggest difference between your college professors and your high school instructors?" Student responses are listed below:

- "College professors require more from you than high school instructors. I like my college professors because they treat you like adults instead of kids."
- "College professors go into detail on almost everything, they are very specific and are not easily strayed off of the subject."
- "College professors make you think more. High school teachers gave you a chance to review and basically told you what would be on the test—college professors don't do that."

Your college instructors are likely to ask you to think more and to do more than your high school teachers—it is their job to challenge you intellectually.

The second question asked was, "What do you like most about your college professors?" and question three was, "What do you like least about your college professors?" Student answers are listed below:

- "What do I like most about college professors? They are *demanding*."
- "College professors are passionate about what they teach—they have a real interest in the subject."

Finally, one student, when responding to the question, "What makes an effective college professor?" indicated that:

- "College professors set higher expectations with little direction, which forces you to become more responsible and devoted to your schoolwork."

In summary, college students expect college professors to be more demanding, and they are. College professors expect you to be able to keep up the pace when you are in their class.

CLASSROOM ETIQUETTE

Classroom etiquette, or knowing how to properly conduct yourself in a college lecture or class, is very important as you begin your journey. One of the most important things about being a good student is realizing that you are not the only person in the room. There may be times when you are not interested in what is being said, but the person next to you may need the information. Being a responsible student means having respect for the other people in your class and respect for the instructor. The points below, although they may seem "preachy," are designed to help you get more from your college experience. Several ways in which you can respect the instructor and other students are:

1. If, for some unforeseen reason, you have to be late for class, you should not make a lot of noise when you enter the room. Never walk in front of the instructor as you enter the room. If you usually sit on the other side of the room, do not worry about your regular seat. Take the seat that is closest to the door.

2. Eating, drinking, or using tobacco products in a classroom setting, unless the professor has given you permission to do so, is rude.

3. If you must leave class early, it is important that you tell the professor before class. If you feel that you have to leave class early once or twice a week, perhaps it is best for all involved if you drop the course, or have your counselor arrange for you to take another section. Attitudes on this matter vary widely. Be aware.

4. Don't start to pack up your book bag or other materials and begin to rustle through your books and papers before your professor has dismissed the class. Few things will make your professor angrier than this. Some even refer to this as "book bag levitation"!

5. Please don't start a conversation with another student during the lecture, regardless of the subject matter. Even if you missed something the professor said, it is better to politely question the professor than to start a conversation with another student. Use the time before and after class to discuss topics with other students.

6. When visiting a professor's office, you should try to make an appointment instead of simply showing up. Many times, the professor will be grading papers, working on school projects, or helping other students. If you must go to the professor without an appointment, never enter the office without knocking. Also, if you did not have an appointment, make your visit short. Have your questions lined up *before* you knock on the door. Ask if this is a convenient time for you to interrupt.

7. Common courtesy dictates that you will not enter a professor's office without permission, even if the door is open. Always knock and wait to be invited in.

8. If you disagree with a grade that you have received, you should make an appointment to talk with the professor and ask him or her to go over the specifics of the grade. Approach the conversation from the perspective that you are trying to understand what you did wrong so that you will learn from your mistakes and not make the same mistake again. Try not to be defensive. Professors like students to be interested enough in their work to question and probe, as long as they do so diplomatically!

You should extend the same amount of courtesy to your professors and fellow students that you expect from them. Your journey will be more enjoyable if you pay attention to being "nice" along the way.

READING THE PROFESSOR'S SCHEDULE

As you begin to learn where your professors' offices are located, you will also notice, should you happen to visit, that most professors post their schedules outside of their door. Reading a professor's schedule is really quite easy. Usually, a professor will post the hours that he or she is teaching, the hours reserved for "office hours," and possibly other important information such as lunch and prep time. A typical professor's schedule might look something like the one shown in Figure 1.1.

Looking at this schedule, when would you want to try to make an appointment with Dr. Doe?

_____

_____

To get to know your professors better, copy the information sheet on the page 21 and use it for each professor you have. Check the schedule for each of your professors and make an appointment with each of them. During the course of your conversation, fill out the information sheet. You will get to

FIGURE 1.1   A typical professor's schedule.

Dr. John Doe   Office 237–B

MON	TUES	WED	THURS	FRI
8:00 Eng 101	8:00	8:00 Eng 101	8:00	8:00 Eng 101
9:00 Eng 102	9:00 Office	9:00 Eng 102	9:00 Office	9:00 Eng 102
10:00 Office	10:00	10:00 Office	10:00	10:00 Office
11:00 Eng 201	11:00 Office	11:00 Eng 201	11:00 Office	11:00 Eng 201
12:00 Lunch	12:00 Lunch	12:00 Lunch	12:00 Lunch	12:00 Lunch
1:00	1:00 Eng 202	1:00	1:00 Eng 202	1:00
2:00 Office	2:00	2:00 Office	2:00	2:00 Office

know the professor a little better and will be able to find the professor's office when you really need to talk to him or her.

Hopefully, this activity will allow you to see your professors as real people and will foster a relationship with this person outside of class. You certainly do not have to be best friends with your professor, but if you understand a little more about her background, it might make it a little easier to understand her views while you are in class.

THE NEXT STEP

Now that you have become more aware of the tangible and intangible resources available on college campuses, it is time for you to do an inventory of what is available on your college campus. An inventory is simply a list. Using Exercise 1.1, make a list of all of the resources available on your college campus. Your college catalog will assist you in completing this exercise.

PROFESSOR INFORMATION

Professor's name:

Professor's office location:

Professor's office phone:

Where did the professor go to school?

Undergraduate:

Graduate:

Graduate:

Postgraduate:

How long has the professor taught at
this school?

If the professor is ranked, what is the rank?

Does the professor have any special research
interests?

If so, what are they?

What are the professor's hobbies?

What advice could the professor give you in
order to be a more successful student?

MILESTONES

NOW THAT YOU ARE HERE . . .

Answer each statement by checking "Y" for Yes, "N" for
No, or "S" for Sometimes.

1. I know how to use the college catalog.	(Y) (N) (S)
2. I know how to find services that I need.	(Y) (N) (S)
3. I am aware of the computer options available to me on the campus.	(Y) (N) (S)
4. I know where to find my academic advisor.	(Y) (N) (S)
5. I know where to go to get help with my classes.	(Y) (N) (S)
6. I am aware of campus organizations and clubs.	(Y) (N) (S)
7. I understand academic freedom.	(Y) (N) (S)
8. I know how to find my professors' offices.	(Y) (N) (S)
9. I know how to approach my professors in their office.	(Y) (N) (S)
10. I know all of my professors' office hours.	(Y) (N) (S)

Now that you have completed this chapter, revisit the Milestones checklist.
How did you do on this inventory after reading this chapter? If you would
like to be a more successful student, you must first know what is available to
you to assist in this endeavor. Utilizing campus services, such as financial aid
when you are concerned about paying for school, talking to your professor
when you are worried about your grade, and using the Internet to complete
research assignments for your classes will all enable you to be more successful. There are a variety of resources available if you ask for help.

Academic:

_____

_____

_____

Financial:

_____

_____

_____

Social:

_____

_____

_____

Physical:

_____

_____

_____

Career:

_____

_____

_____

Religious:

_____

_____

_____

Applying What You Know

Now that you have completed this chapter, refer back to the Case Study about Gwen at the beginning of this book. Based on her situation, answer the following questions:

1. What campus resources did Gwen utilize?

_____

_____

_____

_____

2. Were they advantageous to her? If so, how?

_____

_____

_____

_____

3. If faced with some of the problems Gwen was faced with (not doing well in her English class, having financial difficulty, not understanding her professor) what might you do?

_____

_____

_____

_____

Observations

CHARTING YOUR COURSE

Students who utilize campus resources are more likely to be successful academically, stay involved in the process, make more friends, and stay until graduation than students who do not. You are now aware of what is available on your campus, and you should resolve to take advantage of these services.

Getting There on Time

1. How does knowing your professor's schedule assist you in your management of time?

   _____

   _____

   _____

2. Explain how effective uses of campus resources can assist you in managing your time.

   _____

   _____

   _____

3. What is the effect of not meeting financial aid deadlines?

   _____

   _____

   _____

4. What is the effect of not meeting academic deadlines?

   _____

   _____

   _____

Effective use of campus resources can aid you tremendously in the management of your time. The resources available to you, both on-campus and off-campus, should be used wisely. Your time as a student is valuable—utilize any available resource to make the most of your time and your education.

Exploring Technology

Computers and the Internet are now facets in American society. Americans who refuse to learn how to use them, or who are too scared to use them, are placing themselves at a disadvantage in the marketplace. More jobs now require computer skills. Employers are less likely to hire someone who is computer illiterate due to the time and cost of training. There is also a negative stigma attached to being computer illiterate.

Likewise, individuals who are well versed in computers and the Internet can take advantage of the many benefits available. Some of these benefits include free long distance calling, music, quick and reliable information for research (provided you visit reputable websites), discounts on merchandise, discounts on travel and leisure, and increased contact with friends and family members via e-mail. (Note: If you do not have a computer at home or Internet access, you can probably use a computer free of charge at your public library. You can set up a free e-mail account at "Hotmail," "Yahoo!," and several other sources.)

Your assignment involves sending an instructor an e-mail with an attachment:

1. Send an instructor an e-mail *using proper writing skills*. Include your name in the body of the message. Ensure you write a "proper" e-mail, following the rules of e-mail etiquette. If in doubt, follow the same guidelines as you would when writing a letter.

2. Include an attachment to the e-mail. The attachment can be anything: an assignment, a paper, a presentation, or a picture.

3. The instructor will reply to your e-mail. You are now to reply to the instructor's e-mail message. You must respond using the "reply" feature.

4. Forward the instructor's reply to another student and to the instructor using the "forward" feature. You must use the forward feature; do not simply "reply" back to the instructor.

Web Connections

TRAVELING THE INFORMATION SUPERHIGHWAY

During your journey, you may want to check out some of the following Web addresses to assist you in utilizing campus resources effectively:

www.collegeresource.com
www.lcweb.loc.gov
www.ed.gov

As a result of this chapter, and in preparing for my journey, I plan to . . .

Planning To Reach Your Destination on Time

2

TIME MANAGEMENT

Her name was Alice. Alice was always late. Alice and I became friends during my sophomore year in college. She was a year ahead of me in school and was someone I looked up to. Alice was involved in the Student Government as well as the Student Activity Programming Board. Initially, I just assumed that she had a lot of responsibility and was occasionally late.

Then, after getting to know Alice a little better, her "lateness" became more the rule than the exception. People kidded Alice about "always being late" and we made our jokes about her being "late for her own funeral." No one realized the seriousness of her chronic tardy behavior until one day when she confided to us that she had been late for a final exam in a class, and the instructor would not allow her to enter the room after the prescribed time. As a consequence, Alice failed her political science class and it caused some major problems with her financial aid. The fact that Alice was "always late" finally caught up with her. Unfortunately, it cost her a great deal in terms of financial-aid dollars and in time spent repeating Political Science 101.

The management of time, the act of "getting things done," seems to confuse students who have not yet mastered the technique. The process of time management can be quite simple; yet, if undeveloped, can cause major problems. Another example of a time-management problem that students have expressed over the years is working all day or going to school all day and feeling as if they did not accomplish anything!

Have you ever worked a full day of 8 to 10 hours or spent 6 to 8 hours at your college and felt like you really did not accomplish anything? Did you feel that the day was not productive, that you were busy all day but few, if any, important tasks or goals were completed? Did you feel like the dragon won that day? What is your productivity level for any given day? Are you productive? Are you accomplishing what is important to you on a regular, day-to-day basis? If not, how can you become more productive and achieve your goals?

We usually start our time-management classes with this question: "How many of you are satisfied with your current level of productivity?" Almost no one ever raises his or her hand. However, when we ask, "How many of you would like to be more productive?" almost everyone raises his or her hand. We do not want the dragon to win any day. We can turn this situation around and be productive. With a few simple time-management tools, for example, a prioritized "to-do" list and a calendar, you can be productive every day. You can move forward toward the accomplishment of your goals daily.

"Never before have we had so little time in which to do so much."

FRANKLIN D. ROOSEVELT

We have surveyed hundreds of students over the years and have found that most time-management problems expressed by students are very similar and have common solutions. For example, students have stated that they do not have enough time for work and home; that they do not use a to-do list on a daily or regular basis; and that they have too many distractions or interruptions to have a successful or productive day.

There are many questions, but all can be summarized as follows: How do you balance your time among work, college, family, and friends? How do you maintain a schedule when there are always interruptions? How do you resume a set schedule once interrupted? How do you accomplish what is important to your family and yourself? These and other questions will be answered in this chapter and interwoven throughout the book to give each student an opportunity to learn proven time-management skills, to assess strengths and weaknesses, to practice these effective skills in true life exercises, and to adopt a time-management system that will help make your semester, as well as your life, challenging, goal oriented, and productive.

This chapter is designed to help you learn to manage your time more effectively. After reading this chapter and completing the exercises, you should be able to:

- Understand the concept of time management
- Understand the importance of a balanced life and the choices you need to make on a daily basis
- Identify your strengths and weaknesses relative to time management
- Understand how to build upon these strengths and improve upon the weaknesses
- Understand how to effectively use a calendar, a to-do list, and a daily plan
- Understand how to use a time-management system, to integrate it into your daily life
- Be able to develop a study plan based on your own time analysis

Using the Milestones checklist, take a few moments and determine where you stand in relation to making time-management decisions.

If you have more "No" and "Sometimes" answers to these statements, do not be overly concerned at this point. This chapter will address each statement and provide you with valuable tools that will assist you in becoming a more effective time manager.

MILESTONES

WHERE ARE YOU NOW?

Answer each statement by checking "Y" for Yes, "N" for No, or "S" for Sometimes.

		Y	N	S
1.	I know how to prioritize my responsibilities.	Y	N	S
2.	I manage my time effectively.	Y	N	S
3.	Completing daily goals is important to me.	Y	N	S
4.	Making a daily "to-do" list is necessary for me.	Y	N	S
5.	Writing down all of my assignments helps me.	Y	N	S
6.	I use short- and long-term planning.	Y	N	S
7.	I understand discretionary time or free time and nondiscretionary time.	Y	N	S
8.	My friends control my time.	Y	N	S
9.	I am in control of my time.	Y	N	S
10.	I understand that time management helps me to become a better student.	Y	N	S

COLLEGE SUCCESS STRATEGIES

Numerous strategies may be employed to help you succeed in college. One such strategy is to plot the coming semester on a calendar. Faculty at most colleges are required to provide students with a course syllabus the first day of each class. These syllabi generally contain the course objectives, grading scale, and dates of reports, exams, tests, etc. Using a calendar and the course syllabus, you can plot each test, exam, report, and research paper on your calendar. The calendar becomes a very useful planning document that sets the stage for study, research, and writing time.

A DAILY TIME ANALYSIS

Where does your time go? How much time do you spend at work each day? How many hours do you sleep daily? Do you have family time each day? Do you have spiritual time daily? Do you waste time, not knowing where a good portion of your time goes each day? An easy way to address these and other questions about our daily activities and the use of our 24-hour day is to complete a daily time analysis. There are several very effective daily time assessments that we can use for this exercise. The easiest and least time consuming is the "wheel" approach. Exercise 2.1 offers a personal daily time analysis. A completed "wheel" daily time analysis is presented in Figure 2.1 for your reference as you conduct your individual assessment.

| FIGURE 2.1 | A daily time analysis. |

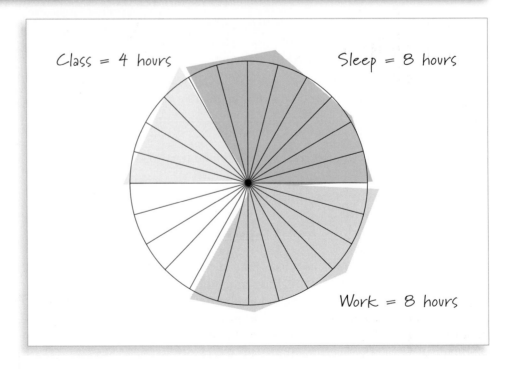

Choose a particular day of the week (e.g., Monday) and write the number of hours you spend that day next to each activity listed. Add any activity that is associated with this particular day. Using a pencil, shade and mark slices of the pie or wheel that represent the same number of hours that you spend doing that activity. Analyze your results. What was your total number of hours for that day?

Sleep	_____	hours
Classes	_____	hours
Study	_____	hours
Work	_____	hours
Meals	_____	hours
Family	_____	hours
Spiritual	_____	hours
Exercise	_____	hours
Commuting	_____	hours
TV	_____	hours
Computer	_____	hours
Telephone	_____	hours
_____	_____	hours
_____	_____	hours
TOTAL	_____	hours

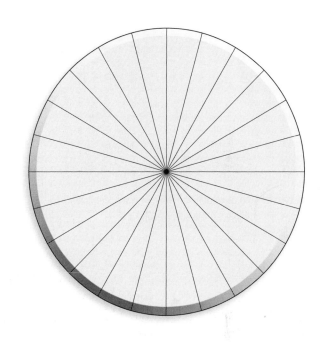

The "wheel" is a circle that is divided into 24 equal parts, like a large pie with 24 slices. Each slice represents an hour of the day. Exercise 2.1 should take about 20 minutes. Its purpose is to open your eyes to the realization that there are only 24 hours in a day and that most students do not really know where all the hours go. To complete Exercise 2.1, follow these three steps:

STEP ONE. Choose a particular day of the week that you want to analyze, for example, a Monday. Once you have chosen a day, review the list of daily activities that are common to most students and write in the corresponding number of hours spent on each activity. You may also want to add one, two, or more activities that are pertinent to your daily life.

"Time is the scarcest resource and unless it is managed, nothing else can be managed."

PETER DRUCKER

Successful time management will help you accomplish your goals and tasks more successfully and with less stress.

STEP TWO. Using a pencil, shade and mark slices of the pie or wheel that represent the same number of hours that you spend in that activity each day. You will need to average some activities as you try to complete the "wheel." In our example, sleep is usually computed at between 6 and 8 hours per day depending on individual needs. Thus, the "wheel" in our example has eight slices shaded and marked to represent 8 hours of sleep. Classes or class time is about 4 hours a day and has been shaded and marked as well. Note that our example has a total of 20 hours of activities, which nearly completes the shading of the "wheel," and there are only three activities listed.

STEP THREE. The final step in this process is to analyze your results. What was the total number of hours for your sample day? Did you exceed 24 hours for that day? What does this exercise tell us? First, most students will exceed 24 hours in a day. Many compute 26, 27, or more hours. What an eye opener! Do we really know where our time goes? Without an effective time-management system or planner that includes a daily plan and "to-do" list, it is very difficult to know where your time goes and what you have truly accomplished for any particular day. This exercise also assists us in determining how much discretionary or free time we have in any given day. Discretionary or free time is the amount of time that you have to yourself each day. It is time to do what you wish. Unlike nondiscretionary time—that is, time spent in class or at work—discretionary or free time is time that you plan and control. How much free time do you have each day? How do you spend that time? Is your free time productive?

Successful Time Management

As educators, and for our own personal professional development, we have attended numerous time-management, self-management, and goal-setting seminars and workshops. A common theme and at least three concepts are presented in the best of these seminars. The common theme is the importance of goal setting, which will be discussed in Chapter 4 and referenced later in this text. The following three things are required to be successful in time management:

- Identify time-management problems.
- Develop solutions for these time-management problems.
- Use a time-management system.

Any of a number of assessment tools can be utilized to assist in identifying time-management problems. The best practices and principles of time management are usually interwoven into these assessment tools to not only identify problems or weaknesses but to identify strengths as well. Once weaknesses are identified, solutions can be selected and implemented.

Time management has long been an issue in this country. Benjamin Franklin, over 200 years ago, was a master of effective time management. Napoleon Hill was very successful in the late 1930s and 1940s and is still quoted today from his book, *Think and Grow Rich*. The point is that there are tried-and-true practices of effective time management that we can all use today to increase our productivity, to get the most out of each day, and to enjoy the time that we have.

One thing that effective time managers use on a daily basis that sets them apart is a time-management system or planner. Hundreds of time-management systems and planners have been produced and marketed. However, today the market is getting less competitive as larger companies are merging with or buying out smaller companies. Later in this chapter we will demonstrate a simple approach to implementing an effective system. You will be able to integrate a planner into your daily life immediately and will see results the first day you start using it.

THREE KEYS TO EFFECTIVE SELF-MANAGEMENT

U p to this point, we have used the term "time management." Time management can be defined as the act of trying to control events through the effective use of time. When we talk about time management in relation to our daily lives, we are really talking about self-management. We cannot really control time or events but we do make choices daily. Self-management is a systematic approach to making choices on a day-to-day basis. What are the three keys to effective self-management?

> *"Even if you are on the right track, you will get run over if you just sit there."*
>
> WILL ROGERS

Daily quiet or planning time is the first essential key of successful self-management. Planning time is that time of day during which you review the current day's activities and tasks, assess your accomplishments, and plan for the next day. The best time of the day to do your daily planning is at the end of the day. If you try to make plans first thing in the morning, something will always happen. The phone will ring. Someone will need to talk to you. Interruptions are inevitable. However, at the end of the day, you have a chance to reflect upon what just happened, review your to-do list and activities, and plan for tomorrow. The next morning when you come to college or go to work, your plan for the day is already in place and you are ready to go! Planning at the end of the day is also less stressful. It gives you closure and a sense of well-being to know that your plan is in place for tomorrow.

When we ask students the question, "How many of you have a to-do list?," we are always amazed at the small number of students who raise their hands. We are more amazed by the students who have a to-do list but do not use it every day. How do you know what to do if you do not have a to-do list? We usually receive no reply to this question. Daily planning and a prioritized to-do list go hand-in-hand with effective self-management. It is not enough to have a to-do list. It must be prioritized and used each day. In the section covering time planners, we discuss in detail, with examples, how to develop, prioritize, and use a to-do list.

A time-management system or planner is the glue that holds self-management together. It is the place for your calendar, your daily plan, your to-do list, and your notes and files. Later in this chapter we will introduce you to time planners. A planner is easy to use and is one of the most effective time-management tools available for students today.

CHANGE AND CHOICES—IS YOUR LIFE BALANCED?

Facts About Time

Several statements apply to everyone about time. A few of the statements may not seem to apply to you, but think about each one individually.

- Few people have enough time, yet everyone has all there is.
- Every man and woman has 24 hours each day, 168 hours each week, 52 weeks per year—no more, no less; the time you are able to control should be the area of time management with which you are most concerned.
- Time cannot be accumulated or stockpiled—it flows at a fixed rate.
- The real problem is not with *time*, but what *you* choose to do with the time that you have available to manage.

The last fact of time presented, the notion that *you* choose the activity that uses your time, is crucial. You are in charge of a large percentage of your time and the choices you make determine how productive that time is going to be. At times, you've probably felt as if you were not in control; everyone experiences this feeling at some point in his or her life. The real key is that you *can* control time that is not typically used for school, work, or commuting. You have to take into account, and schedule appropriate time for, sleeping and eating. Other than that, your time can be divided into the two categories, discretionary or free time and nondiscretionary or required time.

IF I WERE YOUNG, I WOULD FORM GOOD HABITS

n *The Book of Virtues*, William Bennett quotes Aristotle as saying that good habits formed in youth make all the difference in life. Some 50 years earlier, Clovis G. Chappell, in his book *If I Were Young*, devoted a whole chapter to choices and the forming or developing of good habits. Chappell was a Methodist minister and evangelist who concentrated much of his time, energy, and writing to the development of moral, spiritual, and educational growth in young people. "I'd Form Good Habits" is the title of the first chapter in *If I Were Young*, wherein he uses Jesus as an example of a man of good habits living a good life.

To paraphrase Rev. Chappell, habits make the person. If you are a person of bad habits, you are not living a full life. If you are a person of good habits, you are living a better life. For this reason, it is of the highest importance that all of us give earnest and eager attention to the forming of the right kinds of habits. This is especially true for those of us whose habits have not yet been fully formed. Therefore, in all earnestness, when you are young, choose to form good habits. Although this implies that you *have* to be young to form good habits, our experience has demonstrated that one can form good habits at any age. It is a matter of choices. The choices we make day by day gradually form our habits. It is therefore important to have a systematic approach that emphasizes your goals and provides a logical way to make daily choices that move you toward the accomplishment of goals. When most students make a wrong choice, they tend to repeat that choice. Any wrong choice may thus become a habit. To be successful or to do our best educationally, we need desire, discipline, and execution. To have a balanced life, we need to make right choices in all departments of life.

> *"'Tis easier to prevent bad habits than to break them."*
>
> BENJAMIN FRANKLIN

Develop the right kind of study choices, which will lead to good study habits. To further your understanding of free time and where the rest of our time goes, we have developed a weekly time analysis.

WEEKLY TIME ANALYSIS

At the end of a busy day, have you ever looked back at that day and wondered, "Where did my time go?" Where does your time go? A large percentage of our time escapes us without our noticing. Certainly, we know that we spend what seems to be hours on the road, commuting to and from school, events, and work, and more hours at school, at work, and studying. Do you really have any free time or time to yourself? In order to help you answer this question, get a handle on your time, realize where your time is going, and then begin to "manage" your time, you must first complete a weekly time analysis. Our previous time analysis or inventory was a daily time analysis to assist you in understanding what actually happens on any given day in your life. What did you discover? It was probably an eye-opening exercise that caused you to start thinking about the importance of planning and organizing your day.

> *"People often ask me where does time go and I tell them, 'It goes the same place it has always gone and no one has ever known where that is.'"*
>
> ANDY ROONEY

The most common cycle in a series of life cycles is a seven-day period that we call a week. The week is the most common time denominator for most people. The work week usually starts on Monday as you return from some form of time off. Wednesday for many is a hump day, or the middle of the week. Friday is TGIF for a great number of people. The weekend is a time to relax and recuperate for the next Monday. However, what do you do with this week of 168 hours? Where and what has been your emphasis for the week? Did you waste time? Did you maximize your free time? Did you *have* any free time?

Exercise 2.2 is a "Weekly Time Analysis." Before the next class, please take about 20 minutes to complete this exercise and be prepared to discuss your assessment during class. Then, and only then, can you begin to realize how your time is really spent.

Please take about 20 minutes to complete this exercise and be prepared to discuss your personal analysis.

First, add any activities that relate to your personal weekly schedule to column one. Next, fill in the hours you spend doing each activity listed for

	S	M	T	W	T	F	S	WEEKLY TOTAL
PHYSICAL WELL-BEING								
Sleep								
Meals								
Exercise								
Grooming/Bathing								
Subtotal								
MENTAL WELL-BEING								
In Class								
Study Time								
Reading/Computer								
Relaxation								
Quiet Time								
Subtotal								
SPIRITUAL WELL-BEING								
Prayer								
Meditation								
Volunteering								
Church Meetings								
Community Service								
Subtotal								

	S	M	T	W	T	F	S	WEEKLY TOTAL
WORK								
On the Job								
Commuting Time								
Subtotal								
FAMILY/FRIENDS								
Friends Time								
Family Time								
Telephone								
Subtotal								
MISCELLANEOUS								
Bill Paying								
House Maintenance								
Car Maintenance								
Other (List)								
Subtotal								
Daily/Weekly Totals								

each day of the week. Add across to get a weekly total for that activity. Add down to get a subtotal for each category for each day. Next, add each column to get each day's total and a weekly total. Remember there are 24 hours in each day and 168 hours in the week.

The first step in completing the "Weekly Time Analysis" is to review the items listed in the first column and to add any activities that depend upon your weekly schedule. The second step is to fill in the number of hours you spend doing each activity, listed in the first column, for each day of the week. The week starts with Sunday and runs to Saturday. The third step is to add the number of hours in each category and record your subtotal for those activities. The next step is to add each column or day, keeping in mind that there are 24 hours in a day. Add the daily totals to produce your total hours for the week.

Finally, be prepared to answer the following questions at your next class meeting:

1. What am I doing that is totally unnecessary?
2. On what items am I spending too much time?
3. On what items am I spending too little time?
4. Does my schedule allow for flexibility?
5. How can I change my schedule to fit in required items and still have time left over?

How did you feel about completing your personal weekly time analysis? What did you discover? How many hours are in your day? How many hours are in your week? Did you find any discretionary time or free time? How did you use this valuable time? The choices we make about how to spend "free" time can also determine how successful we are. Basically, it all boils down to priorities. Priorities are adopted after certain goals have been established. If your goal is to complete your education, placing a high priority on study time outside the classroom, preparing for class, is paramount.

IDENTIFYING TIME-MANAGEMENT STRENGTHS AND WEAKNESSES

Are you an effective planner? What are your goals? Do goals have any impact on motivation? Do you believe that self-esteem is a building block for success? These and other questions have been formulated in our third exercise that we will use to identify your time-management strengths and weaknesses. This assessment will take about 20 minutes and can be completed in class.

Exercise 2.3 is a three-step exercise. The first step is to read each question and assign a score of 1 to 5 (with 5 being the highest) to each. The next step is to add these numbers to compute an overall score. A score of 100 to 125 is an outstanding score that indicates very effective time-management habits and skills. In the final step, you need to transfer or record the individual question scores from the first page to the corresponding question numbers on the second page. For example, the score for question 1 is transferred to 1 under the self-esteem column. Question 2 from the first page is transferred to 2 under the goal setting/planning column, etc. A score of 20 or higher on any one of the five areas indicates strength in that area. A score of 15 or higher is another strong area that could be improved. Scores of 14 or less indicate a weak area that needs improvement. Once your strong and weak areas have been identified, how do you go about improving in those areas? The first and simplest approach is to go back to the original 25 questions. These 25 questions are based upon the most effective practices of time management and student success. For example, question 1 and every fifth question thereafter deals with self-esteem and its impact on success. Question 2 and every fifth question thereafter represents an effective goal-setting or planning principle. After identifying your strengths and weaknesses, determining possible solutions and ways to build upon your strengths and to improve upon your weaknesses, the next step is to find a planner that you can use on a daily basis to increase your productivity.

"If you don't plan it, it won't happen."

Answer the following questions by writing in a score of 1 to 5, with 5 being the highest.

_____ 1. Do you have high self-esteem?

_____ 2. Do you have a written plan of goals you plan to achieve?

_____ 3. Are you on time to class, work, appointments, etc.?

_____ 4. Do you know what active listening is?

_____ 5. Do you use a study plan?

_____ 6. Are you a positive person?

_____ 7. Do you write a daily list of tasks you plan to do?

_____ 8. Can you quickly find things that you filed or stored?

_____ 9. Do you know what passive listening is?

_____ 10. Do you schedule time to study?

_____ 11. Do you often think about your future?

_____ 12. Do you meet college and work deadlines?

_____ 13. Are your home and work areas clean and orderly?

_____ 14. Do you continue to listen when you don't agree?

_____ 15. Do you know how to read a textbook?

_____ 16. Are you serious about your future?

_____ 17. Do you have a quiet or planning time each day?

_____ 18. Do you have an effective filing system?

_____ 19. Do you know how to get others to listen to you?

_____ 20. Do you know how to highlight a textbook?

_____ 21. Are you a risk taker?

_____ 22. Do you prioritize your to-do list?

_____ 23. Do you keep college and work supplies where they are easily accessible?

_____ 24. Do you continue to listen when you don't like the speaker?

_____ 25. Do you have a suitable place to study?

_____ TOTAL SCORE

A score of 100 to 125 is an outstanding score that indicates very effective time-management habits and skills. Scores below 75 indicate that there may be one or more areas that need improvement. But which areas are strong and which are weak? Please continue to the next page.

The chart below will provide you with an indication of your strong areas where you have effective time-management skills and your weak areas, which will need some improvement. As mentioned earlier in this chapter, you need to record or transfer the scores from the first page to the corresponding question numbers on this page.

SELF-ESTEEM	GOAL SETTING & PLANNING	ORGANIZING	LISTENING	STUDYING
1. _____	2. _____	3. _____	4. _____	5. _____
6. _____	7. _____	8. _____	9. _____	10. _____
11. _____	12. _____	13. _____	14. _____	15. _____
16. _____	17. _____	18. _____	19. _____	20. _____
21. _____	22. _____	23. _____	24. _____	25. _____
TOTAL SCORES				
_____	_____	_____	_____	_____

A score of 20 or higher on any one of the five areas indicates strength in that area. A score of 15 or higher is a fairly strong area that can be improved upon. Scores of less than 14 indicate a weak area that needs improvement. As mentioned earlier, once your strong and weak areas have been identified, you can return to the 25 questions to look for solutions or ways to improve upon any area of strength or weakness. For example, question 2 and every fifth question thereafter deals with goal setting and planning and its impact on success. If you scored low in goal setting and planning, questions 2, 7, 12, 17, and 22 provide effective practices of time management that when implemented will improve your time-management skills.

"Anything less than a conscious commitment to the important is an unconscious commitment to the unimportant."

STEPHEN COVEY

A TIME-MANAGEMENT SYSTEM: A PLANNER FOR STUDENT SUCCESS

A planner must have several common components to be effective. In their book, *Manage Your Time, Your Work, Yourself,* Merrill E. Douglass and Donna N. Douglass identified eight components required to form a truly effective system. A good planner will include these components—a yearly calendar, a monthly schedule, a daily schedule, a to-do list, a "contacts" directory, and specialized forms. In the following paragraphs, we will take you through a simple planner, introducing you to each of these components.*

Please refer to your regular planner or the one that you purchased for this class. We will take you through a systematic approach to time management and the effective use of a planner. In addition, we will explain how a planner can be used to build upon your strengths, improve your weaknesses, and help you to become an effective student and to succeed in all areas of your life. If you use this system correctly, it becomes an integral part of your life.

When you open your planner, you should first come to an information page. This page is for your own personal use and information. Your name, address, phone number(s) are important, as well as a note that states, *"Reward Offered if Lost and Returned."* In most cases, it will be returned if you misplace it. Most planners also display reference calendars in the first several pages. Reference calendars are just that; that is, they may be used to refer to last year, next year, or as a quick reference for any particular month of the current year.

Monthly Planning

The monthly calendar is an important planning document. All appointments, class schedules, work schedules, meetings, and other activities or events should be entered here first. Using a monthly calendar properly will provide you with a week at-a-glance and a month at-a-glance planning document. You can see all activities or events for any week of a particular month. Why do you need such a tool? Used properly, you will be better able to schedule your classes and other events without double scheduling or scheduling events on top of each other, which can be very embarrassing and time consuming.

The monthly calendar should never be used as a to-do list. Having a to-do list, class schedules, meetings, and so on, on the same document is very confusing and can cause a lack of control, as well as add unnecessary stress to your day. Most monthly calendars have a place for additional notes. This section is a good place to list events or activities that will take place in a certain month but not necessarily on any particular day. This note section is a good place to record reminders. For example, a friend or relative in another state may ask you to call them in August. To avoid losing that information, where would you record it? You can record it under the note section on the month of August (see Figure 2.2).

Daily Planning

Daily planning is a key to successful time management. It is the heart of a time planner system. Let's look at an example of a two-page-per-week daily planning concept by reviewing the example in Figure 2.3.

The left side of the daily plan is your daily schedule. All of your activities for any given day, such as Friday, August 25, 2006, are recorded on your daily schedule. Where do these activities and events originate? When do you execute your daily plan? How do you get started?

---

*We recommend that you purchase and use the planner that was designed specifically for use with this textbook. It is *A Planner for Student Success* by Charles T. Muse, ©2005 and published by Pearson Custom Publishing, ISBN 0-536-95943.

FIGURE 2.2

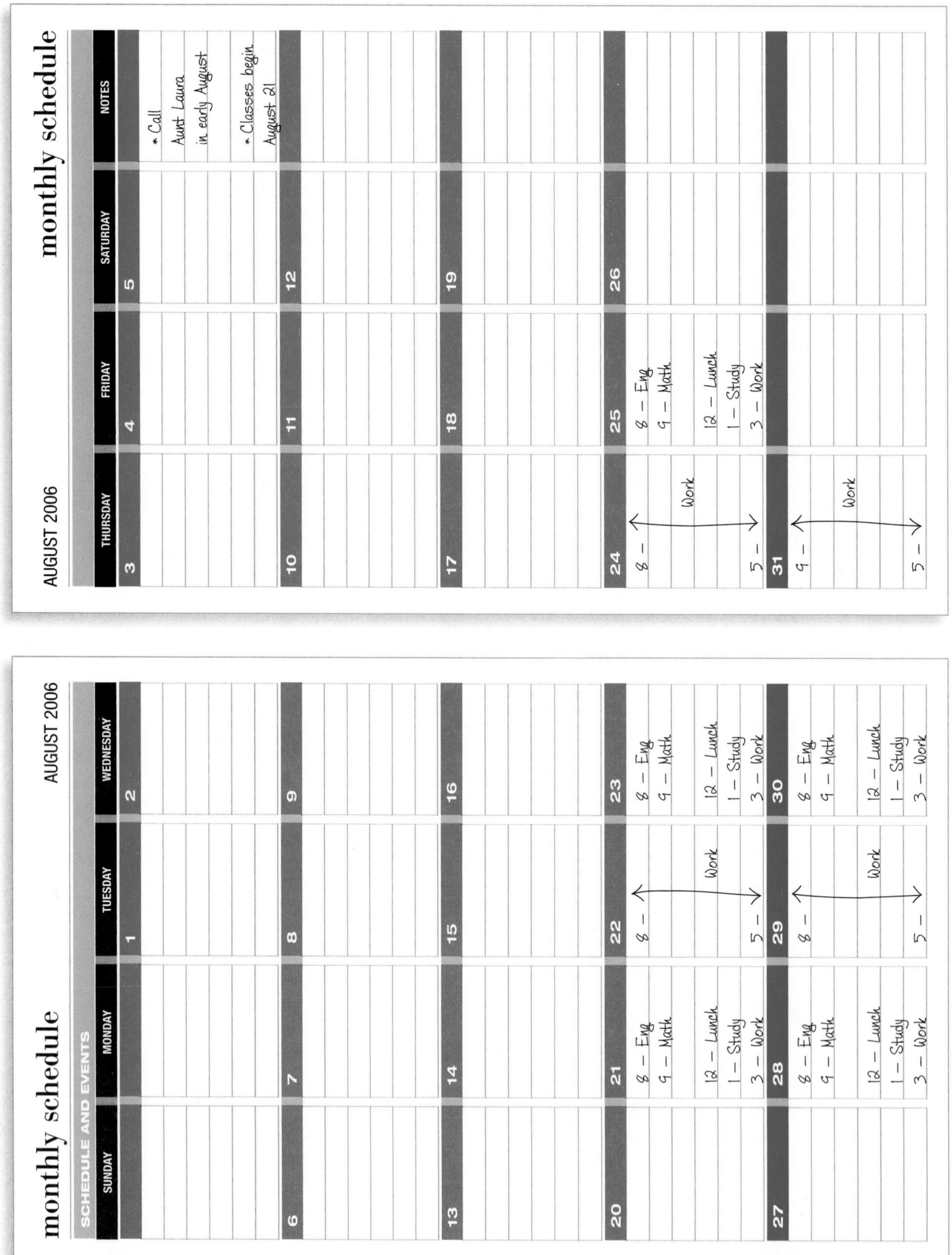

monthly schedule

AUGUST 2006

THURSDAY	FRIDAY	SATURDAY	NOTES
3	4	5	* Call Aunt Laura in early August * Classes begin August 21
10	11	12	
17	18	19	
24 8 – ← Work → 5 –	25 8 – Eng 9 – Math 12 – Lunch 1 – Study 3 – Work	26	
31 9 – ← Work → 5 –			

monthly schedule

AUGUST 2006

SCHEDULE AND EVENTS

SUNDAY	MONDAY	TUESDAY	WEDNESDAY
		1	2
6	7	8	9
13	14	15	16
20	21 8 – Eng 9 – Math 12 – Lunch 1 – Study 3 – Work	22 8 – ← Work → 5 –	23 8 – Eng 9 – Math 12 – Lunch 1 – Study 3 – Work
27	28 8 – Eng 9 – Math 12 – Lunch 1 – Study 3 – Work	29 8 – ← Work → 5 –	30 8 – Eng 9 – Math 12 – Lunch 1 – Study 3 – Work

FIGURE 2.3

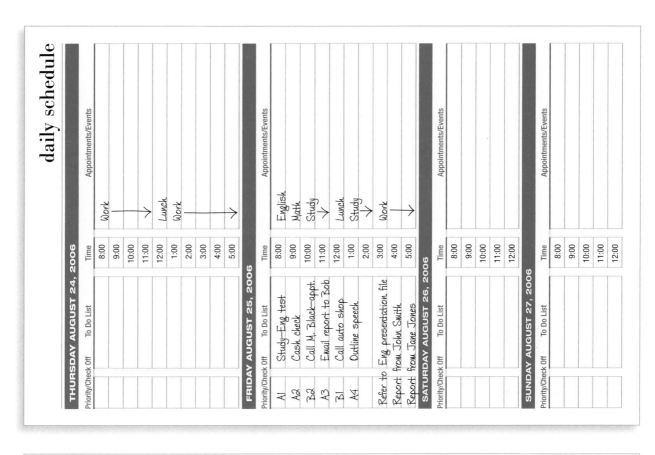

daily schedule

THURSDAY AUGUST 24, 2006

Priority/Check Off	To Do List	Time	Appointments/Events
		8:00	Work
		9:00	→
		10:00	
		11:00	
		12:00	Lunch
		1:00	Work
		2:00	
		3:00	
		4:00	
		5:00	→

FRIDAY AUGUST 25, 2006

Priority/Check Off	To Do List	Time	Appointments/Events
A1	Study—Eng test	8:00	English
A2	Cash check	9:00	Math
B2	Call M. Black—appt.	10:00	Study
A3	Email report to Bob	11:00	→
B1	Call auto shop	12:00	Lunch
A4	Outline speech	1:00	Study
		2:00	→
Refer to Eng presentation file		3:00	Work
Report from John Smith		4:00	
Report from Jane Jones		5:00	→

SATURDAY AUGUST 26, 2006

Priority/Check Off	To Do List	Time	Appointments/Events
		8:00	
		9:00	
		10:00	
		11:00	
		12:00	

SUNDAY AUGUST 27, 2006

Priority/Check Off	To Do List	Time	Appointments/Events
		8:00	
		9:00	
		10:00	
		11:00	
		12:00	

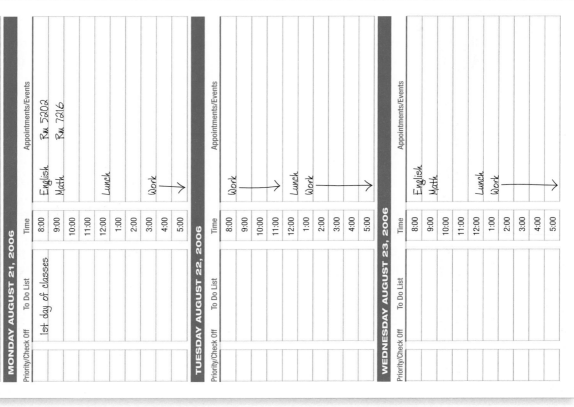

daily schedule

MONDAY AUGUST 21, 2006

Priority/Check Off	To Do List	Time	Appointments/Events
	1st day of classes	8:00	English Rm 5202
		9:00	Math Rm 7216
		10:00	
		11:00	
		12:00	Lunch
		1:00	
		2:00	
		3:00	Work
		4:00	→
		5:00	

TUESDAY AUGUST 22, 2006

Priority/Check Off	To Do List	Time	Appointments/Events
		8:00	Work
		9:00	→
		10:00	
		11:00	
		12:00	Lunch
		1:00	Work
		2:00	
		3:00	
		4:00	
		5:00	→

WEDNESDAY AUGUST 23, 2006

Priority/Check Off	To Do List	Time	Appointments/Events
		8:00	English
		9:00	Math
		10:00	
		11:00	
		12:00	Lunch
		1:00	Work
		2:00	
		3:00	
		4:00	
		5:00	→

First and foremost, set aside about 15 minutes each day for planning. Schedule this time at the end of the day when there are fewer interruptions and you can reflect upon what happened today and what you need to do tomorrow. Start with your monthly calendar and transfer any classes, meetings, and your work schedule for that day to your daily schedule for tomorrow.

For example, if it were August 24th, you would be planning for August 25th and would transfer all classes, meetings, work hours, children's ball games, and so on from your monthly calendar to your daily schedule. Now, you have a schedule of events that you know will happen tomorrow. You also can see whether there is any discretionary or free time on August 25th as well.

The left side of this daily plan is a prioritized daily to-do list. Where did the items on this to-do list originate? These items come from several different places. Some are items that you wrote on the August 25th to-do list that you knew about last week. For example, you have a test or quiz in English on Monday, August 28th. Your instructor announced this test on August 18th. Once the assignment was made, you decided to study for that test on August 25th. Two things must be accomplished at this point. Number one: Do you have any free time on August 25th? If the answer is yes, block off time on your daily schedule, say from 10:00 to 12:00 noon for study, and write on your to-do list, "study for English test."

Three very important things have just happened. You committed to preparing for a test by studying on a particular day, August 25th. To ensure that you have time to study, you blocked off two hours on your daily schedule. Finally, to emphasize the importance of this event and to make it a part of your daily goal for that day, you included "study for English test" on your to-do list with a high priority of A1. You record other items on this to-do list as you are planning for the next day. For example, you want to cash your paycheck tomorrow, which is a high priority and needs to be on your list. Or perhaps you need to talk to two classmates about a project. Tomorrow is a good day to do that task. Again note the amount of free time on August 25th.

Priorities and To-Do Lists

There are several important steps to developing and prioritizing a to-do list. As mentioned previously, tasks that form your to-do list come from several sources. Naturally, the first step is to create the list. The list should consist of the tasks you feel should be accomplished on any given day. You must keep in mind that your to-do list should be long on days with a great deal of free time and short on days with little or no free time. For example, August 25th is a day with several hours of free time. In Figure 2.3, the student has two classes, an English class from 8 to 9 A.M. and a math class from 9 to 10 A.M. From 10 to 12, there is a block of free time. Note that earlier, we filled in a two-hour study time and listed that as a task on the to-do list. Noon to 1 P.M. is lunch, if you choose to go to lunch, and work starts at 3 P.M., which provides another two-hour block of free time.

The next step is to analyze the list, identify the most important items, and assign them an "A" priority. Items that are of lesser importance are assigned a "B" priority. This system of setting priorities was introduced by Allan Lakein in his book, *How to Get Control of Your Time and Your Life*.

Lakein's system is an A, B, and C system with Cs being routine tasks that can be put off indefinitely. We have deleted Cs from our prioritizing process to allow you to concentrate on what is most important to you.

When you end up with more than one "A," you have to prioritize them. If you could only do one of your As, which one would you do? That A becomes your "A1" priority and the next, an "A2" priority.

Once you have completed all "A" priorities, you can move to your "B" priorities. Students can also create a brevity code for their to-do list. For example, X can be used for a task completed or an → for a task moved forward to another day's to-do list.

Once your daily schedule and prioritized to-do list are complete, you have a well-organized plan of action for the next day. You have what is called "closure." You can now forget about your to-do list until tomorrow.

In Figure 2.3, at the bottom third of your to-do list, leave space for an "Assignments Due" section. Usually, planners have a similar space that is designed to help you track special projects at college or at work. For example, let's suppose that you are working on a presentation for one of your classes with two other students. Each of you has researched certain aspects of the presentation and the two other students are to provide you with a report of their findings. How do you remind yourself that these reports are due to you on a certain date? Simply note in the Assignment Due (or similar section of your to-do list) the date that you are to receive the reports (see Figure 2.3). At the end of the day when you are in your planning mode for the next day, you notice that only one of your classmates turned his report in to you. At this point, you should write on your to-do list for the next day, "Call Jane Jones, English Report." This systematic process ensures that you and your teammates do not miss deadlines.

Contacts Directory

The A–Z or contacts directory in most planners is designed to provide you with a quick source of information about your friends, peers, family, and coworkers. By using the monthly calendar, the daily schedule, and the prioritized to-do list with the directory, you have an excellent filing and retrieval system. Let's look at an example to see how this retrieval system works. The presentation for your English class is a major project that requires research, note taking, and several interim reports by your project team. How do you track and file all of this information in a way that you can have it at your fingertips as you need it?

The initial project due date, as well as several other deadlines, are first recorded in the monthly calendar. The monthly calendar becomes a very valuable planning document. You are now in a position to look at any given week or month to see the workflow of this project. Next, you move the planning process to an action process. This process is accomplished by moving tasks that originated from your monthly calendar due dates and deadlines to your daily schedule and prioritized to-do list. When you take notes as part of your project, you file them and reference that information back to your assignment due section of the prioritized to-do list. In our example (Figure 2.3), note that two reports are due from your teammates, John Smith and Jane Jones. Also, note that your notes and your research report are filed in your English Presentation File. Once you receive the other reports on this project, you may file them in the English Presentation File as well. It is also important to have consistency in your note-taking process. (More detailed information on note taking is discussed in Chapter 7.)

YOUR STUDY TIME

Be prepared to take full advantage of time spent studying—be physically and emotionally prepared and use your time wisely.

Time spent studying must be time for which you are physically and emotionally prepared. It is important that you not be tired or hungry.

It is also important that you attempt to let go of distracting emotional issues. You will not be able to use your time wisely if you have not met the needs of your mind and body. (Another barrier to effective study time is procrastination—we will discuss that a little later on in the chapter.)

When choosing your study time, think about your peak times. If possible, select those times for studying. For example, some students prefer to study during the early morning hours, whereas other students prefer evening hours.

As a student, you have to set aside a certain number of hours, *five days a week*, for studying. The amount of time spent will vary from day to day and from student to student. As a rule of thumb, for every hour spent in class, two hours should be spent studying for that class. For example, if your class meets three hours per week, then you should spend six hours outside of class studying. This is a realistic amount of time and should be used as a guide. You should try to remember that some classes will require more time, others not as much. Most students require one to three hours of outside time (per course, per week) to be academically successful.

Of the courses you are now taking, which ones will require more study time?

_____

Why?

_____

_____

Which courses will require the least amount of outside study time?

_____

Why?

_____

_____

This raises a good point for the nontraditional student. Is it realistic to be a full-time student, a full-time employee, and a parent all at once? Students who find that they are able to juggle a variety of commitments will always tell you that it is not easy. Decisions, tough decisions, concerning what is most "urgent" and what can wait must be made on a daily basis. Many successful adult students also indicate that support from family, friends, or spouses helps tremendously with the time-management problem of being a student, an employee, and a parent. Try to remember that the decision to be a student carries with it a significant time commitment.

Now, let's take some time to get a handle on your situation. Use the monthly schedule and the daily schedule in your planner to complete the following tasks:

1. You should have already blocked out the time you're in class, at work, participating in religious/social activities, etc.
2. Examine the time remaining and indicate the time that could be used for studying.

Do you have "free time" that you can dedicate to studying?

_____

If not, what can you eliminate?

_____

_____

_____

Where do free blocks of time exist during the day?

_____

_____

_____

After revising your daily schedule, use the space provided to identify the things that might interfere with your study time.

_____

_____

_____

What do you think you could do to prevent these situations from interfering with your study time?

_____

_____

_____

There are some "concrete" things that you can do to make it possible to juggle your study time and family responsibilities. A few of the suggestions are:

- Schedule study time at a time when your school-age children are studying.
- Develop a "network" of other students with children. Trade babysitting responsibility with the people in this network. Volunteer to watch their children when they are studying and ask them to sit with yours when you are preparing for a big test.
- Predetermine what your peak study times will be for the semester and ask family and friends to help with babysitting responsibilities during these peak times.

YOUR STUDY PLAN AND DAILY PRIORITIZED TO-DO LIST

As mentioned earlier, at the end of each day, make a prioritized to-do list for the next day to help you organize your study time. This plan should enable you to get the most from your valuable time. It is important to list first those assignments that are most difficult to complete. If you save those items until the end, you will not be at your best. This could increase your frustration and you may decide not to complete the assignment. If there are unfinished tasks on your list, the unfinished work should be transferred to your study plan for the next day.

Refer back to the prioritized to-do list example, Figure 2.3, to see what a typical study plan looks like. This example uses a prioritized list of things that must be done today. Using an "A" for the most critical and urgent items and a "B" for the less critical items, as we discussed earlier, generates a system that will work well for your study plan.

IT'S ALL ABOUT PRIORITIES!

By developing a priority system (a system that lets you know what is "most important," "next most important," and "least important") of tasks that must be accomplished, you create a much more efficient use of your time. Many successful people have a time-management system that they have developed over a long period. Talk to successful students and ask them to share their technique for using their planner. Sharing helpful "tips" on time management can help you as well as others.

LEADING TIME WASTERS

Have you ever tried to study, sleep, watch TV, or talk with a friend and been constantly interrupted? No doubt, regardless of your lifestyle, you have distractions that keep you from completing tasks that must be finished or things that you really want to accomplish. Time wasters are a big problem in a time-management system. Recognizing distractions and avoiding them is a major hurdle in the "time management" game. Some of the leading time wasters are listed below:

- friends who call or show up unexpectedly
- television
- the telephone
- trying to get so "organized" that you never get anything accomplished
- computer games and the Internet
- the weather
- a messy house or dorm
- a hobby
- procrastination

What are some time wasters that you have encountered?

_____

_____

_____

_____

What are some of the ways you can eliminate these time wasters?

_____

_____

_____

_____

PROCRASTINATION: THE ENEMY OF THE STUDENT

'll do that in a little while." How many times have you uttered this statement?

Procrastination or "putting off until tomorrow what you could do today" can kill the best study plan. It is easy to procrastinate—even the best time managers have to fight this "enemy" every day. The good news is that *you* are in control. You choose whether to complete or not complete assignments and then, ultimately, you pay the consequences if you have procrastinated. The best way to fight procrastination is to "jump right in" and make an attempt to get started.

You might want to break your study time up into 15-minute segments at first. Tell yourself that "if I finish 15 minutes of productive studying, I will treat myself to a 5-minute break." There are times when 15 minutes might be all of the time you have. Try to begin learning to use this time effectively and efficiently. Later on, as you get more "into" your subject, you may want to increase the time to

> *"Don't put off for tomorrow what you can do today, because if you enjoy it today you can do it again tomorrow."*
>
> JAMES MICHENER

30 minutes with a 5-minute break. Be sure to give yourself a break when you have earned it!

Another way to avoid procrastination and to study effectively when children are around is to have "group study time" set aside for the students in the house. Everyone may want to sit down at the dinner table and begin to "tackle" the day's assignments. If you begin this at the beginning of the academic year, it will become a matter of routine, a habit that will take priority in your home.

Now that you have completed the chapter on time management, take a few minutes to complete the Milestones self-analysis again.

Did any of your "No" and "Sometimes" answers become "Yes" answers as a result of completing the exercises in this chapter? Hopefully, you will begin using the strategies presented in this chapter to develop lifelong habits for effective time management. Your planner is an essential tool that needs to be used now and in the future and made an integral part of your life.

MILESTONES

NOW THAT YOU ARE HERE . . .

Answer each statement by checking "Y" for Yes, "N" for No, or "S" for Sometimes.

1. I know how to prioritize my responsibilities. (Y) (N) (S)

2. I manage my time effectively. (Y) (N) (S)

3. Completing daily goals is important to me. (Y) (N) (S)

4. Making a daily "to-do" list is necessary for me. (Y) (N) (S)

5. Writing down all of my assignments helps me. (Y) (N) (S)

6. I use short- and long-term planning. (Y) (N) (S)

7. I understand discretionary time or free time and nondiscretionary time. (Y) (N) (S)

8. My friends control my time. (Y) (N) (S)

9. I am in control of my time. (Y) (N) (S)

10. I understand that time management helps me to become a better student. (Y) (N) (S)

- Work on your *hardest* subjects first; save the easiest items for last.

- Organize your free time into *usable* chunks—5 minutes here or there is of little or no value.

- Make lists, prioritize them, and *follow* them.

- *Revise* your "to-do" list every night. Items that were not completed one day should be completed the next.

- Find a place that allows you to *study* without interruption. Do not allow others to interrupt your work.

- Utilize your planner as a temporary *filing* system.

Applying What You Know

This chapter on time management has given you the opportunity to determine where your time goes and how much time you spend on various activities and commitments, as well as an opportunity to identify your time-management strengths and weaknesses. Now that you have completed this chapter, refer back to the Case Study about Gwen at the beginning of this book. Based on her situation, answer the following questions:

1. What time-management strategies or techniques should Gwen utilize?

2. How should Gwen utilize the monthly calendar, daily plan, and to-do list to help her address the challenges that she faces?

3. If faced with problems similar to Gwen's (no free time, no time for her friends, and little time for family), what would you do?

Observations

CHARTING YOUR COURSE

We have taken a three-prong approach in presenting time management to you. First, we assisted you in identifying your time-management strengths and weaknesses. Once identified, strengths were emphasized and weaknesses were addressed with proven solutions. Finally, we introduced you to a time-management system that integrated schedules—annual and monthly—with a daily schedule and a prioritized to-do list with established goals for the semester and beyond. This system also integrated the goal-setting process, address and telephone directory, and note-taking skills. The weekly time analysis, we hope, was an eye-opening experience. Through this experience you discovered how to get a good handle on time and where your time goes. You also learned to understand the significance of free time and how to take advantage of it. The 25-question exercise provided you with an understanding of the importance of goal setting, planning, implementation of a plan, evaluation, and follow-up. The time-management system pulled it all together for you based upon your individual situation and goals. It assembled the tools you need to succeed in an integrated format that will continue to assist you in guiding your academic success. You will be able to use this system throughout your academic career and in the world of work.

"Plan for the future, because that's where you are going to spend the rest of your life."

MARK TWAIN

Why do we study time management? Ultimately, because we need more free time to do the things we want to do. Quite simply, if we manage our time effectively, we can do what we want. Time is everyone's resource. Every person has the same amount of time. How one chooses to spend his or her time is a matter of priorities. Having a realistic perception of time enables you to judge the passage of time more effectively. Knowing where your time goes and being able to recognize "free time" and "nondiscretionary time" can allow you to make priorities. Time management is a learned skill, one that will enable you to be a more successful student.

DETOUR — Getting There on Time

This feature reinforces what you will be learning throughout the text related to time and the management of time. This particular exercise focuses on self-management as it relates to time management.

Answer the following questions:

How do you feel about how organized your life is at this moment?

_____

_____

How do you feel when you do not have control of your time?

_____

_____

How do you deal with not having control of your time?

_____

_____

How do you feel about other "things" and people controlling your time?

_____

_____

Exploring Technology

Most students and colleges have access to Microsoft Office, which includes Microsoft Outlook. Features of Microsoft Outlook include e-mail, task or to-do lists, calendars, and a contacts directory. As an introduction to using electronic or computerized calendars and to-do lists, take a few minutes to explore these features and complete the following activity. If you are not currently using Microsoft Outlook as your planner, make sure that you have your manual planner set up and are comfortable with its features. Pick one month and transfer your appointments, meetings, class schedule, work schedule, and so on into the Microsoft Outlook calendar. Use the standard toolbar to view your calendar for a single day, a work week, a full week, or a month. Once you have completed this step, use the Tasks icon in the Outlook Shortcuts to bring up your "Task Pad" or "To-Do" list. Use this feature for the month that you have chosen to track your tasks and to experience an electronic to-do list. You can go back and forth from your Tasks icon to your Calendar icon to update, review, and complete your to-do list. The Microsoft Outlook calendar provides an excellent one-page daily plan, as well as your prioritized to-do list. Once you have tried this form of computerized planner, you may never go back to the manual paper and pencil format.

Web Connections

TRAVELING THE INFORMATION SUPERHIGHWAY

During your journey, you may want to check out some of the following Web addresses to assist with enhancing your time-management skills:

> www.businesstown.com/time/time.asp
>
> www.omega23.com/books/b/si_timemgmt.html
>
> www.prenhall.com/success/StudySkl/timemanage.html
>
> www.ecomagic.org/520PleasureThroughPlanning.html

As a result of this chapter, and in preparing for my journey, I plan to . . .

Fine-Tuning Your Vehicle

3

RECOGNIZING YOUR POTENTIAL AND BUILDING SELF-ESTEEM

I remember walking to the mailbox and getting the letter from my "college of choice." As I walked back toward the house, every dream I had of a college education passed before my eyes. "We regret to inform you that because of your SAT scores and your high school rank, your application has been denied."

I was not the best student in the world. Looking back, I was not even average. I passed senior English with the grade of D minus. My predicted grade point average (GPA) for college was a mere .07. I never knew how to study. I never asked for any assistance. I did not even know how to properly use the library. I now faced having to continue working in the textile plant instead of going to college.

Two days later, another letter came to me from the college. It was signed by the director of the Summer Prep Program. They offered me a second chance. Their letter stated that if I would come to the summer session and make at least a B average, I would be admitted as a temporary student. The weight of the world was on my shoulders. How could I, a D minus high school student, take four classes in college and score a B? Quickly—and I mean very quickly—I learned how to ask for help. I went to the Assistance Lab and the first thing I learned was how to study. I studied and I studied and I studied. At the end of four weeks, I had three As and a B. I had made it!

Those four weeks were the easy part. I had changed and I knew that I could never go back. I had a thirst for something that could only be quenched in college . . . a thirst for knowledge.

Dr. Robert Sherfield, a faculty member at the Community College of Southern Nevada–Las Vegas, wrote this passage. He learned that his dreams could be realized by assuming responsibility for his future and learning how to study.

*T*his book is intended to be a guide to show you how to assume responsibility for your own learning, which will enable you to make the most of your education and your future. It is our hope to show you that learning can be one of the most rewarding and exciting

"Life is about change and about movement and about becoming something other than what you are at this very moment."

experiences of your life. Right now, you may or may not see it that way. You may have had some experiences that were not positive, or you may be in college because your parents or someone else insisted that you enroll. Your interests may lie in getting a quick degree or re-training for a promotion at work—that's okay. The primary concern at this moment is developing the basic skills that will allow you to graduate and move into the world of work, get that promotion, or move on to a four-year degree.

How do you feel about being enrolled in this course? You may be upset at this moment because you were "required" to take this course. Many freshmen feel the same way. They do not want to "waste" their time in classes that may carry only one hour of credit or carry no degree credit at all. It may be that this course does not count toward your graduation credit hours. At some schools, however, it does.

One day, a professor heard a group of students complaining about having to take "developmental" courses. When she came around the corner of the hallway, they froze with fear, knowing that she had heard them talking. They were right; she had heard them. She stopped to ask how they were doing, sat on the bench with them, and told them something that made a huge difference in their lives. "I know that you are upset for having to enroll in classes that won't transfer or count toward graduation,"

she said. "But without these classes, there will be no graduation for you. This program is not a punishment, but a second chance for you. So many people never get a second chance, but this school cares about you. You can look at it as punishment or you can look at it as the first day of the rest of your life. *You* have to make that decision."

Most of the group chose to take her words seriously because they knew in their hearts that they lacked the skills to make it to graduation. As college *graduates*, most students who enrolled in developmental studies courses can tell you, without hesitation, that study skills and orientation courses work. Research case after research case proves how freshmen who enroll in orientation or study skills courses graduate in higher numbers than those who do not take them (Gardner & Jeweler, 1995). This course gives you another chance . . . it makes today the first day of the rest of your life.

Your college cares about you and your success, otherwise this course would not exist. The faculty and administration of your college have devoted countless hours to developing and designing a course that will help you to become the very best that you can be. They believe in you, and they want to provide you with the tools to allow you to believe in yourself. This is their life's work. It is now your responsibility to assume responsibility for your education through the services being offered at your college. If you complete the exercises in this chapter, participate in class, read the additional assignments that may be issued by your professor, and keep an open mind, at the end of this chapter you will be able to:

- Determine why you are in college
- Evaluate your past educational experiences
- Define success and identify successful people in your life
- Use your inner potential
- Assess your value system
- Complete a personal analysis of yourself
- Define self-esteem and describe why it is important
- Use "Roadways for Increasing Self-Esteem"

In the Milestones checklist, you will find 10 questions intended to cause you to think about your potential and self-esteem at this point in your life. Take a moment and answer each statement carefully.

If you would like to turn more of your "No" and "Sometimes" answers into "Yes" answers, you might consider some of the following activities. Maybe you should spend more of your time thinking about your potential and your future and learn to use techniques that will assist you in achieving your goals and dreams. If you happen to have more negative answers to these questions, relax! This text is designed to give you the skills to help you develop your potential and realize your goals.

WHY ARE YOU HERE?

t does not matter if you are just starting college, or if you are in your second semester, or if you are a sophomore—you have probably asked yourself from time to time, "How did I get here?" or "Why am I really sitting in this class?" What answers come to your mind? Your first thoughts might have been:

1. I want to be a better person.
2. I have nowhere else to be.
3. My friends came, so I did too.
4. Job retraining.
5. Personal or professional crisis.
6. To provide a better life for my family.

The first key to success in most endeavors is deciding to take action. You've done that by enrolling in college. Second, you probably have a good idea why you are here and what you want to accomplish.

Using the spaces below, list the reasons why you have chosen to attend college:

1. _____
2. _____
3. _____
4. _____

Was it hard to come up with your list, or did you jot down your thoughts quickly? Why? If it was difficult, perhaps it is because most of us spend so little time actually thinking about our education and what it really means to our future. The next few questions are intended to get you thinking about college on a different level. Take your time responding to each question.

Is learning an enjoyable experience? _____

Why or why not?

_____

How could learning become a more enjoyable experience for you?

_____

_____

_____

What are the major ideas you must consider in making learning and school more enjoyable experiences? Below, list what you feel your school could do to make learning more enjoyable for you.

1. _____
2. _____
3. _____
4. _____

List what you feel your teachers could do to make learning more enjoyable for you.

1. _____
2. _____
3. _____
4. _____

Most important, list the ways that you can bring about change. How can you make learning and school a more enjoyable experience?

1. _____
2. _____
3. _____
4. _____

A great part of your success in college is realizing that *you* can bring about change. You've just begun by spending time evaluating your current situation. Remember, it's hard to play ball when you're not on the field.

WHERE ARE YOU GOING?

"I have learned that success is to be measured not so much by the position one has reached in life, as by the obstacles which they have overcome while trying to succeed."

BOOKER T. WASHINGTON,
AMERICAN EDUCATOR

The famous poet Robert Frost wrote a poem about two roads splitting in a forest and his decision to take "the one less traveled." Today, you are faced with the same decision. There are two roads for you. One will be filled with challenges and hard work. The other will be the road that, unfortunately, many students take: the road that avoids challenge, sidesteps opportunity, and often leads to dropping out of college. Which road will you take? Only you can make that decision, and it will not be an easy one. Whatever your ultimate goal might be, it will be important for you to map out a course to get there and then learn to take the proper roadways. Success seldom happens without a plan. In the coming days, you will begin to realize that your road will look different, ride different, and feel different from that of your friends. Everyone's path to success is different, and only you can map your course.

The following questions are intended to help you begin to develop a philosophy about success and determine what you can do to bring about success in your life.

Write your definition of success:

_____

_____

_____

Describe one person in your life whom you consider to be successful. Why is this person successful?

_____

_____

_____

List the one accomplishment you want to achieve more than anything else:

_____

_____

Why?

_____

_____

How do you plan to achieve this?

_____

_____

_____

What part does your education play in reaching this goal?

_____

_____

_____

What do you need to do to make sure this goal is reached?

_____

_____

_____

What part does this course play in reaching your goal?

_____

_____

_____

One of the most important lessons to be learned about beginning a journey is that the road will sometimes change. Have you ever been driving to a friend's house and decided to do a couple of unexpected things along the way like stop at the store, pick up another friend, or take a different road? Your road to your friend's house changed, didn't it? Keep in mind that when beginning your journey to success, your road will most likely change several times. There is no harm in changing your mind. The harm lies in traveling down a road that no longer suits you and your ideas.

There are probably as many definitions of success as there are people in the world. The poem to the right gives us a look at how many ways we can succeed. Thinking positively and realizing that one failure or one setback does NOT make us failures or unsuccessful is a step toward success. It only means that we have to try harder and concentrate on the many positive aspects of our lives. Our setbacks can help us see our potential.

DISCOVERING AND ACHIEVING YOUR POTENTIAL

Ironically, one of the things we know least about ourselves is what we are capable of and how great our potential can be. It has been said that we use only 1 percent of our brain capacity. It has further been suggested that of the

A DEFINITION OF SUCCESS

To laugh often and much; to win the respect of intelligent people and the affection of children; to earn the appreciation of honest critics and endure the betrayal of false friends; to appreciate beauty; to find the best in others; to leave the world a bit better, whether by a healthy child, a garden patch, or a redeemed social condition; to know even one life has breathed easier because you have lived. THIS IS TO HAVE SUCCEEDED!

Ralph Waldo Emerson

400,000-plus words in the English language, the average educated person uses only 2,000 of them. Discovering your potential is an ongoing process that hopefully lasts for a lifetime.

You are always discovering new things you can do and new ideas that can help you live a productive life. When was the last time that you did something you thought couldn't be done? One of the keys to a successful life is analyzing your potential and setting your goals. Many times, students let other people determine what they will be able to do for the rest of their lives. Because of poor math performance, you may never choose to be an architect or physicist. Math may simply not be your strongest area. This does not mean that you can't do math, it simply means that you may have to try harder in this subject area. Others may find that in the areas of art, music, theatre, English, literature, hobbies, crafts, and people skills, their possibilities are limitless. It does not mean that they will use these skills as their life's work. You have to look beyond what you are capable of at this very moment to discover your true potential. In other words, don't cut yourself short just because problems may arise in certain areas.

> "There is a joke about a man who was asked if he could play the violin and he answered, 'I don't know. I've never tried.' Those who have never tried to play a violin really do not know whether they can or not. Those who say too early in life and too firmly, 'No, I'm not at all musical,' shut themselves off from whole areas of life that might have proved rewarding. In each of us, there are unknown possibilities, undiscovered potentialities—and one big advantage of having an open self-concept rather than a rigid one is that we shall continue to expose ourselves to new experiences, and therefore we shall continue to discover more and more about ourselves as we grow older."
>
> *Alfred Adler*

The first step to discovering your potential is deciding what you value most in your life. Is it playing the violin, becoming a physical therapist, or repairing a car? Do you enjoy working with people, with numbers, indoors or outdoors? All of these endeavors are worthy; you will be the one to make the final decision. To add even more confusion to the situation, you are going to meet people who have very different interests than your own, and they may introduce you to other areas of interests. This can be helpful and confusing at the same time, but if you allow yourself to think and experience these differences with an open mind, you will begin to grow in ways you never imagined possible. You will have given yourself a broader base on which to build. Who ever said that you could do only one thing? You need to decide where your interests lie and how those interests can best be expanded and enjoyed throughout your life and career. Experiencing new challenges and meeting new people will help you discover and evaluate your greatest potential.

The exercise below will help you begin an evaluation of your life and your potential. Some of these questions are going to be a bit difficult because you may have never thought about them and you probably have never written down the answers before. Take as much time as you need to answer these questions truthfully and completely.

List three things you expect of yourself:

1. _____

2. _____

3. _____

List five things that you consider yourself to be capable of, interested in, or talented in:

1. _____
2. _____
3. _____
4. _____
5. _____

Now, list why you consider yourself to be capable, interested, or talented in these things:

1. _____
2. _____
3. _____
4. _____
5. _____

List five things that interest you but that you consider yourself to be less capable of or talented in:

1. _____
2. _____
3. _____
4. _____
5. _____

List why you believe that you are less capable or talented in these areas:

1. _____
2. _____
3. _____
4. _____
5. _____

More than likely, you listed reasons such as: "I do not spend enough time on it," "I am not as committed as I should be," "I am afraid of what people will say," and so forth. Many times our potential is limited by our lack of practice, time, or commitment, or our fear that we may be thought of as different.

When a friend was in elementary school, he took piano lessons and all of the guys found out. It was not easy for him to continue, and eventually the teasing and name-calling led him to quit. He said that he regretted the decision to quit many times. There had always been something inside of him that cried out every time he passed a piano. He said, "I always have to sit down and play." Apparently, his potential in that area had never been realized. He recently said that he bought a piano and discovered that he had talent. He said, "I may never be a famous pianist like Chopin or Beethoven, but that piano has brought me

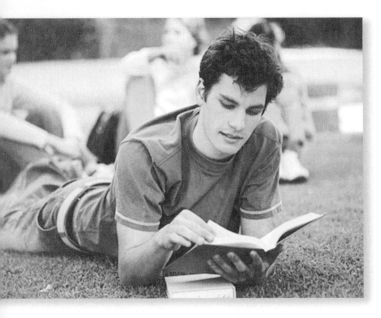

When you take time to get to know yourself, you are better able to realize your potential and find the motivation to reach your goals.

a great deal of pleasure and challenge." Realizing our potential *requires* us to conduct an evaluation of our interests, our values, our dreams, and ourselves. It requires us to take risks. So often in this life, we let others tell us what to do and we let them choose our future. It is only when we go through a self-analysis that we set our goals and begin our journey toward achieving our true potential. Simply stated, when we are sure of ourselves and like ourselves, and if we realize our potential and find the motivation to make our dreams come true, success will most likely follow.

PERSONAL VALUES

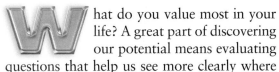hat do you value most in your life? A great part of discovering our potential means evaluating questions that help us see more clearly where we are going—and from where we have come. So many times, we concern ourselves with our friends, our family, or someone else, but spend very little time thinking about our own lives. Has this happened to you? This section in the book is designed to allow you to spend some time with yourself, your values, your ideas, and your life.

In the next section, you will be given an imaginary $100.00. You may spend the money any way that you choose based on your value system. Compare how your values differ from those around you. Your professor will assist you with this exercise.

After the auction is over, your professor will ask you why you bid money on a certain item. Listen carefully to your peers and compare their reasons for bidding on an item or not bidding on an item to your reasons. You'll be surprised how different—and how alike—you may be.

EXERCISE 3.1 *The Values Auction*

DIRECTIONS: Ten items are listed below. You can bid in $5.00 increments. It may be that you want to bid $5.00 on each item, $10.00 on ten items or $100.00 on one item. You cannot spend over $100.00 in total. If someone outbids you, you can move money from any item that you have not purchased. Example: If you have a written bid of $35.00 on "A satisfying religious faith" and someone bids $40.00, you can move money from any item to outbid that person as long as you do not spend over $100.00. Be sure to record the top bid for which the item sold so that you can compare how your views and values may differ from those of your classmates.

The Auction

ITEM TO BE BOUGHT	MY BUDGET	TOP BID
A happy marriage and family	$ _____	$ _____
A chance to be president	$ _____	$ _____
The love of friends	$ _____	$ _____
Self-esteem and confidence	$ _____	$ _____
A healthy life	$ _____	$ _____
A world free of prejudice	$ _____	$ _____
To understand the meaning of life	$ _____	$ _____
Success in a chosen profession	$ _____	$ _____
A satisfying religion	$ _____	$ _____
Unlimited power	$ _____	$ _____

In the Values Auction, what is the item for which you bid the most money?

_____

Why?

_____

_____

_____

For which item did you bid the least amount of money?

_____

Why?

_____

_____

_____

"They are the weakest, however strong, who have no faith in themselves."

CHRISTIAN BOREE

Value systems differ greatly, and it is only when we understand our own values that we can truly begin to appreciate the values of others. This is somewhat complicated by the fact that building self-esteem means knowing our values and ourselves, but it is almost impossible to know what we value without positive self-esteem. We have to work on both issues at the same time and treat both with care and detail.

SELF-ESTEEM

Another area that you will have to consider on the road to achieving your full potential is your self-esteem. Just as you are the only one who can identify and realize your own potential, you are the only one who can give yourself worth. You can be told a thousand times a day that you are kind, gentle, caring, giving, smart, handsome, pretty, or talented, but until you believe in your own strengths, temperament, intellect, looks, or talents, you can never have high self-esteem. The way you feel about yourself determines how you treat other people. Only the very strong people in this world can be sensitive and caring. It is the weak and those with low self-esteem who are cruel and insensitive. Reread that statement and consider it carefully. Often, we think of this situation in the converse, don't we? However, it is only the people who love and respect themselves who can love and respect others. When you begin to discover your potential, you begin to build your self-esteem.

What Is Self-Esteem?

Much research has been done in the areas of self-esteem and self-worth. Basically, self-esteem is the picture or photograph that you hold of yourself in your mind. It is the value you place on "who you are" and "what you are worth." Your self-esteem is learned; you are not born with self-esteem. You develop your self-esteem in part through others in your life. The most important aspect of self-esteem is that no one can give it to you, but many people may try to lower your self-esteem.

Why Is Self-Esteem Important?

Low self-esteem has been linked to many problems in our society. The lack of self-esteem has been traced to poor performance in school, crime, homelessness, teen pregnancy, and even AIDS, to name a few social and academic problems. William Purky, a psychologist, found that there was a direct relationship between self-esteem and academic achievement. Purky also found a relationship between self-esteem and how much people contribute to society. He said, "People with higher self-esteem are more aware of the needs not only of themselves, but of society as a whole. They tend to be more productive members of society and contribute more to the good of the whole population."

Developing Positive Self-Esteem

If you have low self-esteem, you are not going to be able to increase your self-esteem overnight. However, there are ways to begin to develop self-esteem that may have some immediate impact. Building positive self-esteem is a process that takes time. The process should be done in steps. This section of the chapter is designed to help you recognize some important facts about yourself and build a higher self-esteem. Spend some time with these questions and answer them truthfully.

What is the most important statement that you can make about your life?

_____

_____

List three things that you like most about yourself.

1. _____

   Why?

   _____

2. _____

   Why?

   _____

3. _____

   Why?

   _____

Now, list the three things that you would like to improve on or change about yourself and why.

1. _____

   Why?

   _____

2. _____

   Why?

   _____

3. _____

   Why?

   _____

Do you consider yourself to be a positive or negative person? Why?

_____

How do you think others see you?

_____

_____

In the space below, write an advertisement for you as a person.

_____

_____

_____

_____

"Building self-esteem comes with reclaiming that part of ourselves that we put on the sidelines because we felt we didn't deserve to be happy."

ROBINSON

How do you really view yourself? What is the picture you hold in your mind of your life? Many times, you tend to see the bad more clearly than the good, don't you? If you study your responses, you will find that you probably spend much of your time concentrating on the things you like least about yourself, and not nearly enough time concentrating on the things that are beautiful and positive in your life.

Building positive self-esteem is mathematical. It simply requires you to subtract and to add. It requires you to subtract or take away those things in your life that are negative or the things that make you feel bad. It may mean that you have to subtract people, jobs, or even objects from your life. However, building a more positive self-esteem also means that you have to do some addition in your life as well. You have to add things to your life that make you feel good and positive. You can add friends, a new job, a college education, or a new environment.

List three things that make you feel good in your life:

1. _____
2. _____
3. _____

List three things that make you feel bad in your life:

1. _____
2. _____
3. _____

Study the list above. What have you done in the past week to eliminate the bad or negative aspects of your life?

_____

_____

From the list above, what have you done to make sure that you have added positive aspects to your life in the past week?

_____

_____

As mentioned earlier, a child is not born with self-esteem. Children learn their worth from their caregivers. Often, you "learn" what you can or cannot do through your association with other people, not yourself. Many times, you may be told, "you'll never be able to do that" or "you're not smart enough to do that." You've heard the old expression, "tell a child he is dumb long enough, and he'll believe it." All too often, you begin to believe what others tell you about yourself and fail to listen to your inner voice that says, "yes, I can."

When was the last time your negative thoughts came true?

_____

_____

_____

Do you believe that others' actions or words lead you to fail?

_____

_____

_____

_____

Building positive self-esteem is a mathematical process, requiring you to subtract negative aspects from and add positive aspects to your life.

After studying the answers to these questions, you can see how negative thoughts from others or from yourself—from your inner voice—can cause your self-esteem to be lowered. You now must look at ways to build a more positive self-esteem.

It has been said that the only way to conquer fear is to face it head-on. The same is true with building self-esteem. The only way to build a positive self-esteem is to note your shortcomings and do your best to correct them. The best way to correct shortcomings is to take them one at a time. For example, if you listed a fear of public speaking or a lack of public speaking skills as one of the things you would like to improve about yourself, you should develop a plan that allows you to correct the situation slowly. You need to map out a course that will raise your self-esteem in the area of public speaking. For example:

- Choose one person in class whom you do not know very well and begin a conversation with that person.
- Accept an invitation to a party where you know only a few people. You will then be forced to talk with others.

- The next time you have an oral report due in history, biology, or English, look at it as an opportunity, not as a tragedy.
- If you are asked to speak at church or a club meeting, accept the challenge, no matter how difficult it may seem.
- Take a public speaking course as an elective.

This type of planning and risk taking could ease your fear of speaking in public and raise your self-esteem as well. It may not happen overnight, it may take months or years, but at least you are on your way. You can't overcome the fear and raise your self-esteem if you don't start somewhere.

List an area where you would like to feel better about yourself and raise your self-esteem.

_____

_____

Now, plot a course that will help you achieve your ultimate goal and make you feel better about yourself:

Step 1. _____

Step 2. _____

Step 3. _____

Step 4. _____

_____

- Get *involved* in your own life . . . don't let others control you!

One of the easiest ways to maintain low self-esteem is to let other people rule your life. This gives you a sense of helplessness and them a sense of power. When you let other people constantly tell you what to do, you fail to realize your own potential and your self-esteem suffers.

TIP To build high self-esteem, get involved in the decisions that affect your life. Take charge of your future. It is okay to listen to other people's advice, even to ask for their advice, but the decisions that you make should be your own.

- Take negative power *away* from your friends and family.

Many times, you allow other people to create problems and cause your self-esteem to be lowered. You allow them to constantly belittle you, criticize you, and sometimes you join in on the criticism of yourself. This behavior generally is not healthy.

TIP Admit your shortcomings to yourself and tell yourself that you are working on correcting them. If you already know your weaknesses, no one can ever make you feel bad by pointing them out to you. Using this method allows you to take negative power away from those who would hurt you with words.

- Embrace the notion: I am *responsible* for my own life.

When you turn away from your responsibilities and duties in life, you weaken your worth and self-respect. Many times you do not lay claim to your successes or to your failures. When you learn to admit your mistakes, combat your weaknesses, and tell yourself, "I am responsible for me," you begin to build your self-esteem.

TIP Identify an area of your life where you have not taken responsibility, such as your schoolwork, your family chores, or your social duties. Begin to develop a plan or set a goal (Chapter 4) to assume responsibility for your past, your present, and most importantly, your future.

- Focus on your *potential* and your strengths.

So often, you spend your time worrying about what you cannot do and not enough time celebrating your accomplishments and strengths. You beat yourself over the head each time you do not meet a goal or a deadline, but you never pat yourself on the back when you achieve a goal.

TIP Make a list of all the positive things that you know about yourself: "I am smart," "I am a friendly person," "I love my family," "I am a responsible person." Then, post these qualities on your bathroom or bedroom mirror so that you will be able to see them each day. Celebrate your accomplishments in life! Celebrate!

- Control your *"self-talk."*

"Self-talk" is the little voice you hear inside of your head throughout the day. This little voice may very seldom speak positively. Most of the time, the "self-talk" voice is telling you things like: "You're not good enough for that job," "You'll never pass that test," "You're not as smart as Janice," or "John always looks better than you do." Self-talk can be one of the most damaging aspects of your life.

> **TIP**   The next time you hear that little voice go off in your head, make an effort to stop it before it can finish its sentence. Make it a point to mentally say to the little voice, "I am good enough for that job," "I will pass this test," or "I am a nice and caring person." When you learn to control your self-talk, you become one of your own best friends; positive self-esteem will follow.

- Take at least one *positive* risk per week.

So often, you shield yourself from the unknown or from things you fear. This robs you of your potential and steals your self-esteem. Risk taking is one of the most dangerous and one of the hardest things a person can do. However, risk taking is the *only* way to promote growth in your life. It makes you stronger and carries you further than your mind could have imagined. Risk taking builds character.

> **TIP**   Risk taking does not involve putting your life in danger. However, it does involve putting your "comfort zone" in danger. The next time you have the opportunity to do something exciting or new and your little voice (self-talk) begins to chatter negatively, take control of your future and growth and try this new adventure, despite your fear. Once the activity is complete, you will have grown and the fear will not be as great the next time around.

- Stop *comparing* yourself to other people!

Sometimes, you spend your life trying to be as pretty as Judy, as handsome as Tyrone, as smart as Tinaka, or as outgoing as James. When you compare yourself to other people, you are telling yourself that you are not as good as they are and that you do not have as much worth as they do. In time, your little voice begins to believe this and soon, your self-talk reminds you of your "shortcomings" every time you see someone else.

> **TIP**   The next time you begin to compare yourself to another person's looks, intellect, personality, or wealth, remember that every person is different and not all people come from the same background. Celebrate your accomplishments!

- Develop a *victory* wall or a victory file.

Many times you tend to take your accomplishments and hide them in a drawer. You put your certificates or letters of praise in a box and soon you have forgotten a certain accomplishment. When friends send you nice cards of thanks or you receive letters from an old friend, you should keep them in a treasured place so you see them from time to time.

> **TIP**   If you do not have a special place in your residence for cards, letters, certificates, or diplomas/degrees, start one TODAY. When you receive a degree or diploma, a certificate or award of appreciation, frame it and hang it on your wall, or put it on your bookcase so that you can see it often. Start a victory file in a place where you keep good grades, compliments from

teachers, cartoons that make you laugh, and cards that made you feel good. Then, if you have a bad day, go through the file and you'll be surprised how good you feel when you are finished.

- Surround yourself with people who *support* you.

All too often, you keep people in your life who pull you down. You may tell yourself, "I've been friends with Jane since grammar school, and I can't stop being her friend." This is one of the most difficult decisions a person can make, but if Jane is pulling you down and constantly telling you that you are not worthy, Jane has no place in your life.

> **TIP** Send Jane (or anyone who pulls you down) packing! Surround yourself with people who are positive and who support you and your efforts. The smartest and happiest people in this world are those who surround themselves with smart and happy people. Choose your companions and friends carefully.

- Keep your promises and be *loyal* to friends, family, and yourself!

If you have ever had someone break a promise to you, then you know how it feels to have your loyalty betrayed. The most outstanding feature of a person's character is the ability to be loyal and to keep one's word. Few things will make you feel better about yourself and improve your self-image than being a loyal person. Keeping promises and being loyal are trademarks of friendship, maturity, and good citizenship.

> **TIP** If you say that you are going to do something . . . do it. Always check to see if you have the time to do a favor before you say you can. If you can't help, tell them so and ask them to consider you again at a later time.

- Win with *grace* . . . lose with class.

Everyone loves a winner, but everyone also loves a person who can lose with class and dignity. On the other hand, no one loves a bragging winner or a moaning loser. If you are engaged in sports, debate, acting, art shows, math competitions, academic teams, or talent shows, you will encounter winning and losing. We've all heard the old expression, "It's not if you win or lose, but how you play the game." This is one of the hardest things by which to live.

> **TIP** If you win a show or an event, be graceful and tactful. Do not brag to the loser and make them feel worse. This will lower your self-esteem and make you feel bad in the long run. You should always be proud of your accomplishments, but you should never let your "win" overshadow the healthy art of competition. You should always congratulate your opponents and tell them that you are happy to have had the honor to compete with them. If you lose, this does not mean that you were bad or "the worst of them all." It simply means that you had more courage than the 50 percent of the population who would never have tried at all. If you lose, you should never belittle or degrade your opponent. People admire and respect people who can win or lose with grace and style.

- Learn from your *mistakes* . . . move on!

A major sign of maturity and high self-esteem is the ability to admit your shortcomings and mistakes. Part of being human is making mistakes, but few of us know how to admit it when it happens. The most mature and healthy people are those who have learned that mistakes are always going to happen and the best way to deal with them is to admit them, correct what can be corrected, apologize if someone was hurt, and *move on!*

TIP When you make a mistake, never try to blame it on someone else. This can cause your self-esteem to fall. Mature people have learned how to take the "heat" for things they do. Always accept responsibility for your actions and decisions. Never try to overlook a mistake. When you make one, deal with it immediately before it grows into something uncontrollable. Putting off the decision to deal with a mistake only makes it worse. Never take pleasure in calling attention to others' mistakes. If you notice that someone has made an error, show him or her what is wrong, and move on. Never use this as an opportunity to "get the upper hand." Remember, you are human too, and you will make mistakes. Above all, learn from your mistakes. A mistake made over and over again is not a mistake but a lesson never learned.

- See yourself as *successful!*

Just as you need a road map to get to places you've never been, the same is true of your life. You can't be successful if you do not plan your journey and then convince yourself that you *will get there.* You must see yourself as a success before you will ever be one.

TIP Write your goals and objectives on a note card. Post these note cards in your car, on your mirror, on the front of your notebooks . . . anywhere you can see them. When writing your goals, state them as if they are already true. If your goal is to get a well-paying job, your note card might read, "I make $50,000 a year." If your goal is to lose weight, your card might read, "I weigh 120 pounds." This type of statement allows your mind to begin to see the positive effects of your efforts.

Now that you have had the opportunity to reflect on who you are, what your values are, and how they impact self-esteem, complete the Milestones checklist again.

How did you do on this self-analysis? Do you now have a more positive outlook? Are you more positive in the way you view life and your academic goals? Did you learn new ways to increase and enhance your self-esteem? If so, you are well on your journey to becoming a better and more positive student. If not, perhaps you need to spend some additional time going back over the exercises in this chapter and asking a fundamental question: "How do these things affect me today and for the future?"

MILESTONES

NOW THAT YOU ARE HERE . . .

Answer each statement by checking "Y" for Yes, "N" for No, or "S" for Sometimes.

	Y	N	S
1. I am serious about my future.	Ⓨ	Ⓝ	Ⓢ
2. I study at least two hours per week per course hour.	Ⓨ	Ⓝ	Ⓢ
3. I feel better about myself when I manage my time.	Ⓨ	Ⓝ	Ⓢ
4. I enjoy learning.	Ⓨ	Ⓝ	Ⓢ
5. I take risks.	Ⓨ	Ⓝ	Ⓢ
6. I expect a great deal from myself.	Ⓨ	Ⓝ	Ⓢ
7. I often think about my future.	Ⓨ	Ⓝ	Ⓢ
8. I plan for my success.	Ⓨ	Ⓝ	Ⓢ
9. I have high self-esteem.	Ⓨ	Ⓝ	Ⓢ
10. I am a positive person.	Ⓨ	Ⓝ	Ⓢ

Applying What You Know

Now that you have completed this chapter, refer back to the Case Study about Gwen at the beginning of this book. Based on her situation, answer the following questions:

1. Gwen was in college to improve her life and make a better life for her family. What do you hope to gain from your college experience?

2. In Gwen's value system, she saw education as important to her life and to the life of her family. What does your value system tell you about

your own life? How will you apply the reflection you completed in this chapter to your own life?

---

3. Gwen was determined not to let her past educational experiences get her down. What have you learned from examining your past experiences, and how can that help you with the decision to attend college?

Observations

CHARTING YOUR COURSE

Never let anyone put a price tag on you. You are worth more than money, more than cars, and you are worth much more than you probably give yourself credit. Many times you are your own worst enemy and your own worst critic. It is time to start thinking positively about your life and your future. We have all made mistakes and messed things up, sometimes very badly, but as the famous actress Mary Pickford once said, "You can have a fresh start at any point that you please. And suppose that you have tried and tried again and failed and failed again. . . . There is always another chance for you . . . anytime that you choose it."

> *"We are always getting ready to live, but never living."*
>
> R. W. EMERSON

Choose happiness. Choose success. Choose tomorrow. Choose life. Choose to treat others with kindness. Choose to treat yourself with respect. Choose to be the best person you can be. With these mottos, you will realize your potential and your self-esteem will blossom.

Exploring Technology

It might be just as challenging, but surfing the Web is *not* a sport. Americans are becoming more and more sedentary as technology advances. The number of Americans who exercise occasionally increases, but in general Americans are becoming fat and lazy. Sixty percent of all Americans are overweight, and a significant number of children are developing type II diabetes, the type that one normally develops due to inactivity and poor diet. There is no cure for diabetes, just management of the disease. The rise in weight just happens to coincide with the increased popularity of Web surfing. Is there a correlation? There's just so much neat "stuff" on the Internet that people can waste hours and hours a day seeing what's out there. It is fun to be able to locate information on the Web, but a well-rounded person should be involved in a variety of activities.

This assignment should improve your ability to locate information on the Internet and maybe even boost your self-esteem by showing you that you can be technologically "literate." Research the Web to locate the following information:

1. What is the name of the website for the following picture of Andersonville Prison? Name the two locations of Andersonville Prison (provide town and state). Use the "photo" feature of the Excite search engine to do your search.

2. Read about the conditions at Andersonville Prison. What were the daily rations for Union prisoners? What were the daily rations for the Confederate guards?

The following search engines may be helpful:

www.excite.com

www.lycos.com

www.yahoo.com

www.altavista.com

(Adapted from David Eldridge, HSS 205.)

Web Connections

TRAVELING THE INFORMATION SUPERHIGHWAY

During your journey, you may want to check out some of the following Web addresses to assist with enhancing your self-esteem:

www.utexas.edu/student/lsc/handouts/1914.html

www.academicinnovations.com/sesteem.html

www.uwsp.edu/stuserv/counsel/esteem.htm

www.nifl.gov/nalld/nalldmis.htm

As a result of this chapter, and in preparing for my journey, I plan to . . .

Mapping Your Journey

GOAL SETTING AND MOTIVATION

I n the earlier part of this century, a friend's grandfather came to America from Europe. He arrived by ship in the harbor of New York, passing by the Statue of Liberty. After being processed at Ellis Island, he went into a cafeteria in New York City to get something to eat. He sat down at an empty table and waited for someone to take his order. Nobody ever came to his table. Finally, a man with a tray full of food sat down opposite him and told him how things worked in a cafeteria setting. "Start at the end of the line," he said to the old man, "and just go along and pick out what you want. At the end of the line, they'll tell you how much you have to pay for it."

"I soon learned that's how everything works in America," Grandpa told his friend. "Life is a cafeteria here. You can get anything you want as long as you're willing to pay the price. You can even get success. But you'll never get it if you sit at a table and wait for someone to bring it to you. You have to get up and get it yourself."

—FROM *BITS AND PIECES* (V:1)

S hakespeare once said, "nothing will come of nothing." This statement rings true, doesn't it? If there are no plans, there will be no action. If there is no action, there can be no success. This chapter is intended to help you visualize the places where you hope to be in 1, 5, and even 10 years. The exercises in this section are designed to examine your abilities in goal setting and determine your motivational level. Many people in this world have plans and goals, but they do not have the most important things to achieve success—they do not have clear objectives and they do not have motivation.

After reading this chapter and completing the exercises, you will be able to:

- Identify your fears that could hinder you in reaching your goals
- Define internal motivation and external motivation
- Define long-term goals and short-term goals
- Understand what you value most in life and where you are going
- Write down your long-term and short-term goals
- Write specific steps or objectives to reach your goals
- Identify barriers that destroy goals and decrease motivation

"Far better is it to dare mighty things, to win glorious triumphs even though checkered with failure, than to take rank with those poor spirits who neither enjoy much nor suffer much because they live in the gray twilight that knows neither victory nor defeat."

OLIVER WENDELL HOLMES

Using the Milestones checklist, take a few moments to determine where you stand in relation to goal setting and motivation.

If you would like to turn more of your "No" and "Sometimes" answers into "Yes" answers, consider some of the following activities to help you with goal setting and motivation:

- Take some quiet time or uninterrupted time to think about what you value most in life.
- During this quiet time, think also about where you want to go in life and how you are going to get there.
- Once you know what is important to you, where you want to go, and how you are going to get there, you need to develop specific steps to take you there.

If you are not sure how to start these activities, do not be overly concerned. This chapter will help you understand what you value most in life. Your focus or direction in life will be explored and your goals and objectives will be developed. Finally, this chapter will help you learn how to develop motivation.

WHAT DO THESE PEOPLE HAVE IN COMMON?

lbert Einstein was four years old before he could speak and seven before he could read a word.

A newspaper fired **Walt Disney** because he had "no good ideas."

Lorraine Hansberry was raised in a very poor, run-down part of Chicago. She and her family later moved to an upper-class white neighborhood when she was in her teens. She and her family were threatened and called names. Lorraine was almost killed by a concrete slab that was thrown through her window by an angry mob that did not want her family to live in the neighborhood. As a playwright, she went on to become the first black female to have a Broadway show (*A Raisin in the Sun*) and the first black female ever to win the New York Drama Critics' Circle Award.

Abraham Lincoln dropped out of grade school; ran a country store and went broke; took 15 years to pay off his bills; lost a race for the state legislature at the age of 32; failed in a second business; ran for the State House, lost twice; ran for the Senate, lost twice; finally ran for president and won, but was hated by half of the country. Eventually, he became one of the most famous leaders in the world.

Winston Churchill was a poor student who stuttered. He won a Nobel Prize at the age of 24 and became one of the most powerful leaders and speakers in the world.

WHERE ARE YOU NOW?

Answer each statement by checking "Y" for Yes, "N" for No, or "S" for Sometimes.

1. I use goals to guide my actions.	(Y) (N) (S)
2. Goals are important to me.	(Y) (N) (S)
3. I often set goals.	(Y) (N) (S)
4. I write down objectives that shape my goals.	(Y) (N) (S)
5. I face my fears head-on.	(Y) (N) (S)
6. I take responsibility for my life.	(Y) (N) (S)
7. I know where I want to be in three to five years.	(Y) (N) (S)
8. Having more than one goal is important to me.	(Y) (N) (S)
9. When I reach a goal, I celebrate.	(Y) (N) (S)
10. I internalize my goals.	(Y) (N) (S)

Malcolm X was abandoned as a child, was very poor, and spent time in prison as a young adult. He later became one of the most powerful speakers and leaders for the Civil Rights Movement of the 1960s.

What did these people have in common? Luck? A tooth fairy? A genie in a lamp? No. They had . . .

Goals! Objectives! Motivation!

ELIMINATING FEAR

Two Fears That Hinder Growth And Stifle Motivation:

The Fear of Failure • The Fear of Change

Beginning your journey means realizing that every fear you have is learned. That's right, learned! You are born with only two fears: the fear of loud noises and the fear of falling; the rest are learned. Many times, your progress and success are limited because you are afraid to move forward, afraid to take chances, or afraid to set goals beyond what you already know how to do.

Every person has a "comfort zone." You can say that the comfort zone is the "little box" in which you live and feel safe. This is the small space where you feel comfortable and secure. The reason for goal setting, writing objectives, and developing motivation is to *expand* your comfort zone so that you will feel safe and secure in more activities, with more people, doing more things, and traveling to more places. The famous artist Vincent Van Gogh once said, "The best way to know life is to love many things." The best way to love many things, and in the end, know life better, is to take chances, set goals, be motivated, and expand your comfort zone.

> *"Come to the edge," he said. They said, "We are afraid." "Come to the edge," he said. They came. He pushed them . . . and they flew.*
>
> GUILLAUME APOLLINAIRE

This sounds easy, doesn't it? Actually, many people have goals, but they are afraid to move forward, or they do not know how to move forward. Often, your fears rest on very weak ground. If you examine why you are afraid to leave your comfort zone, you realize that the reasons are simple and the solutions to these fears can be even simpler. The first fear that you should conquer is the fear of failure. Goals are meaningless if you are afraid to go after them. Many times, you may have said to yourself, "I could never do that—I'd fail and I don't want to fail." Now you have to ask yourself, "Is it better to try and fail or never to try at all?" The answer, once again, is quite simple. You know in your mind that it is always better to try and fail than never to try at all. Think about where our civilization would be if we had been afraid to deal with fire, afraid to build the first town, afraid to fly, or afraid to build a building with more than one story. Failure is a part of growth.

Think about it. You learn a great deal from your failures, don't you? Remember when you were young and you tried to ride your bicycle for the first time without training wheels? It was scary and you probably wrecked a few times before you were able to ride with success. But you overcame your fear and learned how to ride without training wheels. You mastered your fear.

Some of your strength comes from difficult situations in which your comfort zones were stretched. It is a guarantee that if you take chances beyond your comfort zone, you may get knocked down a few times. You may have a few failures. We've all been there, haven't we? However, it is also a guarantee that if you do not take chances beyond your comfort zone, you may not grow. Remember the old saying, "That which does not kill us, makes us stronger."

The fear of change is another thing that can rob you of your hopes and dreams. Humans are creatures of habit, and in that light, change is neither natural nor desired. Change causes a great deal of frustration and physical reaction. Change can make you feel nervous, tense, afraid, guilty, tired, depressed, and even angry. However, when planning your goals, it is helpful to realize that change is one of the few things in this world that is guaranteed. You can't stop it. The most successful people in this world are those who have learned how to deal with change and accept it as a part of life.

> Change is never easy.
>
> Change is almost always met with resistance.
>
> The person who brings about change is usually not liked very well.
>
> Change creates unfamiliar ground.
>
> Change takes courage.

Just as change can be frustrating and trying, change can also be exciting and rewarding. Change keeps us alive. For us to learn how to communicate with new people, feel comfortable in new situations, and develop new ideas, change must occur. In order to deal with change, remember the words in the box above.

In the questions below, take a moment to reflect on your life and what situations cause you fear and possibly hinder you from growth.

List five activities that you feel comfortable doing:

1. _____
2. _____
3. _____
4. _____
5. _____

List three activities that you would like to do but are afraid to try. Explain why you are afraid to try them. Explain what would encourage you to do this activity.

1. _____

I am afraid because

_____

_____

What would make you do this activity?

_____

_____

2. _____

I am afraid because

_____

_____

What would make you do this activity?

_____

_____

3. _____

I am afraid because

_____

_____

What would make you do this activity?

_____

_____

List three people with whom you feel comfortable and indicate why.

1. _____

    Because _____

2. _____

    Because _____

3. _____

    Because _____

List three people with whom you would not feel comfortable. Explain why you are uncomfortable and what it would take to make you spend time with this person.

1. _____

    Because _____

    What would make you spend time?

    _____

    _____

2. _____

    Because _____

    What would make you spend time?

    _____

    _____

3. _____

    Because _____

    _____

    _____

    What would make you spend time?

    _____

    _____

Review your answers. If you spend some time reviewing your responses to the second and fourth questions, you will find that your fears are probably rooted in family traditions or that you could not come up with many reasons. You may have even written statements like, "I've never done it before," or "I just don't know them very well."

A major part of your education is learning how to expand your horizons through people, places, and things with which you are not familiar. Fear can play a major role in keeping your comfort zone small and stagnant.

- Don't be afraid to fail.
- Don't be afraid to change.
- Don't be afraid to take chances.
- Don't be afraid to go beyond what you know and feel at this moment.

A major part of your education is learning how to expand your horizons through new people, places, interests, and activities.

You'll be amazed at how quickly your comfort zone will grow once you overcome your fears, learn how to set goals, and discover your motivation.

WHAT IS A GOAL?

Webster's New Collegiate Dictionary defines a goal as "the end toward which effort is directed." Have you ever wanted a new car, a CD player, or a new outfit? If you have, then you have had a goal—the goal of getting one or all of these physical, material things. Goals are simply what you want and what you are willing to do to get them.

There are two types of goals that we must discuss—obtainable and unobtainable. We can also call these goals "realistic" and "unrealistic." The obtainable or "realistic" goal is well-defined, well-planned, well-organized, and mapped out carefully. The unobtainable or "unrealistic" goal is one that is not clearly defined, is open-ended, poorly organized, and unmapped. It is a goal that you might say you want, but one to which you have not committed yourself. In other words, you have not developed a plan to reach this goal.

Goals also have timelines. You can have short- and long-term goals. Short-term goals may be things such as:

- I want to purchase a new CD player.
- I want to make an A on my next English test.

Years ago Dr. Albert Einstein was traveling on a train headed west. During the early part of the trip, Dr. Einstein looked up and saw the train's conductor coming down the aisle asking passengers for their tickets. Dr. Einstein began looking for his ticket. He looked in his coat pockets, he looked in his pants pockets, and he looked around his seat but was unable to find his ticket. When the conductor approached him, Einstein stated that he could not find his ticket, at which point the conductor said that he knew who he was and it was no problem. Nevertheless, Dr. Einstein continued to look for his ticket. The conductor assured him several times that he knew who he was and that it was okay if he could not find his ticket. Finally, Dr. Einstein said to the conductor, "Young man, I know who I am, but I don't know where I am going."

DON'T BE AFRAID TO FAIL

You've failed many times,

although you may not

remember.

You fell down the first time

you tried to walk.

You almost drowned

the first time you tried to

swim, didn't you?

Did you hit the ball the first time

you swung a bat?

Heavy hitters,

the ones who hit the

most home runs,

also strike

out a lot.

R. H. Macy

failed seven times

before his store in New York

caught on.

English novelist John Casey

got 753 rejection slips

before he published 564 books.

Babe Ruth struck out 1,330 times,

but he also hit

714 home runs.

Don't worry about

failure.

Worry about the

chances you miss

when you don't even try.

unknown

Long-term goals are more elaborate and planned:

- I want to be a doctor.
- I want to get married and have three children.

Both long-term and short-term goals are important. Today's generation has been accused of having no long-term goals, seeking instant gratification. Goals take sacrifice, planning, and a great deal of hard work; without goals, your life becomes rudderless. A well-known athletic ad states, "No Pain, No Gain!" In other words, if you do not set your goals, sacrifice what is needed to achieve them, and work hard, there will be no gain.

WHY ARE GOALS IMPORTANT?

How do you feel about goal setting? Studies, research, professionals, friends, family, and foes will tell you that goals are one of the most important aspects of life. But why? Why must you have them? Why are they so important? Perhaps nowhere can you find a more powerful answer than that given in a study conducted in 1953 by Yale University. Though the study is old, it is important to look at it because it reveals a very important fact about goal setting.

A survey was given to the senior class. They were asked several questions, three of which dealt with goals. The questions were: "Have you set goals?" "Have you written them down?" and "Do you have a plan to accomplish these goals?" Very few seniors answered "yes" to these questions; only about 3 percent of the entire senior class.

Twenty years later, many members of this class were surveyed again. The research showed that the 3 percent of the class who set goals were happier and more successful than those who did not have goals. However, the most astonishing fact was that the 3 percent who set goals had 97 percent of the wealth of the entire class. In other words, these *goal setters were wealthier than the entire rest of the class combined!* We do *not* want to suggest that money equals success; we do, however, want to suggest that setting goals, for any outcome, can lead to accomplishment.

TYPES OF GOALS

Goals come in a variety of packages. There are as many goals as there are people who set them. People can have many goals in many different parts of their lives. Goals may be in such categories as:

1. Social well-being
2. Academic/mental well-being
3. Physical well-being
4. Spiritual well-being
5. Family/friends
6. Financial well-being

Some examples of the basic goals are listed below.

SOCIAL WELL-BEING GOAL: I will learn how to meet new people by attending two school functions per month.

ACADEMIC/MENTAL WELL-BEING GOAL: I will make an A on my research paper in history by doing the research early, writing a rough draft, and making an appointment with my instructor.

PHYSICAL WELL-BEING GOAL: I will lose 25 pounds by December 31st by watching my fat grams and exercising.

SPIRITUAL WELL-BEING GOAL: I will spend 30 minutes a day in prayer and meditation.

FAMILY/FRIENDS GOAL: I will spend more time with my family by devoting two Saturdays per month to them.

FINANCIAL WELL-BEING GOAL: I will save $1,000 in one year by opening a savings account and contributing $19.23 per week.

Your goals do not have to fall into one of these categories used as examples. In addition to the goals listed, there could be self-improvement goals, career goals, community service goals, artistic goals, etc. The most important thing is that your goal should be your own; it should be internalized.

Goals Work!

"You are never given a wish without the power to make it come true."

RICHARD BACH

"Where there is no vision, the people perish."

PROVERBS 29:18

HOW TO WRITE A GOAL

Goal setting seems rather easy, doesn't it? Actually, it may take some time and thought and preparation for them to come true. An obtainable and realistic goal statement should have the following in order to work:

1. An action statement
2. Objectives
3. Target date (deadline)

"The greater danger for most of us is not that our aim is too high and we miss it, but that it is too low and we reach it."

MICHELANGELO

However, the goal statement is the third part of a four-part process. This four-part process is as follows:

- Values: What do you value most in life?
- Purpose/Focus/Direction: Where are you going in life?
- Dreams/Goals: How are you going to get there?
- Objectives/Activities: What specific steps are you taking to achieve your goals?

You must start with values and focus before you can get serious about writing goals and objectives. Once you have defined your values and your focus or direction in life you can start writing down goals. Exercise 4.2, the Goal Setting sheet on page 98, is a valuable tool to help you plan for your future. The two examples that follow illustrate how this process moves from life values to direction to goals to specific objectives with deadlines. Your values and direction can, but do not need to, be repeated each time you complete a Goal Setting sheet. Each Goal Setting sheet should begin with one value, something that you value most in life. This value should be followed by one direction or focus for your life. The focus leads to one obtainable, realistic goal that is followed by a very specific list of objectives or steps that you need to take to reach your goal within a specific deadline.

Goal Setting: Example One

VALUES. What do you value most in life?

A meaningful, professional career in a health profession.

PURPOSE/FOCUS/DIRECTION. Where are you going in life?

I will focus on becoming a successful registered nurse.

DREAMS/GOALS. How are you going to get there?

Obtain a college degree in nursing.

OBJECTIVES/ACTIVITIES. What specific steps are you taking to achieve your goal?

SEQUENCE	OBJECTIVE/ACTIVITY	DEADLINE
1.	Register for college	August 8
2.	Meet academic advisor	August 9
3.	Select courses to take	August 9
4.	Obtain financial aid	August 11
5.	Attend first class	September 5

Goal Setting: Example Two

VALUES. What do you value most in life?

A meaningful, professional career in a health profession.

PURPOSE/FOCUS/DIRECTION. Where are you going in life?

I will focus on becoming a successful registered nurse.

DREAMS/GOALS. How are you going to get there?

I will get a grade of A in my English class.

OBJECTIVES/ACTIVITIES. What specific steps are you taking to achieve your goal?

SEQUENCE	OBJECTIVE/ACTIVITY	DEADLINE
1.	Develop a study plan for English	August 5
4.	Prepare for presentation	August 12
2.	Report due from John Smith	August 25
3.	Report due from Jane Jones	August 25

Remember that a goal must be one that can be measured. In other words, you must be able to prove that it was completed. See below for an example.

GOAL 1: I will save (*the action statement*) $100 by putting back $10 a week (*the objective*). I will have $100 dollars by January 31 (*target date*).

Some goals will be more complicated and have more steps to complete. See another example below.

GOAL 2: I will lose (*the action statement*) 25 pounds by December 31st (*target date*).

OBJECTIVES:

- Eat the proper number of calories
- Consume less fat
- Walk four miles five days per week

Both goals, however, are obtainable and measurable. You can measure them by having $100 in the bank and by using scales to weigh yourself.

Goals should be written in a positive fashion using action verbs. A poorly written goal might read like this:

I want to try to lose 10 or 15 pounds this summer.

This goal will never be obtained. Why? It has no purpose, it has no action, it has no target date, and it has no objectives.

WHAT IS AN OBJECTIVE?

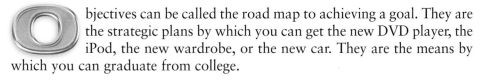 bjectives can be called the road map to achieving a goal. They are the strategic plans by which you can get the new DVD player, the iPod, the new wardrobe, or the new car. They are the means by which you can graduate from college.

Let's look at several goals and work through a few objectives for achieving the goal.

SHORT-TERM GOAL

GOAL: I want to purchase a new DVD player.

OBJECTIVE(S):

1. Find a part-time job
2. Save $10.00 a week
3. Save my income tax refund
4. Shop around for an affordable DVD player
5. Buy the DVD player

LONG-TERM GOAL

GOAL: I want to be a nurse.

OBJECTIVE(S):

1. Enroll in a nursing degree program
2. Study at least three hours per night
3. Maintain at least a 3.5 GPA
4. Complete my degree
5. Pass all national and state boards
6. Begin to practice nursing as a profession

Although some of your goals may not be this big, all goals require objectives and plans. DVD players are never purchased and nurses never practice without goal setting, planning, sacrifice, and hard work.

ROADBLOCKS TO SUCCESS: BARRIERS TO ACHIEVING YOUR GOALS

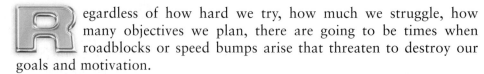egardless of how hard we try, how much we struggle, how many objectives we plan, there are going to be times when roadblocks or speed bumps arise that threaten to destroy our goals and motivation.

Create a list of barriers that could possibly keep you from achieving your goals.

1. _____
2. _____
3. _____
4. _____
5. _____

You may have listed things like money, time, family, transportation, child care, lack of basic skills, peer pressure, alcohol/drug addiction, or lack of motivation.

Using your list, talk with the group assigned by your professor and create some ideas of where you can go to find assistance in overcoming these barriers. Often, we can easily point out to ourselves and others why we *cannot* do something, but we less often take the time to try to resolve the problems and eliminate the barrier.

Create a list of college and community resources that can assist you in overcoming your barriers.

1. *I can find help* _____

   _____

2. *I can find help* _____

   _____

3. *I can find help* _____

   _____

4. *I can find help* _____

   _____

5. *I can find help* _____

   _____

You may have listed some of the places identified in the following box. Review this list because it may give you some ideas of where to find help that you and your group may not have thought of.

CAMPUS AND COMMUNITY RESOURCES

Financial Aid Office	Personal Counseling Center	Campus Health Services
Veterans' Office	Computer Assistance Center	Community Drug and Alcohol Center
Mature Student (Nontraditional) Services	Campus Religious Organization	Community Organizations
Minority Student Services	Student Organizations	Churches, Synagogues, Mosques, Temples
Disabled Student Services	Hall or Residence Counselors	Family and Friends
Career Counseling Office	Professors	Former High School Teachers or Counselors
Academic Assistance Center	Staff Members	
Peer Tutoring Center	The Campus Library	

TRAVELING THE ROAD ON YOUR OWN . . . MOTIVATION

What Is Motivation?

Motivation is a *force*, the driving force that causes you to do something . . . to *act!* Without motivation, you achieve little. You can have all the goals and objectives in the world, but without motivation, not much will happen. You not only have to write goals and set objectives, but you have to work at becoming a motivated person. You have to actually do something with your plans and goals.

> *"It ain't enough to get the breaks, you gotta be willing to use 'em."*
>
> HUEY P. LONG

Why Is Motivation Important?

For many of you, this is the first time in your life that you are on your own. It may be a strange experience for some of you. For others, it may be one of the most exciting things you have ever done. You may be living at school, living in an off-campus apartment, or have a home of your own. Some of you may be completely on your own for the first time in your life. Others of you may have your first full-time or part-time job. Many of you maintain families, relationships, and outside commitments while going to school full time. For some students, this may be the first time that you have left your child in the care of someone else. Many students today have many things "pulling" at them from many directions.

At this point in your life, there may be many people pulling at you but no one is *pushing* you. No one to wake you up and put you on a bus or drag you to the car so that you can make it on time. If you go to class, fine. If you don't go to class, that's okay too! Or is it? You will have some teachers who do not care if you are there or not. You will have some teachers who never take attendance. It may be that you are in a class so large that the instructor never knows your name. More often than not, however, your professors *will* care if you come to class. Many professors *do* take class roll, and lots of professors, regardless of the size of the class, *know* your name. So, it is very important that you not adopt the attitude that it is okay not to attend class. The motivation to go to class and do well in school will have to come from within.

> Nothing in this world can take the place of persistence.
>
> Talent will not;
>
> nothing is more common than unsuccessful people with talent.
>
> Genius will not;
>
> unrewarded genius is almost a proverb.
>
> Education will not;
>
> the world is full of educated derelicts.
>
> Persistence and determination alone are eternal.
>
> The slogan "press on" has solved and always will solve the problems of the human race.
>
> *Calvin Coolidge*

List the things that motivate you in your life.

_____

_____

_____

_____

You may have listed such things as:

Family   Religion or Spirituality

Friends   Money

Learning

INTERNAL VS. EXTERNAL GOALS AND MOTIVATION

Internal (adj.) Existing within the limits or surface of something; situated inside of the body.

External (adj.) Having the outward appearance of something; situated outside of the body.

The most important step in goal setting and objective writing is to determine if your goals and objectives are internal or external. There comes a point when you have to stop, take a moment, reflect, and ask yourself, "Am I doing this for myself or for someone else?" Whether you are setting goals, striving to find motivation, or simply stepping along from day to day, you should develop a clear picture of what you want, why you want it, and *why* you are performing the action to get it. In other words, "Why are you in college?" "Why are you working at that job of yours?" So often, you push yourself from day to day feeling unhappy, dissatisfied, frustrated, and even angry because you have to do certain things. Usually, you are most unhappy or unsatisfied when you are doing something that you do not enjoy or something that someone is making you do.

Realizing that every person must do certain things that are unpleasant or not fulfilling is the first step in finding motivation. However, the happiest person in the world is one who has discovered how to internalize these unpleasant tasks and set additional goals based on internal motivation.

Example: When Ben was going to college, he had to pay all of his tuition. His parents were unable to assist him. He worked in a factory for seven years while working his way through his bachelor's and master's degrees. However, there were two summers after his sophomore and junior years during which he found an additional part-time job with a local sewer district. The hourly pay rate was the highest he had ever made in his life at that time. However, you can imagine how he hated that job. Hot! Nasty! Horrible odors! Disgusting! He dreaded getting up each morning because he knew what the day would bring. He worked in the sewers from 8:00 A.M. until 2:00 P.M. and then went to work in the factory from 4:00 P.M. until 12:00 A.M. It was not an easy or satisfying life.

It was during this time in his life that he learned how to internalize this activity and look at it as a

When completing daily tasks and jobs that may seem unpleasant or boring, internalize your goals to help you maintain motivation to achieve those goals.

stepping-stone. Soon, his bank account grew, he was able to pay off his used car, and finally, he saw enough money in his account to pay for his fall and spring tuition! The days of working in the sewer and the factory were not as hard for him because he internalized his goals. He saw this as an opportunity to get what he eventually wanted, not as a horrible life unfit for living. He began to work for his future and not look at each day as a tragedy. He embraced the fact that he had a job that paid well and that he would use this job to make a better life for himself and his family.

Had Ben looked at it as just a job, he would have never been able to live through it. He often said that he would have quit the sewer job and would have left the factory shortly thereafter had he not internalized those tasks. By quitting, however, he would have robbed himself of a college education. When he internalized this job and looked at it from the perspective of his future, it made the situation bearable.

This is how you should look at your daily tasks that are unpleasant or boring and how you must set your goals. You should look at them in terms of "the end result"—what you eventually want. Internalizing your goals will help you develop motivation and eventually reach your goal.

From the list that you generated previously, divide your motivators into:

INTERNAL MOTIVATORS

_____

_____

_____

_____

EXTERNAL MOTIVATORS

_____

_____

_____

_____

Now that we have discussed goal setting, objectives, roadblocks, and motivation, you are ready to begin planning a goal and working toward it. Exercise 4.1 is a goal-setting exercise that will assist you in plotting your course and setting goals. Use this exercise to develop the skill of goal setting. Once you are comfortable with this process, use the Goal Setting sheet and the tracking system to file and track your goals to their successful completion.

EXERCISE 4.1 *Goal Setting*

For practice, in the spaces provided below, describe a short-term and a long-term goal. Once you are comfortable with this process, use copies of the Goal Setting sheet found in Exercise 4.2 to record and track your progress on each of your goals.

Write a short-term goal.

_____

_____

_____

Why is the goal important to you?

_____

_____

_____

List the objectives:

_____

_____

_____

Target date: _____

Barriers to overcome:

_____

_____

_____

Write a long-term goal.

_____

_____

_____

Why is the goal important to you?

_____

_____

_____

List the objectives:

_____

_____

_____

Target date: _____

Barriers to overcome:

_____

_____

_____

EXERCISE 4.2 *Goal Setting Sheet*

VALUES. *What do you value most in life?*

_____
_____
_____
_____

PURPOSE/FOCUS/DIRECTION. *Where are you going in life?*

_____
_____
_____
_____

DREAMS/GOALS. *How are you going to get there?*

_____
_____
_____
_____

OBJECTIVES/ACTIVITIES. *What specific steps are you taking to achieve your goal?*

SEQUENCE	OBJECTIVE/ACTIVITY	DEADLINE

Now that you have had the opportunity to think about what you value most in life, to determine where you are going in life, to write goals and specific steps or objectives for reaching your goals, and to internalize motivation, complete the Milestones checklist again to see how much you have improved.

How did you do this time on the self-analysis? You should have more "Yes" answers this time and should be more self-confident and more motivated. In addition, you should have a written plan of where you are going and how to get there.

MILESTONES

NOW THAT YOU ARE HERE. . .

Answer each statement by checking "Y" for Yes, "N" for No, or "S" for Sometimes.

1. I use goals to guide my actions.	Ⓨ Ⓝ Ⓢ
2. Goals are important to me.	Ⓨ Ⓝ Ⓢ
3. I often set goals.	Ⓨ Ⓝ Ⓢ
4. I write down objectives that shape my goals.	Ⓨ Ⓝ Ⓢ
5. I face my fears head-on.	Ⓨ Ⓝ Ⓢ
6. I take responsibility for my life.	Ⓨ Ⓝ Ⓢ
7. I know where I want to be in three to five years.	Ⓨ Ⓝ Ⓢ
8. Having more than one goal is important to me.	Ⓨ Ⓝ Ⓢ
9. When I reach a goal, I celebrate.	Ⓨ Ⓝ Ⓢ
10. I internalize my goals.	Ⓨ Ⓝ Ⓢ

ROADWAYS

- Carefully *examine* your life to determine what you value most.

- Determine where you are *going* in life.

- Seek *advice* from people who have achieved your goal. Ask them how they got it and if it was worth going through what they had to endure.

- Set your goals *high,* but be realistic.

- Set goals that can be *measured*.

- Set *both* long- and short-term goals.

- Develop a plan to *achieve* your goals or objectives.

- Write clear *objectives* that can be reached in steps.

- Look at your goals and objectives *one step* at a time.

- *Internalize* your goals so that they become your own.

- Find something that *motivates* you and stick with it.

- Tell people about your goals, ask for their *help* in reaching them.

- Don't let setbacks cripple you. Look at it as a lesson and *move on*.

- Don't let *others* dictate your goals to you. Set your own goals.

- Write your goals and objectives utilizing the Goal Setting sheet and *track* them until success-fully obtained.

- Use a *planner* to track your goals.

- Think *positively*. Good things come to those who wait . . . and work hard.

Applying What You Know

Goal setting is a difficult task for many people. There is some fear involved as well as a commitment of time and energy to accomplish a realistic goal. Goal accomplishment in many cases involves the whole person: mind, body, and spirit. Now that you have finished this chapter on goal setting and motivation, refer back to the Case Study about Gwen at the beginning of this book. Based on her situation, answer the following questions:

1. What goal-setting and motivational strategies or techniques should Gwen utilize?

2. What internal and external motivators should Gwen rely upon to inspire her to address her new challenge that going to college creates?

3. How can Gwen use the Goal Setting sheet presented in Exercise 4.2 to assist her in achieving her goals?

Observations

CHARTING YOUR COURSE

The remaining chapters in this book will be useless to you if you have not mastered the art of goal setting, objective writing, and motivation building. The most important aspect of this chapter is that it can't really be taught to you. Your instructor can show you how to write down a goal and how to construct an objective list, but beyond that, your instructor has no control or power. *You are in control!*

No one can write your goals for you. No one can live your life for you. No one can finish your education for you. No one can motivate you except yourself. Remember that you are never given a wish without the power to make it come true.

DETOUR

Getting There on Time

A logical and effective way to track your goals and your Goal Setting sheets is to file and reference them to your planner. Please refer to the sections on using a time planner in Chapter 2 for a review of this process. Once you have completed a Goal Setting sheet, you can file this sheet and reference it in your planner. However, please understand that this is only the first step in effectively tracking your goals.

It is very important to complete all four sections of the Goal Setting sheet. Once you have determined what you value most, where you are going, and what goals and means to achieve those goals you have, then you must add specific objectives and set deadlines for the accomplishment of each objective. The deadlines are used to record the objectives or activities in sequence in your planner. Where do you record these objective deadlines? The best place to record and track your deadlines is on an "Assignments Due" section in your planner. Naturally, you need to write this objective on the date that it is due. For example, in Chapter 2 in the sections on "Daily Planning" and "Priorities and To-Do Lists," two teammate reports for a joint presentation are discussed and recorded in the "Assignments Due" section on August 25th. Please refer to the two "Goal Setting" examples in this chapter to understand where these two objectives originated.

In the first "Goal Setting" example, it was stated that a meaningful, professional career in a health profession was one thing of greatest value in life. The focus of this value was to become a successful registered nurse. The goal that was listed was to obtain a college degree in nursing. Finally, in the objectives section, registering in a college, meeting with an academic advisor, selecting specific courses, obtaining financial aid, and attending classes were listed as objectives with specific deadlines. The second example of goal setting was more specific and detailed. In this example, a specific course grade was the goal with several objectives. Two of these objectives were the reports from John Smith and Jane Jones.

Where is the best place to record and track the reports due from John Smith and Jane Jones? This question has already been answered. "Report from John Smith" and "Report from Jane Jones" are recorded on the date due, August 25th, in the planner on the "Daily Schedule" page. This systematic approach will ensure that you stay on track, that you do not forget any reports, projects, papers, etc., and that your objectives and final goals are met.

Exploring Technology

In Chapter 2, Time Management, you had an opportunity to experiment with the Microsoft Outlook calendar and task pad. Some of the tasks that you must accomplish each day are really objectives or activities that support the accomplishment of your goals. Review one of your major goals and its objectives/activities, look at the month that you chose in the Microsoft Outlook calendar and task pad, and record your objectives for this goal on the various days that you feel you will be able to address them. Update the task pad at the end of each day and carry forward any tasks that were not completed to another day. At the end of the month, assess where you are in achieving your goal and carry forward to the next month those objectives or tasks that can be accomplished in that month. By participating in this activity, you are taking your time-management and goal-setting skills to the next level; that is, the electronic or computerized level.

Web Connections

TRAVELING THE INFORMATION SUPERHIGHWAY

Numerous websites deal with goal setting and motivation. Check out the following Web addresses to assist you in achieving your goals and motivating yourself to excellence.

www.mygoalmanager.com

www.selfgrowth.com/

www.topachievement.com

www.mindtools.com/page6.html

As a result of this chapter, and in preparing for my journey, I plan to . . .

Sights, Sounds, and Sensations

5

INFORMATION PROCESSING AND LEARNING STYLES

Math. How Andre hated that subject! It didn't matter how hard Andre studied—he couldn't get it. He could remember his parents, teachers, and friends getting on his case about studying. Andre did study! He even had tutors! But, nothing seemed to work. He was discouraged and frustrated, and Andre knew he was doomed to never make a grade better than a D (and that was on a good day).

One day, all that changed. It was Andre's freshman year in college. He never forgot that first class with Mr. Lane. Mr. Lane explained that math was about to become everyone's favorite subject. Andre thought he was crazy! That'll be the day, he thought.

Lo and behold, Mr. Lane was able to change Andre's attitude toward math. He first explained how important it was that we think positively and believe that we could master numbers. Sure, some students would have to work hard, but Mr. Lane explained that in order to really understand math we needed to see it, hear it, and touch it. For example, he told us to use our fingers when counting and to remove our shoes and use our toes if we had to.

He was an excellent teacher. He really did show the class how to see, hear, and touch math. For the first time in his life, Andre understood what he was doing. It was as if someone had unlocked a door that was blocking his way. Andre got an 88 out of 100 on his first test. He even managed to pass the class with an 82!

Perhaps Andre's fear of math sounds familiar to you. The story about Andre is quite common. Many students share these same fears, anxieties, and academic frustrations over math and other subjects. Fortunately, Mr. Lane was there to show this student how to master a tough subject.

Students often give up or quit learning new material because they do not comprehend it right away. What they do not realize is that they may not have been processing information correctly. Andre's story is a perfect example of how learning involves seeing, hearing, and touching the information in order to understand it.

The intention of this chapter is to show you how to become a successful student by applying information-processing theory and learning-style theory when trying to master information. This chapter will teach you how to use a holistic approach to process information with all five senses, thus pointing

"He who has no inclination to learn more will be very apt to think he knows enough."

JOHN POWELL

the way to academic success. Being a student means accepting responsibility for learning the information presented to you. In a nutshell, when you understand how material is processed by your brain and how to use your preferred learning style, you can overcome academic barriers.

At the end of this chapter, if you complete the exercises, participate in class, read the additional assignments that may be issued by your instructor, and keep an open mind, you will be able to do the following tasks:

- Define information-processing and learning-preference theories
- Identify your preferred learning style
- Create and use learning-style strategies to learn and recall information
- Use a global and analytical approach to processing information
- Use mnemonic devices, or "memory tricks," to store and recall information

Studying is not necessarily a natural or easy activity for everyone. It is, however, a learned skill in which you can become proficient if you are aware of your own individual learning style. In the box at right, you will find 10 questions intended to cause you to think about how you learn and process information. Please consider carefully each statement and then answer each one as honestly as possible.

How did you do with the self-analysis? Are you familiar with any of the terms presented? Do you understand that there are different ways in which we learn? If you are unfamiliar with any or all of the terms used, do not despair—this chapter is intended to teach you as much as possible about learning styles and the various ways in which people learn.

WHERE ARE YOU NOW?

Answer each statement by checking "Y" for Yes, "N" for No, or "S" for Sometimes.

1. I understand how the brain processes information.		Ⓨ Ⓝ Ⓢ
2. I know my preferred learning style.		Ⓨ Ⓝ Ⓢ
3. I use a variety of senses when studying and learning.		Ⓨ Ⓝ Ⓢ
4. I enjoy learning.		Ⓨ Ⓝ Ⓢ
5. I know how a visual learner processes information.		Ⓨ Ⓝ Ⓢ
6. I know how a kinesthetic learner learns.		Ⓨ Ⓝ Ⓢ
7. I know the characteristics of a global thinker.		Ⓨ Ⓝ Ⓢ
8. I know how an auditory learner learns.		Ⓨ Ⓝ Ⓢ
9. I use mnemonic devices.		Ⓨ Ⓝ Ⓢ
10. I know how to store information in long-term memory.		Ⓨ Ⓝ Ⓢ

INFORMATION PROCESSING THEORY

Learning and processing information are primarily functions of the brain. The human brain is divided into two halves, called the left and right hemispheres, that deal with information in different ways. The human brain functions best when both sides are able to work together. The left hemisphere is the part of the brain that does the thinking and reasoning. It exhibits most of the characteristics associated with analytical thinking. The right hemisphere controls mostly feelings and actions. It gives us most of the characteristics associated with "global" thinking. The two styles of thinking are of equal importance, each balancing the other and contributing to learning and information processing.

If you discover how you learn best, you can apply that knowledge to each class—you may even be able to help your instructors teach you more effectively.

Traditional school settings are designed to meet the needs of students who think analytically (i.e., those likely to find reading, writing, and math easy to learn). However, there are many students who fail to learn in school or experience difficulties understanding new information. Many of these students are global thinkers and need to use this strength to master the analytical skills. When students use analytical and global thinking together (i.e., using both halves of the brain), learning becomes easier. As a student, it may be useful to figure out what type of thinker you are (analytical or global) and how to use both types of thinking at the same time.

It is important that you understand that you have strengths associated with both types of processing. Everyone, however, has a dominant style. The inventory on the following page will help you to identify the style of thinking that is dominant for you. Stop reading now and complete the inventory before going on.

Most individuals spend about 70 percent of their time completing and participating in analytical activities and only about 30 percent of their time in global activities. By learning how to develop both styles of processing or thinking, students can significantly improve their ability to learn.

Because everyone has a preference for one style of thinking or the other, the key to successful learning is to use both styles of thinking at the same time. For example, if you are unorganized and always forgetting assignments, then writing down assignments would be very helpful to you as a student. In addition, when taking notes, you might find it helpful to use colored pens and pencils. The color is helpful because it stimulates global processing while you are completing the analytical skill of taking notes. When learning vocabulary, you might use index cards. Flashing through the cards is a global activity that helps the analytical processing needed to develop vocabulary.

When you learn to use both styles of thinking at the same time, retaining and understanding information become much easier. Albert Einstein and Pablo Picasso, along with many other scientists and artists, saw the value of using both styles of thinking. These individuals had well-developed analytical and global thinking skills.

DIRECTIONS: First, read through the following statements. After you have read all of the statements for both "A" and "B" traits, check the statements that most apply to you. Please keep in mind that there are no right or wrong answers.

"A" TRAITS	"B" TRAITS
_____ I am good at remembering faces.	_____ I am good at remembering names.
_____ I remember how to perform a task better when someone shows me how to do it.	_____ I remember information best when I can read about it.
_____ I like expressing my feelings.	_____ I do not like expressing how I feel.
_____ I enjoy doing many things at once.	_____ I like to work on one thing at a time.
_____ I can sense how someone feels.	_____ I usually cannot tell how someone is feeling.
_____ I can create funny things to say or do.	_____ I find it difficult to create funny things to say or do.
_____ I like having fun when I am doing things.	_____ I like to be serious when doing things.
_____ I like studying in groups.	_____ I prefer to study alone.
_____ I am easily distracted.	_____ I am not easily distracted.
_____ I am disorganized.	_____ I am organized.
_____ I enjoy art, music, and/or dance.	_____ I enjoy reading, math, and/or science.
_____ I prefer essay tests.	_____ I prefer multiple-choice tests.
_____ I like meeting new people.	_____ I am uncomfortable meeting new people.
_____ I make decisions with my heart.	_____ I make decisions with my head.
_____ I like to answer questions by guessing.	_____ I like to think through questions before answering them.
_____ I don't pay attention to details.	_____ I pay attention to details.
_____ I learn best by seeing or doing.	_____ I learn best by hearing about things.
_____ I have difficulty following directions.	_____ I can follow directions.
_____ I use my hands when I talk.	_____ I rarely use my hands when I talk.
_____ I lose track of time.	_____ I can keep track of time.

Now, count the number of checks you made for "A" and "B" and record the totals below:

Total A Traits = _____

Total B Traits = _____

"A" traits are characteristics associated with _global thinking_.

"B" traits are characteristics associated with _analytical thinking_.

Characteristics of Analytical and Global Thinkers

Analytical Thinkers	Global Thinkers
concerned with details	concerned with the big picture
organized	disorganized
predictable	spontaneous
auditory	visual and kinesthetic
consecutive	random
aware of time	unaware of time
math (algebra)	geometry (shapes, etc.)
reading, spelling, writing	music, art, drama, dance
practical	creative
logical	instinctive
focused	easily distracted

The following information describes strategies for activating analytical and global processing:

ANALYTICAL PROCESSING OR THINKING

When learning, analytical thinkers prefer:

- Bright light
- Quiet study environment
- Working on one activity at a time
- Studying alone
- Formal or traditional learning environment

GLOBAL PROCESSING OR THINKING

When learning, global thinkers prefer:

- Short breaks
- Low lighting
- Eating/drinking while learning
- Music or sound in the background
- Informal learning environment
- Working on many activities at a time
- Studying in groups

Brainteaser

This activity does not measure your intelligence, your fluency with words, or your mathematical ability. It will, however, give you some indication of your mental flexibility and creativity. It will require that you draw from both styles of thinking in order to achieve success. Few people can solve more than half of the items, so don't get discouraged if you have trouble.

EXAMPLE: 4 W on a C   Four Wheels on a Car
13 O C   Thirteen Original Colonies

1. SW and the 7 D   _____
2. I H a D by M L K   _____
3. 2 Ps in a P   _____
4. HDD (T M R U T C)   _____
5. 3 S to a T   _____
6. 100 P in a D   _____
7. T No P L H   _____
8. 4 Q in a G   _____
9. I a S W A A   _____
10. 50 S in T U   _____

LEARNING PREFERENCE THEORY

Many of you have undoubtedly wondered how information gets into your brain. This information travels along several very common avenues or pathways. When you are learning or processing information, you are in fact using one or more of your five basic senses (sight, touch, sound, smell, or taste) to gather information for your brain to process. Successful learning of new information occurs when you use as many of your senses as you can to transmit the new material to the brain.

Everyone has a preferred learning style or dominant sense that they use to learn information, especially information that they find difficult. For instance, have you ever asked someone to write something down, to repeat what they said, or even to let you try your hand at something in an effort to understand? If you've made these comments, chances are you were trying to get the information presented in such a way that you could best understand it.

Most students use a combination of senses to help guarantee that the brain will understand the material. If you are learning a new song, for instance, your sense of _hearing_ is challenged more than the other senses. Sight may also play a part in the learning process because you feel as though you can "see" the musical notes. In addition, by using a musical instrument to play the song, you are using _touch_ to learn the song. These examples reveal that you can use a combination of senses to experience a new song. In all likelihood, your chances of mastering the song are increased if you involve several of your senses.

Another illustration of how you might combine your senses in learning might occur if you were studying a new type of flower. You may first examine it closely. Next, you may smell its scent. You may also be able to taste the flower if it is edible, and finally you may even observe how it feels. Once again, you would be using several of your senses (sight, smell, taste, and touch) to identify the new flower.

If information is received through as many of the senses as possible, you are more likely to understand a new concept. _Using the five senses, explain how you would teach the following items to someone who has never been exposed to that item before. Be creative and have fun._

Lesson #1. *A vocabulary word: beautiful*

Sight _____

_____

Smell _____

_____

Taste _____

_____

Touch _____

_____

Hearing _____

_____

Lesson #2. *A math problem: 2 + 2 = 4*

Sight _____

_____

Smell _____

_____

Taste _____

_____

Touch _____

_____

Hearing _____

_____

Lesson #3. *To spell a word: success*

Sight _____

_____

Smell _____

_____

Taste _____

_____

Touch _____

_____

Hearing _____

_____

Lesson #4. *An object: a lemon*

Sight

Smell

Taste

Touch

Hearing

After completing the activity, answer the following questions:

Were you able to use all of the senses each time? Why or why not?

Which senses were harder to use? Why do you think they were harder to use?

Which senses do you feel students use when they are learning new information? Why?

HOW DO YOU LEARN?

As you have discovered, effective learning involves a range of senses. We all learn differently, and some students must use specific senses in order to learn. Students generally use one or more of the following senses when learning a new skill: visual (sense of sight); auditory (sense of sound); and/or kinesthetic (sense of touch). Each student has a preferred style that he or she uses regularly to achieve academic success. Which style do you think you use most often? Circle your preferred style:

VISUAL   AUDITORY   KINESTHETIC

It is important that you know your preferred style and how to use the other styles to reach your academic potential. Knowing about other learning styles can also help when the material seems difficult to learn. The inventory that follows will identify your preferred learning style.

Learning Preference Inventory

Before completing this activity, read each statement in each category. For each of the following categories, check (✓) the appropriate number for each statement. Please keep in mind that there are no right or wrong answers.

1 = least like me   2 = sometimes like me   3 = most like me

"A" LEARNING PREFERENCE

① ② ③   In my spare time, I enjoy watching TV or reading a magazine.

① ② ③   When putting something together, I need to look at a diagram.

① ② ③   I like teachers who write on the board and use visual aids.

① ② ③   I need to see things in order to remember them.

① ② ③   When I solve math application problems, I draw pictures.

① ② ③   I need a map in order to find my way around.

① ② ③   I can tell how someone feels by the expression on his face.

① ② ③   At a meeting, I prefer to watch people.

"B" LEARNING PREFERENCE

① ② ③   In my spare time, I enjoy listening to music or talking on the phone.

① ② ③   When putting something together, I need someone to explain how to do it.

① ② ③   I like teachers who lecture on the course's subject.

① ② ③   I need to hear things in order to remember them.

① ② ③   When I solve math application problems, I need to talk them out.

① ② ③   When getting directions, I need to hear them.

① ② ③   I can tell how people feel by the sound of their voices.

① ② ③   At a meeting, I prefer to listen and talk to people.

"C" LEARNING PREFERENCE

① ② ③ In my spare time, I enjoy physical activities (running, playing ball, etc.).

① ② ③ When putting something together, I need someone to show me how to do it.

① ② ③ I like teachers who provide classroom activities and encourage student involvement.

① ② ③ I need to write things down in order to remember them.

① ② ③ When I solve application problems (in math), I prefer that someone show me what to do.

① ② ③ When getting directions, I need to write them down in order to remember them.

① ② ③ At a meeting, I prefer to take part in the conversation or activities.

Total points for "A" Learning Preference = _____

Total points for "B" Learning Preference = _____

Total points for "C" Learning Preference = _____

"A" learning preference is Visual, the sense of sight.

"B" learning preference is Auditory, the sense of sound.

"C" learning preference is Kinesthetic, the sense of touch.

It is important to note that there are *no* right or wrong answers. We are all different, and we all learn differently. One style is not more important or better than the other, and you may see a little of yourself in all of the preferences. This inventory indicates the style you prefer when learning new material. The following information describes the three types of learners and strategies for using each style.

Visual Learners

Visual learners learn information through their sense of sight. They need to see in order to understand and remember. This learning style is the most common. The following activities help to develop visual strengths:

- Reading or studying the written word, pictures, or charts
- Taking notes (especially in color)

Visual learners, who learn primarily through their sense of sight, may be challenged in college, where much material is presented through lectures and discussions.

- Drawing pictures or diagrams
- Visualizing information in your mind

Auditory Learners

Auditory learners learn information through their sense of hearing and through sound. They need to hear something to learn and remember it well. Approximately 80 percent of the material presented in college is taught in this way. Therefore, it is extremely important that you develop this learning style in order to achieve academic success. The following activities help to develop auditory skills:

- Stop talking and listen
- Focus on what your teachers are saying
- Make audiotapes of class lectures and discussions
- Talk to yourself or others about the information
- Study in a group

Kinesthetic Learners

Kinesthetic learners learn best through their sense of touch. Students who learn in this way must physically experience the information to understand and remember it. The following activities help to develop the kinesthetic sense:

- Acting out the information (role-playing)
- Using your hands
- Making models, charts, diagrams, etc.
- Taking notes
- Adding movement when studying (e.g., walking, tapping a finger, or rocking in a chair)
- Chewing gum
- Studying in a group

Learning new information can sometimes be difficult. It may sometimes be easy. Regardless of its difficulty level, to successfully master new material, students should involve as many of their senses as possible. Learning new information can be easier and more fun with the help of your senses.

USING MNEMONIC DEVICES

People forget about 98 percent of what they learn. This is an alarming statistic, especially when you consider the enormous amount of time and effort that many of you put into studying. Understanding human memory and applying memory techniques can help increase the chances that you will be able to recall the information you have studied for an exam.

According to psychologists, there are three types of human memory:

1. Sensory memory
2. Working memory
3. Long-term memory

Sensory memory stores information gathered from your five senses. This memory is usually temporary unless it is important to you. Working memory is the information gathered from your senses that you feel is important. You can only store a limited amount of information in your working memory. If you want to ensure that you remember this information, you must store it in your long-term memory. Long-term memory stores information permanently. How you organize and remember information is extremely important.

In many ways, your brain is like a room with file cabinets along the walls. On the floor in the middle of the room is a huge pile of papers. Each sheet of paper contains a separate and distinct piece of information. This pile of papers is your working memory. As the pile gets larger and larger, pieces of information get covered up and forgotten. The only way to move this pile of working memory into long-term memory (where it will not be forgotten) is to organize it and to place it into one of the file cabinets

"Our ability to retrieve information from our memory is a function of how well it was learned in the first place."

JOSH R. GEROW

along the wall. You can, for example, put equations into a folder in the math file cabinet. (This folder in the math file cabinet may hold equations that solve certain types of math problems.) You can also put the definition of a word into a folder in the language file cabinet.

One way to organize this information is to use mnemonic devices or "memory tricks." Mnemonic devices help you to store information in your long-term memory by associating that information with information you already know (i.e., putting it into a folder).

There are five basic types of mnemonic devices:

1. JINGLES/RAP. You can create jingles and rhymes to remember information.

> EXAMPLE: In 1492 Columbus sailed the ocean blue.

2. ASSOCIATIONS. Create associations by putting words, ideas, and symbols together to remember information.

> EXAMPLE: Lightbulb = an idea
> Apple = Macintosh

3. SENTENCES. Create a sentence using the first letter in each word from a list of information that you want to remember.

> EXAMPLE: To remember the order of operations in math, use "Please excuse my dear Aunt Sally." This stands for Parentheses, Exponents, Multiply, Divide, Add, and Subtract.

4. WORDS. Create a word to represent the information you need to remember.

> EXAMPLE: To remember the colors in the spectrum, use the name Roy G. Biv (this stands for Red, Orange, Yellow, Green, Blue, Indigo, and Violet).

5. VISUALIZE. Create a picture in your mind of what you want to remember.

EXAMPLE: Italy looks like a boot on a map.

Create a mnemonic for the following concepts:

1. *Parts of speech (nouns, pronouns, verbs, adverbs, adjectives, prepositions, conjunctions, and interjections)*

_____

_____

_____

_____

_____

2. *The five Great Lakes (Michigan, Erie, Superior, Huron, Ontario)*

_____

_____

_____

3. *The first five presidents of the United States (Washington, Adams, Jefferson, Madison, and Monroe)*

_____

_____

_____

_____

4. *The seven continents (North America, South America, Europe, Asia, Africa, Antarctica, and Australia)*

_____

_____

_____

_____

5. *The nine planets (Mercury, Venus, Earth, Mars, Jupiter, Saturn, Uranus, Neptune, and Pluto)*

_____

_____

_____

_____

_____

Now that you have completed this chapter, take a few moments to complete the Milestones checklist to the right.

How did you do with the questions this time? Do you understand more about how the brain works and how learning is affected by individual preferences? What changes might you make in the way you approach studying now that you are aware of how you learn? Certainly, much can be gained by focusing on your individual learning preferences and how they affect the way in which you approach academic material.

MILESTONES

NOW THAT YOU ARE HERE . . .

Answer each statement by checking "Y" for Yes, "N" for No, or "S" for Sometimes.

1. I understand how the brain processes information. (Y) (N) (S)

2. I know my preferred learning style. (Y) (N) (S)

3. I use a variety of senses when studying and learning. (Y) (N) (S)

4. I enjoy learning. (Y) (N) (S)

5. I know how a visual learner processes information. (Y) (N) (S)

6. I know how a kinesthetic learner learns. (Y) (N) (S)

7. I know the characteristics of a global thinker. (Y) (N) (S)

8. I know how an auditory learner learns. (Y) (N) (S)

9. I use mnemonic devices. (Y) (N) (S)

10. I know how to store information in long-term memory. (Y) (N) (S)

ROADWAYS

- Become *actively* involved when studying, reading, and taking notes. Ask yourself questions to keep yourself focused. Draw visual diagrams, study with friends.

- Get organized! Develop a note-taking *system,* record assignments, and keep an organized notebook.

- Your study environment should be *quiet* and free of distractions (phone, friends, etc.).

- Use colored pens and pencils when taking *notes* and studying.

- Create *movement* when studying. Walk, march, tap a finger, etc.

- Use mnemonics to store and *retrieve* information.

- Get *involved!* Use both styles of thinking and as many senses as possible when learning.

Applying What You Know

This chapter was designed to teach you as much as possible about learning styles and the various ways in which people learn. Applying the strategies suggested in this chapter allows you to take charge of your learning since you are ultimately responsible for your academic success.

Now that you have finished this chapter on information processing and learning styles, refer back to the Case Study about Gwen at the beginning of this book. Based on Gwen's situation, answer the following questions:

1. How would you explain to Gwen what the differences are between global and analytical thinking?

2. If we assume that Gwen is a global thinker, what would you suggest she do to improve her grades in ENG 101?

3. What strategies would you suggest that Gwen implement to improve her grades in MAT 101 if she is a visual and kinesthetic learner?

Observations

CHARTING YOUR COURSE

Your academic success is your responsibility. Your instructors might not teach in the way that is best for you. There also may be academic subjects that you find difficult. Although you may have to face either one or both of these situations, you are ultimately responsible for mastering the information. Do not let your academic subjects get the better of you.

Learn to take charge! Remember to learn and to study new information using both styles of thinking. In addition, use as many senses as possible when learning and studying. Because success is within your reach, you must grasp it by applying the techniques mentioned in this chapter. You can achieve academic success. The road is yours to travel.

Getting There on Time

Once you have mastered techniques related to learning styles, you will learn that you can save a great deal of time spent studying. For example, consider how the use of mnemonic devices will help you. If you become proficient with the use of mnemonic devices, you will be able to recall facts more readily and more easily, focusing more of your time on studying theory and logic as it relates to your particular subject.

Exploring Technology

This exploring technology assignment is about your vehicle's "brains." Computers, computers, computers. Computers and computer chips are part of every aspect of life: television sets, cell phones, toys, and of course our automobiles. Many of us are not aware of the degree to which state-of-the-art technology is used in vehicles. Fuel injectors and exhaust emissions are just two of the ways we use technology to improve the performance of our cars. Computer chips are also used to diagnose and troubleshoot vehicles. In fact, many cars now either keep a record of problems or allow an operator to take a "snapshot" of the vehicle at the time of trouble.

Provide the name of the computer chip that controls your vehicle, or the computer that troubleshoots your car. (Be sure to include the make, year, and model of your vehicle.)

HELPFUL REFERENCES:

- automobile manual
- automobile shop (e.g., Auto Zone, NAPA)
- friendly neighborhood mechanic

  THE FOLLOWING WEBSITES MAY BE HELPFUL:
  www.autoalliance.org/economic/info.htm
  www.fulllogic.com/

Web Connections

TRAVELING THE INFORMATION SUPERHIGHWAY

During your journey, you may want to check out some of the following learning style Web addresses:

www.chaminade.org/inspire/learnstl.htm

www.ncsu.edu/felder-public/learning-styles.html

www.ldpride.net/learningstyles.MI.htm

As a result of this chapter, and in preparing for my journey, I plan to . . .

Scanning the Radio 6

Freshman year! Day one! First class! The History of Western Civilization! Instructor, Ms. Wilkerson! "Your life will never be the same after you leave here," were her first words. She meant it. Ms. Wilkerson had been an award-winning basketball coach for almost 20 years and had retired to teach college history. She was tough in class, tough in the hallway, tough in her office, tough in the parking lot, tough while giving notes, tough when reviewing for a test, and even tougher when test day arrived. She was really, really tough, man!

Usually, on the first day of classes the instructor would go over the syllabus, talk about the class, and let the students go. "Don't expect to leave here one second before my time is up," she said. "You paid for history, and that is exactly what you are going to get." She reviewed the syllabus, spoke briefly about the class, and began to lecture on Mesopotamian Civilization. The entire class scrambled for notebooks and pens. Most of us would have written on anything so as not to miss a word of what she was saying. For the next 37 minutes, we listened, she talked. Our hands were aching from the speed at which we had to take notes as she lectured, wrote on the board, and used the overhead projector.

Shortly before our 50-minute period was over, she closed her book and said the words that I remember verbatim 18 years later. "You'd better get ready. Do not come to this class unprepared. Bring your notebook, textbook, five pencils or two pens with you daily. I shall not stop this class for you to sharpen or borrow an instrument.

"You will come to this class ready to listen to me. You will not talk to your friends during my class. If you stick with me, listen to me carefully, and take your notes, you'll learn more about history than you ever dreamed possible. If you come to me unprepared, you will not know if you are in Egypt, Mesopotamia, or pure hell! Class dismissed!"

With horror and fear running through our bodies, my friend and I left the class bewildered and exhausted. We had never seen anything like it before. She was a tornado . . . a 65-year-old tornado!

"It is the province of knowledge to speak, and it is the privilege of wisdom to listen."

OLIVER WENDELL HOLMES

You will possibly run into a "Ms. Wilkerson" from time to time. You may have already encountered her or professors like her who speak so rapidly that you have to have a "sixth sense" just to keep up the pace. The nation's campuses are full of Ms. Wilkersons. She was a fantastic teacher, but she moved through the centuries at the speed of sound. The students had to learn how to listen as quickly as she spoke, and to either keep up with her or withdraw from the class.

How do you feel about the importance of listening skills to your success as a student? A key step in becoming a good student is knowing how to listen and evaluate the information you hear. This chapter is intended to help you develop your listening skills. In becoming a more active listener, you will be able to take better notes in class, participate more, and retain more information. Upon completion of this chapter, you will be able to:

- Distinguish the difference between listening and hearing
- Explain the listening process of receiving, focusing, interpreting, and responding
- Define effective listening
- Recognize and eliminate the roadblocks to effective listening
- Identify active and passive listening characteristics
- Use the four-step process for "Getting Others to Listen to Me"
- Understand and use the Roadways to Effective Listening
- Understand the fundamentals of written communication

The Milestones checklist includes statements to help you assess where you are as a listener at this moment. Take your time and evaluate each question carefully.

If you would like to turn more of your "No" and "Sometimes" answers into "Yes" answers, you might consider some of the following activities. Maybe you should spend more time watching network news to see if you can remember details of a particular news report. You could possibly have a friend read a passage from a book to you and then ask you to paraphrase the text to see what you retained. Other exercises in this chapter will assist you in further developing your listening skills. If more of your answers were "No" or "Sometimes," don't despair—this chapter is included to help you increase your listening skills and become a more active listener.

MILESTONES

WHERE ARE YOU NOW?

Answer each statement by checking "Y" for Yes, "N" for No, or "S" for Sometimes.

		Y	N	S
1.	I know how to listen with my whole body.	Y	N	S
2.	I enjoy listening.	Y	N	S
3.	I know how to listen for cues.	Y	N	S
4.	I ask questions when listening.	Y	N	S
5.	I know how to listen in different settings.	Y	N	S
6.	I can identify the process of listening.	Y	N	S
7.	I usually keep listening when I don't agree.	Y	N	S
8.	I usually keep listening even if I don't like the speaker.	Y	N	S
9.	I know the difference between active and passive listening.	Y	N	S
10.	I know how to get others to listen to me.	Y	N	S

TO BE A CAPTAIN, YOU FIRST HAVE TO BE A SAILOR

There are many connections and relationships that have to be made to survive in this world. You've already figured out many of them or you wouldn't be in college. As the heading of this section states, to be a captain, you have to know how to be an effective sailor. You may have even read the quote by the poet Ralph Waldo Emerson, "The only way to have a good friend is to be one." The same connection can be made between listening and note taking. If you do not have the necessary listening skills, it is very unlikely that you will be able to take useful notes in class.

To all animals, including humans, listening is a necessary survival skill. For many animals, it is necessary to avoid predators and to sustain life. For others, it is necessary for hunting or gathering food. For humans, listening is necessary for the establishment of relationships, growth, survival, knowledge, entertainment, and even health. It is one of the most important and widely used tools humans possess. How much time per day do you think you spend in listening situations? Research suggests that we spend almost 70 percent of our waking time communicating (Adler, Rosenfeld, & Towne, 1989). Fifty-three percent of that time is spent in listening situations. Effective listening skills can mean the difference between success or failure, As or Fs, successful relationships or strained ones.

For students, listening is a skill critical to success. Much of the information that you will receive over the next two to four years will be provided to you in the lecture format. Cultivating and improving your active listening skills will assist you in understanding lectures, taking accurate notes, participating in class discussions, and communicating with your peers.

Listening is a skill critical to success in school, in work, and in life.

THE DIFFERENCES BETWEEN LISTENING AND HEARING

We usually do not think much about listening until a misunderstanding occurs or something goes wrong. You've probably been in a situation in which someone misunderstood you or you misunderstood someone. These misunderstandings often occur because we tend to view listening as an automatic response, when in actuality, listening is a *learned, voluntary* activity just like driving a car, painting a picture, or playing the piano. Having ears does not necessarily make us good *listeners*. Making this assumption is as illogical as believing that because we are given hands, we should be able to paint the *Mona Lisa*. True, we *may* be able to paint the *Mona Lisa*, but not without practice and guidance. Good listening likewise takes practice, time, guidance, and active participation before one can become an active listener.

Hearing is not learned. It is *automatic and involuntary*. As a matter of fact, if you are within the range of the sound that is made, you will probably hear it. This does not mean, however, that you will listen to it. Just because we heard the sound does not guarantee that we know what the sound was or from whence it came. To be actively listening, we have to make a conscious effort to focus in on the sound and determine what the sound was.

Listening is a four-step process. It can be remembered by using the mnemonic **R O A R.**

R Receiving the information

O Organizing the sounds heard and focusing on them

A Assigning meaning

R Reacting

This cycle is discussed in more detail below.

RECEIVING. Receiving simply means that you were within the range of the sound that was made. It may have been a baby crying, a dish breaking, or a human voice speaking. Receiving the sound does not necessarily mean that you are listening.

To become an active listener, when *receiving* the information, make an effort to:

1. Tune out distractions other than the conversation at hand.

2. Avoid interrupting the speaker.

3. Pay close attention to nonverbal communication such as gestures, facial expressions, and movement.

4. Focus not on what will be said next, but on what is being said at the moment.

5. Listen for what is *not* said.

Take a moment and determine what sounds you are receiving at this exact moment. List them.

_____

_____

_____

_____

ORGANIZING AND FOCUSING. This is when we choose to listen actively to the sound and pay attention to its origin, direction, and intention. Your mind begins to organize the information that was heard. You just did this in the exercise above.

Spend the next few moments talking with your partner in the class. Put your pen down and just listen carefully and actively. Do not take notes on the conversation. Spend at least four to five minutes talking to your partner. Ask your partner about his or her goals, dreams, plans, major, and life's work.

Now, paraphrase what your partner said to you.

_____

_____

_____

_____

If you were actively listening, you would be able to write about his or her goals, major, dreams, and careers. How did you do? Were you actively listening?

To become an active listener, when *organizing and focusing* on the information, make an effort to:

1. Sit up straight or stand near the person speaking so that you involve your entire body.
2. Make eye contact. Listen with your eyes and ears.
3. Try to create a visual picture of what is being said.

ASSIGNMENT. Assignment occurs when we mentally "assign" a name or meaning to what we have been hearing. We may have to pay special attention to some sounds to assign them the correct name or meaning. Have you ever been sitting in your room and you heard a crash? If so, you might have to hear it again before you could identify the sound of the crash as being dishes falling, books dropping, or static on the radio. Your brain is trying to establish a relationship between what you just heard and what you have heard before. It is trying to associate one piece of information with another. When this is done, you will be able to identify the new sound by remembering the old sound.

To become an active listener, when *assigning meaning to* information, make an effort to:

1. Relate the information to something that you already know.
2. Ask questions to ensure that there are no misunderstandings.
3. Identify the main idea(s) of what is being said.
4. Try to summarize the information into small "files" in your memory.
5. Repeat the information to yourself (or aloud if appropriate).

When you are listening in class and taking notes, you will find information that is similar to or related to information previously heard. For instance, if you hear about *Oedipus Rex* in theater class, you might immediately relate it to the Oedipus Complex in psychology class. If you hear about Einstein in history, you will probably make the connection to science. Active listening allows us to make associations, thus assisting us in creating learning patterns for long-term memory. Simply hearing the information will not allow you to make these relationships.

Listen carefully to the sounds made by your professor. He or she will ask you to close your eyes and listen actively. Try to identify them without asking him or her to repeat them.

Sound #1 _____

Sound #2 _____

Sound #3 _____

REACTING. This stage is nothing more than our response to the sound that was heard. If we hear a crash, we may jump; if we hear a baby crying, we may pick him up; if we hear a voice, we may turn to face the person speaking. Our reaction can also be a barrier to active listening. Have you ever "tuned out" or ignored someone because they were boring or because you did not agree with their point of view? If so, it is important to note that this is also a reaction to the information. It is highly unlikely to have no reaction at all.

To become an active listener, when *reacting* to information, make an effort to:

1. Leave your emotions behind. Do not prejudge.

2. Avoid overreacting.

3. Avoid jumping to conclusions.

4. Ask yourself, "How can this information help me?"

PRACTICAL DEFINITIONS OF LISTENING

Perhaps the drawing of the Chinese verb "to listen" is the most comprehensive and practical definition that can be given. To speakers of Chinese, listening involves many parts of the body: the ears, the eyes, the mind, and the heart. Do you make it a habit to listen with more than your ears? The Chinese view listening as a whole-body experience. Western cultures might seem to have lost the ability to effectively involve the whole body in the listening process, favoring the ears and sometimes not even using them at all.

The *American Heritage Dictionary* defines listening as "to make an effort to hear something, to pay attention, to give heed." Although this definition is standard, it does not offer us a great deal of concreteness or direction. Listening must be personalized and internalized. In order to understand listening as a whole-body experience, we will define listening on three levels:

Ear   Eyes

Heart   Undivided attention

- Listening with a purpose
- Listening objectively
- Listening constructively

Listening with a purpose suggests that we have to recognize the different types of listening situations in which we might be involved, such as class, worship, entertainment, and relationships. We do not listen the same way in every situation. When we go to a concert, we turn on our "concert ears"; we are listening for the sake of pleasure. Unless we are musicians, we do not take a pen and pad with us to take notes on the music. When you go to class, you are listening to gain a deeper understanding of the materials presented. Have you ever listened to a friend who needed advice? If so, you were listening with "different ears" than you would in a classroom or in an entertainment setting. This may sound a bit elementary, but unless you understand the difference between various listening situations, you will find listening to be a more difficult adventure. Each situation demands that we know which type of listening will be required. This is called "listening with a purpose."

List some different listening situations in which you will be involved this semester:

1. _____
2. _____
3. _____

How do they differ?

1. _____
2. _____
3. _____

Listening objectively means that we are listening with an open mind. Few gifts that you give yourself will be greater than knowing how to listen without bias or prejudice. This is perhaps the most difficult aspect of listening. Have you ever had someone cut you off in the middle of a conversation or sentence because the person disagreed with you? Has anyone ever left the room when you were giving your opinion of a situation? If so, you have experienced people who do not know how to listen objectively, with an open mind.

Many times, we tend to shut out or ignore things with which we do not agree or information that appears obscure or irrelevant. Listening objectively requires us to listen with an open mind and then make our decisions. So often, we do the reverse; we make judgments and then try to listen. Have you ever done that?

List three situations in which you might be involved this semester that would require you to listen with an open mind:

1. _____
2. _____
3. _____

Why would you have to listen objectively in each of these situations?

1. _____

_____

2. _____

_____

3. _____

_____

Listening constructively suggests that we listen with the attitude, "How can this be helpful to my life or my education?" It simply asks us to evaluate the information being given and determine if it has meaning to our lives. Sound easy? Actually, it is more difficult than it sounds because, once again, we tend to shut out information that we do not see as immediately helpful or useful. To be constructive listeners, we need to know how to listen and to store information for later dates.

John was a student who disliked math intensely. He could never understand why, as a history major, he had to learn algebra. So, he would automatically tune out the math professor when she presented information that he did not see as necessary. From time to time, we've all probably felt this way about some piece of information or another. However, when we tune out because we cannot see, or refuse to see, the relationship to our lives, we are not constructively listening.

When was the last time you "tuned out" for any reason? Why?

_____

_____

_____

_____

Looking back, could you have benefited from the information or the source of the information, had you not tuned out of the listening situation? Why or why not?

_____

_____

_____

_____

OBSTACLES TO LISTENING

 here are several major obstacles to becoming an effective listener. In order to start building active listening skills, you first have to remove some barriers.

Obstacle One: Prejudging

Prejudging is one of the biggest obstacles to active listening. Prejudging means that you automatically shut out what is being said for several reasons. You may prejudge because of the content, or you may prejudge because of the person communicating. Prejudging can also evolve from environment, culture, social status, or attitude.

Willistine enrolled in a religion class at her college. The course was entitled "Faith, Doubt, and Reason." Shortly after the class began, the instructor began asking questions and making statements that challenged what Willistine had believed all of her life. The instructor was trying to get the class to explore thoughts beyond what they held at that moment. After two weeks in the class, Willistine decided to drop the course because she did not want to hear the instructor's comments. Willistine was prejudging. She shut out what the instructor was saying because it went against what she believed. It is almost impossible to prejudge and then actively listen. The best approach is to listen with an open mind, and then make judgments.

Do You Prejudge Information or the Source?

Answer "Yes" or "No" to the questions below:

YES NO   1. I tune out when something is boring.

YES NO   2. I tune out when I do not agree with the information.

YES NO   3. I argue mentally with the speaker about information.

YES NO   4. I do not listen to people whom I dislike.

YES NO   5. I make decisions about the information before I understand all of the implications or consequences.

If you answered "Yes" to two or more of the questions, you might be inclined to prejudge a listening situation.

TIPS FOR OVERCOMING PREJUDGING

1. Listen for information that may be valuable to you as a student. Some material may not be pleasant to hear, but it may be useful to you later on.

2. Listen to the message, not the messenger. If you do not like the speaker, try to go beyond personality and listen to what is being said, not to the person saying it. This is a double-edged sword as well. You may dislike the speaker so much that you do not listen objectively to what is being said. You may accept the material or answers just because you *do* like the person.

3. Try to remove cultural, racial, gender, social, and environmental barriers. Just because a person is different from you or holds a different point of view does not make him or her wrong. If someone is just like you and you hold the same points of view, this does not make that person right. Sometimes, we have to cross cultural and environmental barriers to learn new material and see with greater clarity.

Obstacle Two: Talking

No one, not even the best listener in the world, can listen well and talk at the same time. Take a moment the next time you are talking with a friend and try it. Speak to them while they are speaking—see if you remember what they said. In order to become an effective listener, we must learn the power of silence. Silence gives us the opportunity to do several things: think, listen, and consider. By remaining silent, we allow ourselves to think about what is being said before we respond. This small amount of time can be invaluable to effective listeners. Silence also allows us to listen. The near-impossibility of trying to listen and talk at once illustrates the importance of silence, which allows us to consider what others are saying and to reflect on what they have said.

Are You a Talker Rather Than a Listener?

Answer "Yes" or "No" to the questions below.

YES NO   1. I often interrupt the speaker so that I can say what I want.

YES NO   2. I am thinking of my next statement while others are talking.

YES NO   3. My mind wanders when others talk.

YES NO   4. I answer my own questions.

YES NO   5. I answer questions that are asked of other people.

If you answered "Yes" to two or more of the questions, you may not fully appreciate the importance of silence.

TIPS FOR OVERCOMING THE URGE TO TALK TOO MUCH

1. Force yourself to be silent at parties, family gatherings, and friendly get-togethers. We're not telling you to be antisocial, but do force yourself to be silent for at least 10 minutes. You may be surprised at what you hear. You may also be surprised how hard it is to do this. Test yourself.

2. Ask questions and then allow the other person to answer the question. Many times, we ask questions and either answer them ourselves or cheat the other person out of a response. Force yourself to wait until the person has formed a response. By asking questions and waiting for an answer, we force ourselves to listen.

Obstacle Three: Bringing Your Emotions to the Table

A barrier to active listening is bringing your emotions to the listening situation. Our worries, problems, fears, and anger can prevent us from listening to our greatest advantage. Have you ever sat in a lecture and, before you knew what was happening, your mind was a million miles away because you were angry or worried about something? If so, you have experienced Obstacle Three—bringing your emotions to the table.

Do You Bring Your Emotions to the Listening Situation?

Answer "Yes" or "No" to the questions below.

YES   NO   1. I get angry before I hear the whole story.

YES   NO   2. I look for underlying or hidden messages in the information.

YES   NO   3. Sometimes, I begin listening in a negative frame of mind.

YES   NO   4. I base my opinions on what others are saying or doing.

YES   NO   5. I readily accept as correct information from people whom I like or respect.

If you answered "Yes" to two or more of the questions, you tend to bring your emotions into the listening situation.

TIPS FOR CONTROLLING EMOTIONS THAT INTERFERE WITH LISTENING

1. Know how you feel before you begin the listening experience.
2. Focus on the message and determine how you can use the information.
3. Try to create a positive image about the message you are about to hear.

ACTIVE AND PASSIVE LISTENING CHARACTERISTICS

Active Listeners	Passive Listeners
Lean forward and sit up straight	Slouch and lean back in chairs
Give the speaker eye contact	Look around the room
Listen for what is not said	Hear scattered information
Are patient	Get frustrated easily
Leave emotions outside	Get angry at the speaker
Avoid jumping to conclusions	Make immediate assumptions
Ask questions	Urge the speaker to finish quickly
Focus on the topic	Daydream
Have an open mind	Prejudge the speaker
Do not argue mentally	Create mental arguments
Empathize	Criticize
Tune out distractions	Are distracted easily
React to ideas	React prematurely to the person speaking

Listening is hard work. It is a voluntary, learned skill that few people ever truly master. Active listeners seek to improve their skills by constantly involving themselves in the communication process.

HOW DO I GET OTHERS TO LISTEN TO ME?

As a college student, employee, leader, spouse, or caregiver there will be times when you want people to listen to your views and opinions. There will be times when you want to speak out at a club meeting, a civic group meeting, or the PTA, and you want people to hear what you are saying. Here are several "roadways" that you can use to help other people listen to you.

REPETITION. Make an effort to state your main ideas or points more than one time during your conversation. We need to hear things as many as 14 times to have them placed in our long-term memory. Repetition helps.

MOVEMENT. When you are speaking, use some degree of movement with your body, such as your gestures and facial expressions. If you are standing in front of a group of people, you might want to move from one side of the room to the other. However, it is important to remember *not* to pace needlessly.

ENERGY. When you are speaking and trying to get others to listen to you, be energetic and lively with your words. It is hard to listen to someone who speaks in the same tone all of the time. Be excited about what you are saying and people will listen to you more readily. This is perhaps the single most important way to get people to listen to your views.

CREATIVITY. This simply means that you need to have something to say when you are speaking and you should say it in a way that is creative, fresh, and new. Do you know how hard it is to listen to people who never say a thing? They talk all the time, but seldom say anything important. When you speak, make sure that you are making a contribution to the conversation.

LISTENING FOR KEY WORDS, PHRASES, AND HINTS

Learning how to listen for key words, phrases, and hints can help you become an active listener and a more effective note taker. For example, when the English professor says, "There are 10 basic elements to writing poetry," you should jot down the number "10" under a heading labeled "Poetry," or number your page 1–10, leaving space for taking the actual notes. If the professor completes the lecture and you only have six elements to writing poetry, you know that you have missed some elements of the lecture. At this point, you should ask questions.

THE TOP 10 REASONS FOR ACTIVELY LISTENING

Once you have learned how to listen actively, several key benefits will help you as a student, as an employee, and as a citizen. They are:

1. You are exposed to more information and knowledge about the world, your peers, and yourself.

2. You can help others because you have listened to their problems and fears. You can have a greater sense of empathy.

3. You can avoid more problems at school or work than people who do not listen.

4. You will be able to participate in life more fully because you will have a keener sense of what is going on in the world around you.

5. You will grow to have more friends and healthy relationships because people are drawn to those they can talk to and whose sincerity they can sense.

6. You will be able to ask more questions and gain deeper understanding of subjects that interest you or ideas you wish to explore.

7. You will be a more effective leader. People follow those who they feel genuinely listen to their ideas and give them a chance.

8. You will be able to understand more about different cultures from around the world.

9. You will be able to make more logical decisions on difficult issues in your life and studies.

10. You will feel better about yourself because you will know in your heart and mind that you gave the situation the best effort possible.

Some key phrases and words that may help you become an active listener are:

on the other hand	as stated earlier	in contrast
another way	the main issue is	characteristically
in addition	for example	moreover
most importantly	to illustrate	such as
specifically	because	due to
once again	in comparison	finally
therefore	nevertheless	above all
as a result		

Knowing how to pick up on transition words will help you filter out information that is less important, thus listening more carefully to what is most important. It is also very helpful to know when the information is important, and you should be listening with careful attention when the professor:

Writes something on the board.

Uses an overhead.

Draws on a flipchart.

Uses computer-aided graphics.

Speaks in a louder tone or changes vocal patterns.

Uses gestures more than usual.

TEST YOUR LISTENING SKILLS

The following is a series of activities that test your active listening skills. You will be assisted by your professor. The activities found in this section test a variety of listening situations. You will have to use several types of listening skills.

Circles and Lines    EXERCISE **6.1**

Respond to the directions given by the professor, using the diagram below.

Close your book, listen to the professor's story, and then follow the professor's directions.

_____ 1. A thief approached a cabdriver at a traffic light.

_____ 2. The thief demanded money.

_____ 3. The thief was a man.

_____ 4. The cabdriver's window was down all the way when the thief approached the cab.

_____ 5. The cabdriver gave the thief the money.

_____ 6. Someone sped away with the money.

_____ 7. The money was on the dash of the cab.

_____ 8. The amount of money was never mentioned.

_____ 9. The story mentions only two people: the cabdriver and the thief.

_____ 10. The following statements are true: Someone demanded the money; the money was snatched up; a person sped away.

EXERCISE **6.3** **The Accident**

Listen to the scenario read by your professor. Follow the professor's directions after hearing the scenario.

LISTENER	ADDITIONS	DELETIONS
1.		
2.		
3.		
4.		
5.		

Listen to your peers and draw the design they verbally create for you.

Whispers

EXERCISE **6.5**

Write down what the person next to you whispers in your ear.

Answer questions asked by the professor after listening.

1. _____

_____

_____

2. _____

_____

_____

3. _____

_____

_____

4. _____

_____

_____

5. _____

_____

_____

- Make the decision to listen. Listening is *voluntary;* you must choose to listen.

- Approach listening with an *open* mind.

- Leave your *emotions* at the door.

- *Focus* on the material at hand; how can it help you?

- Listen for *key* words and phrases.

- Listen for *how* something is said.

- Listen for what is *not* said.

- Stop *talking*.

- Eliminate as many *distractions* as possible.

- Listen for *major* ideas and details.

- Take *notes;* this makes you actively involved in listening.

- Paraphrase the speaker's *words* in your notes.

- *Relate* the information to something you already know.

- Encourage the speaker with your body *language* and facial expressions.

- Don't give up too soon; *listen* to the whole story.

- Avoid *jumping* to conclusions.

WRITTEN COMMUNICATION

Besides all of the aspects of listening that we have just discussed, an equally important aspect of communication is the written word. Just think, if our ancestors had not developed their writing skills, much of the history we know today might not be known to us—someone had to write all of this information down and do it in a format that we can now understand. Good writing skills are essential for the successful student. Much of what you will be expected to do in college involves writing. Therefore, it is very important that you develop the positive writing skills today that will serve you well in the years to come. Learning the difference between proper references and plagiarism, learning something about the various research styles used in completing scholarly work, conducting research, and editing your written work are the concepts covered in this section.

What Is Plagiarism?

Plagiarism, as defined by *Webster's New World Dictionary,* is "to take . . . from another." In this situation, "take" literally means to steal. When you plagiarize, you steal ideas and work from another person without his or her permission. Often, the student who plagiarizes is not aware of the difference between compiling similar thoughts and ideas and actually stealing ideas. It is always good practice to let the reader know where a particular point comes from if you include the point in your work. This is called a "reference" and can be noted in your written work in a number of ways. References give credibility to the ideas and thoughts that you have developed and can often help you prove a point in your writing.

An example of a reference is included in the paragraph just prior to this one. The paragraph begins by telling the reader where the author found the information—in this case, it came from *Webster's New World Dictionary.* There are many ways in which you can reference thoughts and ideas that you include in your written work. Very often, when you read your college text, you will see that the author(s) have referenced work in a variety of ways—either within the text or at the end in a reference list.

Select a textbook that you are using this semester. How are references handled in the text?

_____

_____

_____

_____

Are most of the references

- *Within the text? or*
- *At the conclusion of the chapter/article/book?*

Either way, the author has taken great care to give credit to the people who originally presented the ideas. Always be aware of this simple idea: Give credit where credit is due. That assures the reader that you are not stealing someone else's ideas or thoughts. There are some students, on the other hand, who think that if they have properly "referenced" the paper, they do not have to add any additional thought or original ideas. Professors like to see what *you* think about the material based on information that you have gathered. A good rule of thumb is that your paper should be at least two-thirds original thought supported by one-third fact that is properly referenced. Remember, the professor wants to know if you understand the topic and what thoughts you might have regarding the topic.

Search your college's catalog or handbook to find out what the policy on plagiarism is on your campus. Summarize the policy below.

_____

_____

_____

_____

Review your syllabi for this semester—how many of your professors included information about plagiarism?

What are the consequences?

_____

_____

_____

Writing Styles

Various professional organizations (e.g., the American Psychological Association) have developed "styles" of writing that enable research articles to be consistent in their appearance. Whether or not a paragraph is indented, how the references are listed (both within the text and at the end of the text), and how thoughts are divided and subdivided are all considered elements of "style." Without going into great detail here, it is worth noting that there are several styles that various faculty members may prefer. Before beginning *any* written assignment, make sure that you are aware of which style your professor prefers. Then, go promptly to the Internet or to your campus library and find that particular style manual. Styles change periodically, so make sure that you have the most current and relevant manual.

Examine the syllabi for your other courses this semester.

Do any of them require written papers? _____

If so, what style will you be using? _____

If your syllabus does not indicate which style your professor prefers, you must ask—better safe than sorry!

Even though the Internet is an important research tool, getting to know the library and the research librarian can be a great help in your academic career.

Conducting Research

You've been given an assignment in your psychology class to write a research paper. Where do you start? The first and most obvious task is to determine your research topic. Is the topic preassigned or can you select your own? If you select your own topic, is it necessary to have the instructor approve the topic? Once those basic questions are answered, you are ready to complete the research phase of your assignment. Research can be exciting and fun or it can be pure drudgery. If at all possible, find a topic in which you are interested. Once you've selected an exciting topic, it is time to get to work finding all that you can about the topic.

Obviously, the library is one of your greatest resources here. *Use the library and get to know the reference librarian.* The reference librarian's job is to point you in the direction of as many difference resources as possible. Use this person's vast knowledge of research journals and indices to move your research in the right direction.

The Internet can be a fabulous means for conducting research as well. Use as many search engines as you can to find out what is available. Remember, always give proper credit or "reference" to any resource you find. Later in your academic career, you may be asked to conduct experimental research, but that is a much more advanced topic—one that is discussed in the class at greater length. Spending your time reading about the topic on which you will write is invaluable research time. Don't skimp on devoting enough time here—if you do, writing and compiling the paper will be much more difficult.

Editing Your Work

Each year, more and more faculty complain that students do not adequately edit their written work. One can assume that most students believe that with today's technology, if the paper *looks* professionally typed and presented, then it must be good. Nothing can be farther from the truth. Nothing replaces editing—spell check can't, grammar check can't, and word processors won't! *You must spend adequate time editing your work before it is turned in.* If nothing else, find a good student with whom you can share your work and ask that student to help you edit. Sometimes, when you spend so much time writing, you lose sight of the bigger picture and you overlook the mistakes (both in writing and in logic) that may make your paper a disaster. Don't be embarrassed to ask someone else to help you edit. In this case, the old cliché is true—"two heads are better than one."

We've covered just a few of the elements to effective writing. Nothing can replace the written word. You should develop your writing skills just as you would your listening, public speaking, and study skills—all are essential if you are to continue your journey to be a successful student.

MILESTONES

NOW THAT YOU ARE HERE . . .

Answer each statement by checking "Y" for Yes, "N" for No, or "S" for Sometimes.

1.	I know how to listen with my whole body.	Ⓨ Ⓝ Ⓢ
2.	I enjoy listening.	Ⓨ Ⓝ Ⓢ
3.	I know how to listen for cues.	Ⓨ Ⓝ Ⓢ
4.	I ask questions when listening	Ⓨ Ⓝ Ⓢ
5.	I know how to listen in different settings.	Ⓨ Ⓝ Ⓢ
6.	I can identify the process of listening.	Ⓨ Ⓝ Ⓢ
7.	I usually keep listening when I don't agree.	Ⓨ Ⓝ Ⓢ
8.	I usually keep listening even if I don't like the speaker.	Ⓨ Ⓝ Ⓢ
9.	I know the difference between active and passive listening.	Ⓨ Ⓝ Ⓢ
10.	I know how to get others to listen to me.	Ⓨ Ⓝ Ⓢ

Applying What You Know

Now that you have completed this chapter, refer back to the Case Study about Gwen at the beginning of this book. Based on her situation, answer the following questions:

1. One possible reason that Gwen failed in her earlier academic pursuits is that she might not have known how to be an effective listener. How does listening affect your academic success? Describe the link between the two:

2. Active and passive listening were explained in the chapter. What situations can you identify that would be categorized as "passive" listening in your own life?

Observations

CHARTING YOUR COURSE

Listening to others and getting others to listen to us is constant hard work. It takes a great deal of practice and time to master the skills of active listening and effective communication. Listening is a voluntary, learned skill that few master. Effective listeners always seek to improve their skills by actively involving themselves in the total communication process. To be an excellent note taker, your listening skills have to be sharply focused. Perhaps the most exciting thing about having superior listening skills is that you can learn new things and grow as a student and citizen.

Getting There on Time

This particular section focuses on listening as it relates to time management. When was the last time you missed some important information because you were not an active listener? When you completed Exercises 6.1 to 6.6, how did you do?

Your time is affected by how well you listen. Below, list some "time wasters" that are a result of poor listening.

> **EXAMPLE.** You are driving and have received verbal directions. You did not listen carefully and you are late getting to your final destination.

Because your time is so valuable, it is important that you master the art of listening in order to make the most of your time. It is costly to have to repeat certain activities because you did not spend adequate time listening at the beginning of an activity. By becoming a better listener, you can become a better time manager.

Exploring Technology

The cell phone has been likened to the bubonic plague: it's everywhere. You're eating in a restaurant: a cell phone rings. You're watching the latest movie: a cell phone rings. You're sitting in the emergency room: a cell phone rings. You're in class taking notes and listening intently: a cell phone rings. In fact, people love their cell phones as much as they love their cars. You have probably seen people talk on their cell phones while *driving* their cars! Even children have cell phones today. Cell phones are an important communication tool and are becoming as commonplace as televisions and DVD players. This is another example of how technology affects our lives, whether or not we want it to.

Cell phones are a reliable, convenient, and fairly reasonable means of instant communication. The cost continues to drop due to market forces and improved technologies. Wireless companies now sell calling plans that include 4,000 "anytime" minutes, no long-distance charges, and unlimited weekend calling. Advancements in cell phone technology are quite impressive. Cell phones now can connect laptop computers to the Internet, send pictures, download MP3s, and play video games. With continued reliability and lower costs, it is reasonable to assume that many homes will replace their traditional "hard-line" phone with cell phones.

This is a three-part assignment dealing with cell phone technology:

1. What is the full name for a cell phone?
2. What makes an "all-digital network" so great? List the benefits.
3. What is the alternative to an "all-digital network"? (Please don't say "a non-all-digital network.")

HELPFUL REFERENCES:

- cellular telephone store
- cellular telephone sales representative
- books on communication (see library or bookstore)
- select magazines

THE FOLLOWING WEBSITES MAY BE HELPFUL:

www.alltell.com

www.cingular.com

www.sprint.com

www.spring.net

www.bell-labs.com/technology

www.lucent.com

Web Connections

TRAVELING THE INFORMATION SUPERHIGHWAY

During your journey, you may want to check some of the following Web addresses to enhance your listening skills:

www.itstime.com/aug97.htm#listening

www.va.gov/adr/listen.html

http://7-12educators.miningco.com/education/7-12educators/
gi/dynamic/offsite.htmsite=http://bbLL.com/ch02.html

As a result of this chapter, and in preparing for my journey, I plan to . . .

Charting Your Journey

THE PROCESS OF NOTE TAKING

William loved to play pool. Pool was his passion, his hobby, his job, and his first love. Few things ever got in the way of William's pool game. On more than one occasion, William cut class to go to the pool hall with his buddies. "I'll just get the notes from Wanda," he said. "She's always there."

When class met on Monday morning, William asked Wanda for her notes. She explained to him that her handwriting was not very good and that she took notes in her own "shorthand." "Oh, that's alright," William said. "I'll be able to get what I need from them." Wanda agreed to make a copy of her notes for William and bring them to him on Wednesday.

Wanda kept her promise and brought a copy of her notes. William put them into his backpack just before class began. The notes stayed in his backpack until the night before the midterm exam. He had not taken them out to look at them or to ask Wanda any questions about the notes. When he unfolded the notes and smoothed out the wrinkled pages, he was shocked at what he found. The notes read:

Psy started as a sci. disc. from Phi and Physio. Wihelm Wundt/GERM and Will James/US=fndrs. in lt. 19th cent. APA est. by Stanley Hall in US.
5 mjr Pers in PSY=   Biopsy. Per   Cog. Per.
Psychodyn. Per   Beh. Per.
Humanistic. Per
Psy wk in 2 mjr. areas   1. Acad.   2. Practicing

Needless to say, William was in big trouble. He could not understand Wanda's shorthand and had not bothered to ask her to translate her notes. To add insult to injury, William had lost his book a few weeks earlier. After trying to make sense of Wanda's notes, he gave up and went to the pool hall to relax and have fun before the test. William failed his midterm.

"The pen is the tongue of the mind."

MIGUEL DE CERVANTES

We've all missed a few classes from time to time, haven't we? There are very few students who have not missed a class for one reason or another. There are two important reasons for attending almost every class meeting: First, if you are not there, you will not get the information presented; second, even if you get class notes from someone else, there is no substitute for your own notes. William had several problems, including setting priorities, but one of his biggest problems was that he was not in class to take his own notes. His other problem was that he did not bother to review the notes with Wanda to make sure he understood them.

This chapter will help you to develop a system of note taking that works for you. At the end of this chapter, you will be able to:

- Identify key phrases and words for effective note taking
- Understand why note taking is essential to successful students
- Use the "L-STAR" system
- Develop and use a personalized shorthand note-taking system
- Use the outline technique
- Use the mapping (or webbing) technique
- Use the Cornell (split-page or modified) technique
- Put into practice "Roadways to Effective Note Taking"

The 10 Milestones questions are intended to make you think about your ability to take effective notes. Take a moment to answer each statement carefully.

How many of your answers were either "No" or "Sometimes"? If you want to change more of your "No" answers to "Yes" answers, this chapter will help you achieve that goal. Consider this—taking notes effectively is one of the most important skills you can develop. This is also one of the easiest skills to learn. Effective note taking can help you record all of the information your instructors present, and will be the basis for later review. Think of note taking as a tool that will help you achieve academic success.

WHY TAKE NOTES?

Is note taking really important, you might ask? Actually, knowing how to take useful, accurate notes can dramatically improve your life as a student. If you are an effective listener and note taker, you have two of the most valuable skills any student could ever use. It is important to take notes for several reasons:

1. You become an active part of the listening process.
2. It creates a history of your course content.
3. You have written criteria to follow when studying.
4. It creates a visual aid for studying the material.

As mentioned previously, listening is a learned skill, and so is note taking. Simply writing information down does not constitute good note taking. There are note-taking systems and helpful clues that enable students to become more effective note takers. This chapter will discuss, review, and analyze these systems and methods and help you determine which works best for you. Just because your friend uses an outlining method does not make that method right for you. If you are a visual learner, you may need to consider the mapping system. A note-taking system is personal and individualized. You will discover the best style for you as we move through this section of the chapter.

DO I NEED TO WRITE THAT DOWN?

College professors hear this question daily: "Do we need to write this down?" If it were up to most professors, they would have students write down the majority of what is said in class, but they know this is practically impossible. With that in mind, students who are effective listeners and note takers have figured out how to actively listen and distinguish the most important material covered. As discussed in the chapter on listening, they know how to listen for key words and phrases. To recap from the chapter on listening, some of the most important key phrases professors may use are:

in addition	as a result of	above all
because	finally	in contrast
due to	most importantly	to illustrate
the main issues are	you'll see this again	specifically
such as	nevertheless	characteristics
another way to	for example	in comparison
on the other hand	therefore	as stated earlier

Generally, when these phrases are used, you can be assured that the professor is making a major point and you should listen carefully and write it down. Usually, if material is presented on an overhead, chalkboard, slickboard, or other media, you should take notes on it.

PREPARING TO TAKE NOTES

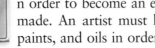In order to become an effective note taker, some preparations have to be made. An artist must have materials such as a brush, palette, canvas, paints, and oils in order to create a painting. Likewise, the student must

have certain materials and make detailed preparations for note taking. For example:

• **Attend class.** This may sound completely elementary and out-of-place, but you will be surprised how many college students feel that they do not have to go to class. "Oh, I'll just get the notes from Wanda," they say, like William in the opening story of this chapter. The only trouble with getting the notes from Wanda is that they are *Wanda's notes.* You may be able to copy her words, but you may very well miss the meaning behind them. If Wanda has developed her own note-taking style, you may not be able to read many of her notes. She may have written something like this:

Come to class prepared. It is easier to take notes when you have a preliminary understanding of the material.

G/Oke lvd in C/SC for 1yr ely 20c.

Can you decode Wanda's notes? How would you ever know that these notes translate to mean: "Georgia O'Keeffe lived in Columbia, South Carolina, for one year in the early part of the twentieth century"? In order to be an effective note taker, class attendance is very important. There is no substitute for it.

• **Come to class prepared.** Do you read your assignments nightly? College professors are constantly amazed at the number of students who come to class and *then* realize that they should have read the homework materials. Reading your text, handouts, and workbooks, or listening to tapes is one of the most effective ways to become a better note taker. It is always easier to write and take notes when you have a preliminary understanding of what is being covered. Few student tasks are more difficult than trying to take notes on material that you have never confronted before. Preparing to take notes involves doing your homework and coming to class ready to listen.

Coming to class prepared also means that you have brought the proper materials to take notes. This means that you have your textbook or lab manual, at least two pens, enough *sharpened* pencils to make it through the lecture, a notebook, and a highlighter. Some students may also bring a tape recorder. If you choose to use a recorder, always get permission from the instructor before recording, and don't rely solely on the tapes you record.

• **Bring your text to class.** Many students do not feel as if they need to bring their text to class if they have read the homework. You will find that many professors will refer repeatedly to the text while lecturing. Always bring your text to class with you. This will assist you in your note-taking endeavors, especially if the professor asks you to highlight, underline, or refer to the text in class. Following the professor in the text as she lectures may also help you in organizing your notes.

• **Ask questions and participate in class!** One of the most critical actions a student can perform in class is asking questions and actively participating in the class discussion. If you do not understand a concept or theory, it is imperative that you ask questions. It is not wise to just leave class with a feeling of being lost. Many professors use student questions as a way of teaching and reviewing materials. Your questioning and participation will definitely help you, but it could also help others who did not understand. Asking questions moves you from a passive learner to an *active* learner.

NOW WE'RE READY TO BEGIN THE BUILDING PROCESS

At this point, you have been exposed to several thoughts about note taking. First, you know that you have to cultivate and build your active listening skills; second, you must overcome the obstacles to effective listening such as prejudging, talking during the discussion, and bringing emotions to the table; third, you have to be familiar with key phrases used by professors; fourth, you must understand the importance of note taking; fifth, you should prepare yourself to take effective notes; sixth and finally, you must realize that scanning, reading, and using your texts helps you understand the materials to be discussed.

THE L-STAR SYSTEM

One of the most effective ways to take notes begins with learning the L-STAR system. L-STAR stands for:

Listening

Setting It Down

Translating

Analyzing

Remembering

This five-step process allows you to compile complete, accurate, and visually oriented notes for future reference. By using this system, you will greatly improve your ability to take accurate notes, participate in class, help other students, study more effectively, and perform well on your exams and quizzes.

LISTENING. As mentioned in the listening chapter, one of the best ways to become an effective note taker is to become an active listener. It is also important to sit near the front of the room so that you will be able to hear the professor and see the board and/or overheads. It is best to sit where you will be able to see the professor's facial expressions and mouth. If you see that the professor's face has become animated or expressive, you can bet the information he is presenting at that time is important. Write it down. If you sit in the back of the room, you may not be able to hear or see certain expressions.

SETTING IT DOWN. The actual writing of notes can be a difficult task. Some instructors are very organized in their delivery of information, others are not. Your listening skills, once again, are going to play an important role in determining what needs to be written down. In most cases, you will not have time to take notes word for word. You will have to be more selective about the information you choose to "set down." One of the best ways to keep up with the information being presented is to develop a shorthand system of your own. Many of the symbols will be universal, but you may use some symbols, pictures, and markings that are uniquely your own. Some of the more common symbols are:

w/	with	w/o	without	etc	and so on
=	equals	≠	does not equal	e.g.	for example
<	less than	>	greater than	vs	against
%	percentage	#	number	esp	especially
@	at	$	money	"	quote
&	and	^	increase	?	question
+	plus or addition	−	subtract	. . .	and so on
*	important				

These symbols and abbreviations can save you valuable time when taking notes. You may wish to memorize them because you will use them frequently. As you become more adept at note taking, you will quickly learn how to abbreviate words, phrases, and names.

Using the symbols listed above and your own shorthand system, practice reducing the following statements. Be sure that you do not reduce them to the extent that you will not be able to understand them at a later date.

1. *It is important to remember that a greater percentage of money invested does not necessarily equal greater profits.*
   Reduce: _____

   _____

2. *She was quoted as saying, "Money equals success." Without exception, the audience disagreed with her logic.*
   Reduce: _____

   _____

3. *He found a greater number of books at the new store than he thought possible. For example, there were over 1,000 dictionaries available; a far greater number than at any other store.*
   Reduce: _____

   _____

4. *The increase in scholarship money has allowed a greater number of students to attend college.*
   Reduce: _____

   _____

TRANSLATING. One of the most valuable things that you can do as a student is to translate your notes immediately after each class. This can save you hours of work when you begin to prepare for exams. Many students feel that this step is not important and leave it out—*don't*. Many times, students take notes so quickly that they make mistakes or use abbreviations that they may not remember later.

After each class, go to the library or some quiet place and review your notes. It may not be possible to do this immediately after class, but before the day ends, you should have rewritten and translated your classroom notes. This gives you the opportunity to put the notes in your own words *and* to incorporate your text notes into your classroom notes. You also have a chance to correct spelling, reword key phrases, spell out your abbreviations, and prepare questions for the next class. Sounds like a lot of work, doesn't it? Well, it is a great deal of work, but if you try this technique for one week, you should see a vast improvement in your grades and understanding of material.

Translating your notes helps you to make connections between previous materials discussed, your own personal experiences and readings, and new material presented. Translating aids in recalling and applying new information. Few things are more difficult than trying to reconstruct your notes the night before a test, especially when the notes may have been taken several weeks ago. Translating your notes daily will be a precious gift when exam time comes.

When you are translating your notes, ask yourself, "What does this mean and why is it important?"

ANALYZING. This step happens when you are translating your notes from class. When you analyze your notes, you are asking yourself two basic questions:

1. What does this mean?
2. Why is it important?

If you can answer these two questions about your material, you have almost mastered the information. It is true, some instructors want you to "spit" back the exact same information you were given; most professors, however, will ask you for a more detailed understanding and application of the material. When you are translating your notes, begin to answer the two questions using your notes, textbook, supplemental materials, and information gathered from outside research. Again, this is not simple or easy, but it is important to test yourself to see if you understand the information. It is important to note that many lectures are built on past lectures. If you do not understand what happened in class on September 17th, you may not be able to understand what happens on September 19th. Analyzing your notes while translating will give you a more complete understanding of the material.

REMEMBERING. Once you have listened to the lecture, set the notes to paper, and translated/analyzed the material, it is time to study, or commit the material to memory. The next chapter on studying will assist you in this endeavor. Some of the best ways to remember information are to create a visual picture, read the notes out loud, use mnemonic devices, and find a study partner.

PUTTING IT ALL TOGETHER: NOTE-TAKING TECHNIQUES

There are as many systems and methods of note taking as there are people who take notes. Some people write too small, others too large. Some write too much, others not enough. Some write what is really important, while others miss key points. This section is provided to help you use the L-STAR system as a formalized note-taking technique. The L-STAR system can be used with any of the techniques about to be discussed.

Before we examine the three most commonly used note-taking systems, we need to review a few principles about basic note taking.

- Date your notes and use a heading.
- Keep notes from each class separate by using a divider or separate notebook system.
- Use 8-1/2" × 11" paper with a three-hole punch.
- Copy any information that is written on the board, used on the overhead, or shown with charts and graphs.
- File your notes in a three-ring binder.
- Organize and review your notes the same day they are taken.
- Try not to "doodle" while taking notes.
- Use your own shorthand system.
- Clip related handouts to appropriate notes.

THE THREE MOST COMMON NOTE-TAKING SYSTEMS ARE:

The Outline Technique
The Cornell or Split Page System (also called the T System)
The Mapping System

The Outline Technique

Although the outline technique is one of the most commonly used note-taking systems, it is also one of the most misused systems. Outlining your notes in class can be a difficult thing to do, especially if your professor does not follow an outline while lecturing. When using the outline system, it is best to get all the information from the lecture and then *combine* the lecture notes and text notes to create an outline after class. Most professors would not advise you to use the outline system of note taking in class. You may be able to use a modified outline while taking notes in class, but the most important thing to remember is not to get bogged down in a "system"; it is much more important that you concentrate on getting the

FIGURE 7.1	Sample outline style notes.

Study Skills   Oct. 18
                                                Wednesday

Topic: Listening
I. The Process of Listening (ROAR)
    A. R = Receiving
        1. W/in range of sound
        2. Hearing the information
    B. O = Organizing & focusing
        1. Choose to listen actively
        2. Observe the origin, direction & intent
    C. A = Assignment
        1. You assign a meaning
        2. You may have to hear it more than once
    D. R = Reacting
        1. Our response to what we heard
        2. Reaction can be anything
II. Definitions of Listening (POC)
    A. P = Listening w/ a purpose
    B. O = Listening w/ objectivity
    C. C = Listening constructively

ideas down on paper. You will always be able to go back after class and "arrange" your notes accordingly.

If you are going to use a modified or informal outline while taking class notes, you may want to consider grouping information together under a heading as a means of outlining. It is easier to remember information that is logically grouped rather than scattered throughout the pages. If you are in an economics class and the lecture is on taxes, you might outline your notes using the headings *Local Taxes*, *State Taxes*, and *Federal Taxes*, for example.

After you rewrite your notes using class lecture information and materials taken from the text, your pages may look something like Figure 7.1.

The Cornell (Modified Cornell, Split Page, or "T") System

The Cornell system was developed by Dr. Walter Pauk of Cornell University. The basic principle of this system is to split the page into three sections. Each section will be used for different information. Section "A" will be used for questions that summarize information found in section "B." Section "B" will be used for the actual notes from class, and section "C" will be used for a summary. Your blank note page should look like Figure 7.2.

When using the Cornell method, you should choose a technique that is most comfortable and beneficial to you. You might use mapping (discussed

Sample note page using the Cornell system.   **FIGURE 7.2**

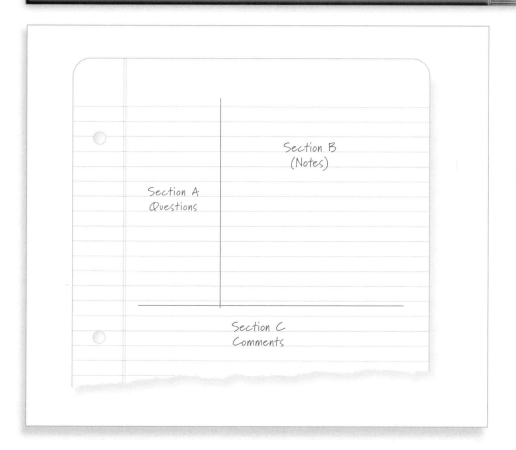

next) or outlining on a Cornell page. A page of notes using an outline with the Cornell method will look like Figure 7.3.

The Mapping System

If you are a visual learner, it might be important to review this section carefully. This note-taking system creates a picture of your information. It may be easier to recall for those who learn best by visualization. The mapping system is just that; it creates a "map" or web of your information that allows you to see the relationship among certain facts, names, dates, and places. Your mapping system might look something like Figure 7.4. Mapping using the Cornell system might resemble Figure 7.5.

The most important thing to remember about each note-taking system is that it *must* work for you. Do not use a system because your friends use it or because you feel that you have to use a certain system. Experiment with each system to determine which one you like. A combination might work best for you.

Always remember to keep your notes organized, dated, and neat. Notes that cannot be read are no good to you or to anyone else. An example of a note-taking system that is inappropriate for anyone is shown in Figure 7.6.

FIGURE 7.3

Outlining using the Cornell system.

Study Skills 101   Oct. 20
                                                    Friday
Topic: Listening

                          *The Listening Process or (ROAR)
                              A = Receiving
What is the   1. Within range of sound
listening process?   2. Hearing the information
(ROAR)   B = Organizing & focusing
                                 1. Choose to listen actively
                                 2. Observe origin
Definition   *Listening Defined
of listening   A. Listening w/ a purpose
(POC)   B. Listening w/ objectivity
                              C. Listening constructively
Obstacles   *What interferes w/ listening
(PTE)   A. Prejudging
                              B. Talking
                              C. Emotions

The listening process involves Receiving, Organizing, Assigning &
Reacting—Talking, Prejudging & Emotions are obstacles.

FIGURE 7.4

Sample notes using the mapping system.

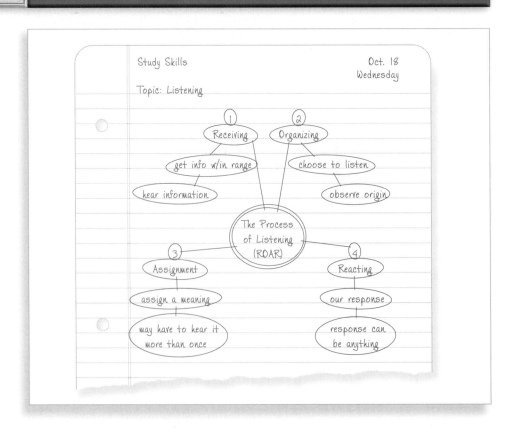

Study Skills   Oct. 18
                                                    Wednesday
Topic: Listening

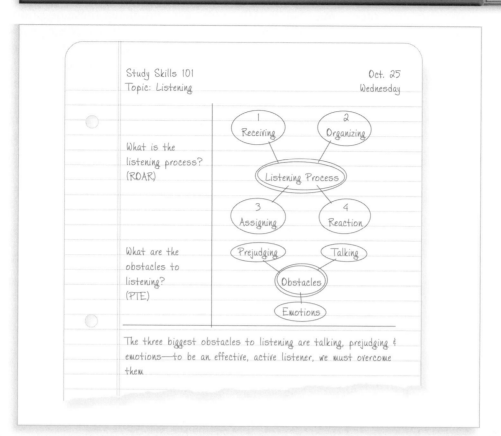

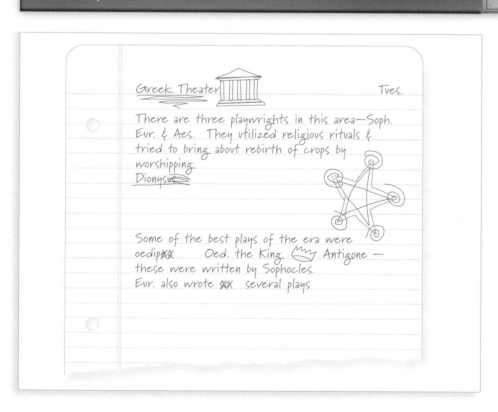

Below, you will find a few questions that you should ask yourself about your present note-taking system. After you have completed these questions, your professor will assign a lecture to which you should listen. Your professor will give you the details for taking notes in the spaces provided. When listening to the lecture, you will take notes using the outline system, the Cornell system, and the mapping system. This is the only way to determine which is the most effective for you.

1. *What system of note taking do you currently use?*

_____

_____

2. *Does it work well? Why or why not?*

_____

_____

3. *What advantages do you see in using the outline system?*

_____

_____

4. *What advantages do you see in using the Cornell system?*

_____

_____

5. *What advantages do you see in using the mapping system?*

_____

_____

Use the spaces provided below to practice your note-taking skills.

THE OUTLINE METHOD

_____

_____

_____

_____

_____

THE CORNELL METHOD

_____

_____

_____

_____

_____

Take a moment to complete the Milestones checklist again.

Hopefully, you have turned some of your "No" and "Sometimes" answers to "Yes" answers as a result of this chapter. Have you effectively utilized the Cornell and mapping strategies? Which system of note taking works best for you? How does taking notes effectively assist you in your studying? Do you take advantage of using a note-taking partner? Why or why not? All of these questions relate to your ability to use new techniques to tackle study tasks. *None* of these techniques will be successful for you if you do not try them. Take some time to get acquainted with each of the methods. You will find that your overall note-taking ability will improve, directly affecting the grades you earn.

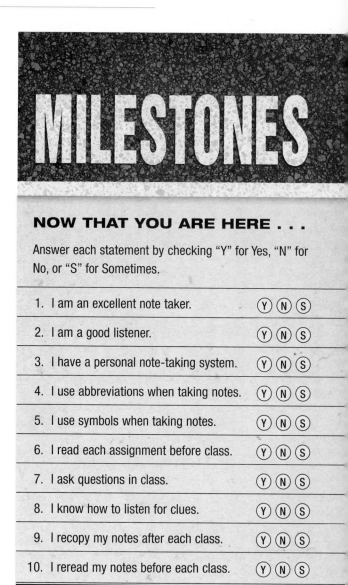

MILESTONES

NOW THAT YOU ARE HERE . . .

Answer each statement by checking "Y" for Yes, "N" for No, or "S" for Sometimes.

1. I am an excellent note taker.	Ⓨ Ⓝ Ⓢ
2. I am a good listener.	Ⓨ Ⓝ Ⓢ
3. I have a personal note-taking system.	Ⓨ Ⓝ Ⓢ
4. I use abbreviations when taking notes.	Ⓨ Ⓝ Ⓢ
5. I use symbols when taking notes.	Ⓨ Ⓝ Ⓢ
6. I read each assignment before class.	Ⓨ Ⓝ Ⓢ
7. I ask questions in class.	Ⓨ Ⓝ Ⓢ
8. I know how to listen for clues.	Ⓨ Ⓝ Ⓢ
9. I recopy my notes after each class.	Ⓨ Ⓝ Ⓢ
10. I reread my notes before each class.	Ⓨ Ⓝ Ⓢ

ROADWAYS

- Attend *class.*

- Be prepared for every class by doing *homework* assignments.

- Sit where you can *see* and hear the professor.

- *Recopy* your notes after each class.

- If it's on the board or overhead, *write* it down.

- Use loose-leaf paper and a three-ring *binder.*

- Keep your notes for each course *separate* from other class notes.

- Keep good, straight *posture* when in class.

- Develop your listening abilities and *tune out* chatter.

- Ask *questions.*

- Use *abbreviations* and special notes to yourself.

- Keep your notes *neat* and *clear;* do not doodle on your notes.

- *Participate* in class.

Applying What You Know

Developing the art of taking notes can be challenging; however, with practice you can become an effective and efficient note taker. Hopefully, this chapter afforded you the opportunity to improve your note-taking skills.

Now that you have finished this chapter on the process of note taking, refer back to the Case Study about Gwen at the beginning of this book. Based on Gwen's situation, answer the following questions:

1. What note-taking technique would you suggest that Gwen implement?

   _____

   _____

   _____

   _____

2. How would you explain to Gwen how to use the L-STAR method in her MUS 105 class?

   _____

   _____

   _____

   _____

3. How would you convince Gwen that taking notes would help her to improve her grades in all her classes?

   _____

   _____

   _____

   _____

Observations

CHARTING YOUR COURSE

If you remember the concepts of the L-STAR system (Listening, Setting It Down, Translating, Analyzing, and Remembering), use this system as a study pattern, and find a note-taking system that is comfortable and useful to you, then you will begin to see drastic changes in your abilities as a note taker and in your performance as a student.

Getting There on Time

Once again, it is important to realize the impact that time management has on the study skill of note taking. Not using a system of note taking can directly affect the amount of time you need to spend preparing for an exam. How much time do you usually spend with your notes before a test? If you've been an effective note taker, the time spent reviewing notes can be the most effective use of your time. Filing your notes in your three-ring binder is another time-saving technique.

Do you feel that the time you spend taking notes and reviewing them is time well spent? Why or why not?

_____

_____

_____

_____

How does not having any notes affect the time you have to spend preparing for an exam?

_____

_____

_____

_____

Effective note taking is a combination of listening, recording, and efficiently using a valuable resource: time.

Exploring Technology

In this assignment, you will visit an instructor's website and print the lecture notes. Many instructors use course websites to provide you with valuable course information, including the syllabus, lecture notes, and resources. To complete this activity, begin your journey at www.fdtc.edu. Click on "online college," then "WebCT," and finally "Login to WebCT." Username: public. Password: public. Under "my courses," select "The American Civil War." Now that you have arrived at the American Civil War course taught by Mr. David Eldridge, take a few minutes to browse the contents.

In this exercise you will:

1. Locate the instructor's lecture notes, then print a set of lecture notes that you find most interesting. What note-taking method does the instructor use?

2. Review the notes and convert them to the Cornell system.

Web Connections

TRAVELING THE INFORMATION SUPERHIGHWAY

During your journey, you may want to check out some of the following note-taking Web addresses:

www.sheridanc.on.ca/career/tips/classrm.htm

www.csbsju.edu/academicadvising/help/lec-note.htm

www.yorku.ca/cdc/isp/notesonline/note1.htm

www.ucc.vt.edu/stdysk/notetake.html

As a result of this chapter, and in preparing for my journey, I plan to . . .

Driver Training

LEARNING HOW TO STUDY

How well Lisa remembers her first semester at college. It was great being on her own. Everything was going well until her economics professor returned the first exam. She remembers it having twenty-five multiple-choice questions and three discussion questions. Lisa also remembers the shock she received when the test was returned with a failing grade. She was devastated! Lisa couldn't believe it! She couldn't figure out how it had happened. She remembers hoping that maybe her professor had made a mistake. But he had not. She remembers feeling scared and doubting if she belonged in college at all.

There was a note on her exam from the professor that said to see him after class. Lisa waited fearfully to speak to him. During their discussion, he shared with Lisa that he felt she hadn't studied for the test. Lisa explained that she had indeed studied. She explained that she reviewed her class notes for almost an hour before the exam. The professor felt that an hour wasn't enough. He offered to work with her during his office hours. Lisa faithfully attended the study sessions, and she learned a variety of strategies designed to help her learn the material. At first, she was overwhelmed with the amount of study time, but as she became proficient using the studying skills, the amount of time she had to spend decreased. Even though Lisa only made a C in this class, she learned how to study. As a result, the classes she took after economics were much easier.

HOMEWORK? STUDYING? WHO NEEDS IT?

Some students think that homework and studying consist merely of writing or glancing at notes. This is a myth. Achieving success in school requires more. Unfortunately, many students are less than successful in school because they have never learned how to study.

In this chapter, you will "learn how to learn." It is extremely important that you keep an open mind when implementing the suggested techniques.

"The only man who is educated is the man who has learned how to learn; the man who has learned how to adapt and change; the man who has realized that no knowledge is secure, that only the process of seeking knowledge gives us a basis for security."

CARL ROGERS

You will be encouraged to try new things that will make a difference. Learning the skills, however, will require commitment, dedication, and time. The more you use the study skills the better you will become at using them. Eventually, you will be able to spend less time and get better grades.

After completing this chapter, you will be able to:

- Understand the importance of class attendance
- Explain and use various organizational strategies
- Use various textbook reading skills
- Apply techniques to learn vocabulary words
- Describe how to study math
- Understand the importance of critical thinking

The Milestones checklist will help you assess where you are with your current study habits. Answer each question as truthfully and honestly as possible.

How did you do? Are your study habits where you think they should be? If not, don't despair—this chapter will help you develop study habits and skills that can serve you for the rest of your academic life. At the conclusion of this chapter, you should have all of the skills necessary to make the most of your valuable study time.

MILESTONES

WHERE ARE YOU NOW?

Answer each statement by checking "Y" for Yes, "N" for No, or "S" for Sometimes.

	Y	N	S
1. I am organized.	Y	N	S
2. I use a study plan.	Y	N	S
3. I know how to study math.	Y	N	S
4. I schedule time to study.	Y	N	S
5. I know how to read a textbook.	Y	N	S
6. I always attend class.	Y	N	S
7. I know how to learn vocabulary.	Y	N	S
8. I know how to use the SQ3R study method.	Y	N	S
9. I highlight my notes and textbook.	Y	N	S
10. I have an appropriate place to study.	Y	N	S

ATTENDING CLASS

Studying includes being organized and using a variety of study techniques. Before we begin discussing these skills, we must discuss the importance of attending class. Some students fail to take class attendance seriously. Attending class is crucial for effective studying and learning. Your instructor may guide you by providing course outlines, instructions, and suggestions. By making every attempt to attend class, you are aiding your success. If you are unable to attend class, you are still responsible for the material covered.

TECHNIQUES FOR SUCCESSFUL STUDYING

Getting Organized

To do a good job of studying you have to be organized. You should develop a notebook system that allows you to store class notes, handouts, and assignments. Being organized also involves having an appropriate study environment, having accessible study supplies, planning time to study, and developing a study plan.

What Note-Taking System Do You Use?

It is very difficult to study the material in a history class if you do not record what was presented during class. Taking notes during class gives you valuable information to review or study prior to an exam. Chapter 7 thoroughly addresses appropriate note-taking systems and gives you information on how to take notes.

When Do You Study?

To study effectively, you must set aside a time specifically for the purpose of studying. If you fail to schedule a time to study, you will most likely not have *enough* time to study. Because it is recommended that students spend two hours studying for every hour spent in class (this varies from student to student), organizing your time is critical. Chapter 2, Time Management, discusses how to manage time effectively.

Where Do You Study?

Choosing the best study environment can determine how successful you will be when you are studying. The appropriate study place is different for everyone. It must be a place where you are comfortable. Therefore, paying attention to the physical condition of the room is important. Proper lighting and temperature, for instance, should be considered. When the lights are low and the room is warm, you may have an urge to take a nap. Some students need some level of noise in the background to concentrate, while others do not. It is, therefore, okay to play soft music when studying. But choose a station or recording that is *not* your favorite—it will be less likely to distract you from your studying. When you are at home, you should choose a room that is relatively quiet (except, perhaps, for the music) and free of distractions. Perhaps the dining room table or your bedroom might be good choices, provided in the latter case that your bedroom has a desk on which you can work. If you find that you cannot concentrate at home, you should choose a place outside of your home for studying. A great choice is the school library or student study center.

Describe your study environment.

_____

_____

_____

_____

Do you feel your study place is appropriate? Why or why not?

_____

_____

_____

List potential study environments that you could use.

_____

_____

_____

_____

Study Supplies

Once you have identified where you plan to do most of your studying, the next step is to be prepared for studying. Each time you study, you should have all of your study supplies at hand. It is amazing how much time is wasted due to poor preparation. Therefore, you should have everything you regularly use in a portable basket or box. Your study supplies should include, but not be limited to, the following items:

pencils/pens	computer disks/CDs
sharpener	highlighters
notebook paper	stapler
staples	folders
thesaurus	dictionary
index cards	colored pencils
scientific/graphing calculator	paper clips

List additional supplies that you feel you may need.

_____

_____

_____

_____

A STUDY PLAN

Now that you have chosen a note-taking system, decided on a place to study, put all of your study supplies in a basket, and identified specific times for studying, you must create a study plan. Making a to-do list will help you organize your study time. This plan will enable you to get the most from your valuable time. List the most difficult assignments to be completed first. If you save those items until the end, you will not be at your best. By waiting until the end to complete difficult tasks, your frustration will be increased and you may decide not to complete the assignment at all. If you do not complete everything on your list, the unfinished work should be transferred to your study plan for the next day.

Using the academic subjects that you are taking this semester, create a study plan using the to-do list below.

TO-DO LIST

1. _____
2. _____
3. _____
4. _____
5. _____

ROADWAYS TO EFFECTIVE STUDYING

Roadways to effective studying involve being organized and studying. The first step, not surprisingly, is to be *organized*. The tips mentioned at the beginning of this chapter describe ways to become organized. The second step is to *study*. Studying is what you do to learn a new skill and to reinforce prior knowledge. This section covers six areas:

1. Learning vocabulary
2. Reading and using textbooks
3. The SQ3R method
4. Reviewing class and textbook notes
5. Studying math
6. Identifying tips for studying math effectively

> *"Learning is not a task or a problem; it is a way to be in the world. Man learns as he pursues goals and projects that have meaning for him."*
>
> SIDNEY JOURNARD

Learning Vocabulary

You must have an understanding of words in order to effectively communicate with those around you. How well you speak, write, read, and understand words may influence how successful you will be in school.

Students with weak vocabularies are at a disadvantage. These students have trouble understanding their college textbooks and their instructors' class lectures. It is, therefore, important that you make a commitment to build your vocabulary.

Perhaps one of the best strategies to improve vocabulary and reading comprehension is (to put it simply) *reading*. When you read, it is crucial that you not skip over words that are unfamiliar to you. Doing so affects your ability to understand what you have read. Instead, use *context clues* and *word analysis* to define the unfamiliar words.

Context Clues

The sentence or paragraph that a word appears in is known as the *context* of the word. In a text, nearby phrases can be very helpful in figuring out the meaning of a word you are unsure of. For instance, what does the word "capricious" mean? By itself, it may be difficult to define the word; however, in the following sentence, the word should seem clearer: "Her capricious or impulsive nature caused her to make many mistakes." In this context, the word *capricious* means "impulsive." The sentence itself defines the meaning of the word.

Context clues usually give you at least a vague meaning of a word and allow you to continue your reading without stopping to look up a word in a dictionary. Look for three basic context clues as you read through a sentence or paragraph:

- One context clue that a sentence can offer is a *definition of the word*. The sentence may actually define the unfamiliar word; for example: "The apartment was so spacious and beautiful it could be called *palatial*."
- Another clue to look for in the context is *opposition*. In this case, the context may explain what the word does *not* mean; for example: "She was not *egocentric* because she cared deeply for other people."
- The third clue to look for in the context is an example of what the word means. Here the context gives you a synonym for the word used; for example: "*Horticulture*, or gardening, has become a very popular way to reduce stress."

You may find that using context clues when reading helps you to understand what you have read and limits the interruption of having to look up something in a dictionary. The dictionary is a valuable resource that should be used when you cannot determine the meaning of a word. It is also a good idea to highlight the unfamiliar words in your dictionary and/or put the word and its definition on index cards.

Practice using context clues to define the italicized word in each sentence.

1. Many *kinesthetic* learners find that they must move during the learning process.

   Kinesthetic means _____

   _____

2. It's amazing that John is always *immaculately* dressed, yet his car is often dirty.

   Immaculate means _____

   _____

3. I was *mortified* and embarrassed when my voice cracked during my speech.

   Mortified means _____

   _____

4. Lisa *procrastinates* instead of getting her work done on time.

   Procrastinates means _____

   _____

5. You can save money by buying *generic* brands of food.

   Generic means _____

   _____

6. The South's warm and sunny climate is very comfortable or *hospitable* to many Northerners.

Hospitable means _____

Word Analysis

Another technique that can be used to decode an unfamiliar word is word analysis. Word analysis involves examining parts of a word to determine its meaning. Words can be made up of a root or "base" word, prefixes that come before the base word, and/or suffixes that come after the base word.

An example is the word *disconnection*.

The root of this word is *connect*.

The prefix of this word is *dis*.

The suffix of this word *-tion*.

Becoming familiar with common prefixes and suffixes can help when you come across an unfamiliar word.

Some common prefixes are:

PREFIX	MEANING	EXAMPLE
un-	not	unusual
in-	not	incomplete
pre-	before	prenuptial
post-	after	posttest
re-	again	restart

Some common suffixes are:

SUFFIX	MEANING	EXAMPLE
-ness	full of	usefulness
-less	lack of	useless
-ful	full of	hopeful
-able	full of	knowledgeable
-ward	in the direction of	backward

Reading and Using Textbooks

Every textbook is filled with a variety of features designed to guide you through the material you are reading. In order to successfully use your textbooks, you must become familiar with all the features in your textbooks. Every time you receive or purchase a new textbook, you should spend 20 to 30 minutes becoming familiar with the special features of the text, such as a table of contents or glossary. See Figure 8.1 for a sample table of contents.

Sample table of contents.

FIGURE 8.1

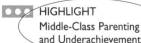

List the features most commonly found in a textbook.

_____

_____

_____

Your list might include the following: table of contents, chapter headings and subheadings, key vocabulary words, section questions, chapter introductions and summaries, study questions, glossary, index, appendix, preface, etc.

Using one of your textbooks, list some of the features and their purpose.

1. *Feature* _____

   Purpose _____

   _____

2. *Feature* _____

   Purpose _____

   _____

3. *Feature* _____

   Purpose _____

   _____

4. *Feature* _____

   Purpose _____

   _____

5. *Feature* _____

   Purpose _____

   _____

The SQ3R Method

After you have previewed your textbook, reviewed the table of contents, and identified chapter features, it is now time to begin reading and learning the chapter information. Some students find reading textbook material difficult. One of the best ways to read, learn, and study a chapter in your textbook is to use the SQ3R method. This stands for:

Survey

Question

Read

Recite

Review

The process for using the SQ3R method is as follows:

STEP ONE: SURVEY. The first step of the SQ3R method involves surveying, or pre-reading, the assigned chapter in your textbook. You begin surveying by reading the title and introduction of the chapter. This gives you an overview of the chapter. As you survey the chapter, read the headings, subheadings, and key vocabulary (usually in bold print) and look at any graphs, tables, and pictures. Finally, read the chapter summary, if any, and the review questions. After surveying the chapter, you should be familiar with the information. Reading, learning, and studying the chapter becomes easier when you take 15 to 20 minutes to survey the contents.

STEP TWO: QUESTION. The second step of the SQ3R method is to form questions. Take each heading and subheading and turn it into a question. Questions beginning with "why," "what," or "how" are the most effective. Creating questions establishes a purpose for reading and enables you to stay focused.

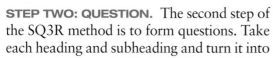

The second step of the SQ3R method is to form questions from headings and subheadings. These questions will help you stay focused as you read.

STEP THREE: READ. The third step of the SQ3R method is to read with the purpose of finding the answers to the questions you have formed. Do not read passively. Become actively involved in what you are reading by highlighting key phrases that answer your questions and by making notes in the margin. When you read actively, you are reading effectively.

STEP FOUR: RECITE. The next step in this method is to recite what you have learned. After you have read the entire chapter, go back and recite the answers to the questions. This strategy is an important step in remembering what you have read.

STEP FIVE: REVIEW. The final step is to review the entire chapter. This step is very similar to surveying. Once again, go back and read the introduction, headings, subheadings, vocabulary, the special notes that you made in the margins or in the text, the summary questions, and the study questions. Any questions you still cannot answer or information that is not clear should be noted so that you can ask your instructor for clarification.

The SQ3R method is a thorough way to read, to study, and to learn new information. If you complete all of the steps in the SQ3R method, you will, in all likelihood, be thoroughly learning the material, just as you set out to do. You will be amazed at how easy it is to understand your textbooks when you use the SQ3R technique. The results will be far-reaching: you will feel better prepared for class, class lectures will be clearer, and most of all, your performance on tests will improve.

Highlighting Your Textbook

Highlighting your textbook or an article is a technique to use when you are reading, learning, and studying. Keep the following suggestions in mind when highlighting:

1. Highlight approximately one-third of a paragraph (main ideas and supporting details).
2. Label main ideas and supporting details by using different colored highlighters.
3. Make margin notes using special notations such as RR for re-read; DEF for definition; 1, 2, 3 for enumeration; and !!!/*** for important.
4. Take notes on the highlighted material and add them to your class notes.
5. *Never* rely on highlighting that someone else has done in your text.

EXERCISE 8.1   *Practicing SQ3R*

DIRECTIONS: Using the sample chapter in Figure 8.2 from *Understanding Plays* by Millie Barranger (1994), practice using the SQ3R method. Answer the questions provided below.

Survey the chapter.

1. *What is the title of the chapter?* _____
2. *How many major headings are found in this chapter?* _____
3. *Are there any graphs, tables, or pictures?* _____
4. *Is there a chapter summary?* _____

Form **Questions** from the chapter headings.

Choose three of the headings and turn them into questions for review.

1. _____

2. _____

3. _____

Read the chapter, highlighting key phrases that answer the questions you developed.

Understanding Plays

The manuscript, the words on the page, was what you started with and what you have left. The production is of great importance, has given the play the life it will know, but it is gone, in the end, and the pages are the only wall against which to throw the future or measure the past.

—Lillian Hellman[1]

DRAMA AND PERFORMANCE

We are bombarded daily with television, videos, newsprint, films, and dramatic events. Terrorists threaten the lives of airline passengers, battles are fought in faraway places, nations negotiate peace treaties, nuclear accidents threaten lives, and a famous boxer divorces his glamorous actress-wife. All are subjects for novels, films, miniseries, and plays. The larger subject is human experience (real or imagined), but the means of representing experience in artistic forms differ with the artist and with the medium. A play, or the dramatic text, is one of the theatre's principal media. It is at once a text to be read and a script to be performed.

Plays are read daily by individuals as diverse as stage directors, designers, actors, technicians, teachers, students, critics, scholars, and the general public. In contrast to novels and poetry, a play is often the most difficult type of prose or poetry to read because it is written not only to be read, but also to be performed by actors before audiences. Like a screenplay, a play is also given life by actors although the medium and technology are significantly different. Kevin Kline acts Shakespeare's Hamlet or Derek Jacobi performs Richard II on a stage before audiences for the time of the performance. In contrast, their film performances in *The Big Chill* and *I, Claudius*, respectively, are contained, unchanging, on videotape for all time.

Reading plays is a unique challenge. As readers, we must visualize all of the elements the playwright has placed on the page to convey a story to us: its characters in action and conflict, its happening in time and space, and, at the end, the completed meaning of all that has happened.

Plays have been formally analyzed since the days of classical Greece. Aristotle's *Poetics* (c. 330 B.C.) is our first record of a critical assessment of plays presented in the ancient Greek festivals. Since Aristotle, there have been many approaches to "understanding" plays. For our purposes, we will approach the analysis of plays from the viewpoint and techniques of the playwright who creates the dramatic text. As Lillian Hellman said, the words on the page are the playwright's measure, after all is said and done, of the future and the past: "The manuscript, the words on the page, was what you started with and what you have left."[2]

Although we call the playwright's words on the printed page "drama," we also use the words "drama" and "dramatic" to describe many events ranging from riots to parades, from sports events to political speeches. That these current events are "real" rather than "fiction" is the essential distinction between life's "dramas" and dramatic "texts." Martin Esslin wrote that "a dramatic text, unperformed, is literature."[3] Like a novel or poem, drama, as written words, is considered a literary text. The chief ingredient that distinguishes drama from other types of literature is, precisely, its potential for being performed or enacted. The very origin of the word "drama" implies its potential for becoming a performable script. We use the words "text" or "script" to describe this written form that becomes the basis for theatrical performance.

Drama comes from the Greek *dran*, meaning "to do" or "to act." Since the word is rooted in "doing" or "enacting," we have come to understand drama as a special way of imitating human behavior and human events. Drama is like narrative in that it tells a story; but unlike narrative, or story telling, it requires enactment before an audience. The story's events must be represented in drama, not merely told or narrated as in epic poetry. The word *"theatre"* has its roots in the Greek word, *theatron*, meaning "a place for seeing," or that special place where actors and audiences come together to experience a performance of the playwright's raw materials—the drama. The dramatic text is not wholly realized until the theatre's artists complete for audiences what the playwright began. As Hamlet, Kenneth Branaugh must breathe life into Shakespeare's character for the text to come alive in the imagined world of Elsinore Castle.

All dramatic texts are constructs. They have in common the fact that they set forth events taking place in an imagined or fictional world, whether it be ancient Thebes or contemporary Manhattan. The dramatic text is the playwright's blueprint for setting forth physical and psychological experience—to give shape and meaning to the world as the playwright sees and understands it. Over the centuries, these blueprints have related a variety of stories not as narrations, but as imitations of imaginary actions. Sophocles wrote

FIGURE 8.2   Continued.

of a king confronted by a plague-ridden kingdom (*Oedipus the King*), Sam Shepard depicted American midwesterners confronting their lost connections with the land and with one another (*Buried Child*), and Samuel Beckett presented worlds in which human beings "wait out" lifetimes (*Footfalls*).

Drama, then, is a special written way of imitating human experience. It is both a literary and a performance text. The fictional character, Hamlet, is played by the living actor Kevin Kline. It is our purpose here to learn to *read* plays, to understand the how and why of the dramatic text, without ignoring the fact that the playwright's words have the potential to be performed in the theatre. We must learn to analyze the pattern of words and conventions that have the potential for "becoming" living words and actions. The playwright provides us with dialogue—words arranged in a meaningful sequence—intended to be spoken aloud and enacted by actors before audiences. Often the playwright includes descriptions of scenes, characters, and activities in stage directions and dialogue. However, the actor remains the playwright's essential intermediary in that complex relationship between the drama and the performance.

DRAMATURGY

In its original Greek meaning, a *dramaturg* was simply a playwright. The word "dramaturgy" defines the playwright's craft. It involves the elements, conventions, and techniques the playwright uses to delineate general and particular truths about the human condition. Those elements involve plot, action, character, meaning, language, spectacle, space, and time. We must develop skills for understanding a writer's dramaturgical skills, which deal with plot, character, language, and so forth, so that we can read plays from all periods of theatrical, cultural, and social history. Styles, conventions, language, and techniques differ among playwrights depending on the physical theatre, the writing conventions of the historical period, and the society or universe mirrored in the writer's work. Also applicable are the ever-changing cultural, social, and technological conditions under which plays have been written, produced, and performed in western society for 2500 years.

DRAMATIC SPACE

Drama is unique among the arts in that it imitates reality through representation rather than narration. The playwright creates a fictional universe with human beings, familiar objects, and recognizable environments. Beckett's characters' feet hurt; August Wilson's hero idolizes his baseball bat; Shepard's Dodge lives out his last days on a frayed green sofa surrounded by pills and whiskey bottles. Like Beckett, Wilson, and Shepard, playwrights use "real" human beings in particular spaces and times to create the illusion of fictional worlds in which recognizable events take place in time and space. We distinguish between the *performance space* (the stage) and the *dramatic space* (the playwright's fictional locale). Dramatic space—or the play's environment—is usually described in dialogue or in stage directions found in modern texts. What is exhibited in the performance space is an interpretation, or staging, of the play's physical requirements set forth in those directions.

Dramatic space has essentially two characteristics. First, it is a "fictional" space—the characters' environment—described by playwrights in dialogue and stage directions. The fictional space may be the palace of Thebes (*Oedipus the King*), an eighteenth-century drawing room (*The School for Scandal*), or the neglected living room of a modern midwestern family (*Buried Child*). The fictional space may encompass simultaneously more than one space, such as palaces and battlefields or apartments and streets. Shakespeare's plays require locations that are miles apart, but the characters must appear in those locales within seconds. Hamlet moves from battlements, to chambers, to graveyards. Dramatic space is magical in its ability to present several locales simultaneously. Bertolt Brecht's Galileo travels many miles and journeys to many cities in his pursuit of truth and reason.

Second, dramatic space always assumes the presence of a stage and an audience and a relationship between the two. As we read plays, we are aware that they are written to be performed. While the stage where a play is produced may be almost any type—proscenium, arena, thrust, environmental—the characters may or may not be aware of the audience. In modern realistic plays, the characters are not aware that an audience is present. The pretense, or stage convention, is that a "fourth wall" exists through which the actors-as-characters cannot see, although audiences can. No character in Henrik Ibsen's *Hedda Gabler* ever acknowledges the audience. In other plays, characters directly address the audience, establishing an invisible flow of space between actor and audience. Sheridan's *The School for Scandal* has many asides where characters speak directly to the audience to comment briefly on some situation. As readers, we need to be sensitive to the "look" of the characters' environment and to the intended relationship of the dramatic space to the audience.

Continued.

FIGURE 8.2

DRAMATIC TIME

Dramatic time is a phenomenon of the text. Jan Kott wrote that "theatre is a place where time is always present."[4] Once begun, the time of a performance is one-directional. It follows a linear path for the two or more hours of its duration. Dramatic time, in contrast to performance time, is free of such constraints.

Within the fictional world of the play, time can be expanded or compressed. Unlike the film editor's manipulation of images in films, the playwright does not have the advantage of editing and splicing film to carry us forward or backward in time. Rather, dramatic time can be accelerated by using gaps of days, months, and even years; or, it can be slowed down by using soliloquies and flashbacks. Whereas real or performance time moves in one direction (present to future) and the past can never be recaptured, dramatic time can violate the relentless forward motion of performance time measured by the clock. For example, events may be shown out of their chronological sequence, or they may be foreshortened so they occur more swiftly than they would in nature. Shakespeare's battles, requiring only a few minutes of swordplay on stage, would ordinarily require days or even months in real time. In Samuel Beckett's plays, characters experience the relentless passage of time because there are no major events or crises. An unchanging sameness characterizes their lives. In Samuel Beckett's *Waiting for Godot*, Vladimir and Estragon wait for Godot's arrival which is always postponed by the messenger's announcement that "Mr. Godot told me to tell you he won't come this evening but surely tomorrow." In Beckett's plays the experience of dramatic time is cyclical—day becomes night and night becomes day—while his characters wait out their uneventful lives in patterns that are repetitive and are experienced as "waiting." In his plays, nothing happens in the traditional sense, but time erodes lives in a relentless journey toward death.

Time and space in the fictional universe of drama are highly malleable and unlike the actual time we experience in our daily lives. Consideration of dramatic time and space has always played a large part in the different theories and rules of drama. In his *Poetics*, Aristotle briefly suggested that the *amount of time it takes the actors to tell the story* should ideally be concurrent with the actual time it takes to perform the play. This attention to a *unity of time*, as it was later called, is still found in modern realistic plays. However, in the many words written about drama over the centuries, the most attention has been given to the playwright's meanings and messages.

DRAMA'S MEANINGS AND MESSAGES

The reader's greatest temptation is to concentrate on the general meaning of the literary work—the novel, poem, or play—overlooking the fact that meaning is generated as the work is experienced. A play's complete meaning does not emerge in the early pages of a text or in the first moments of a performance, but quite often the seeds of the message can be found there. Shepard's statement about the decay of American family values is evident in the first moments of *Buried Child*.

In creating the dramatic text, the playwright connects the reader (and audiences) with a common humanity through the progression of the play's events. Great plays confront us with life's verities, conveying the hope, courage, despair, compassion, violence, love, hate, exploitation, and generosity experienced by all humankind. They show us the possibilities of losing our families and property through accidents, catastrophes of war, or tyranny. Plays show us ways of fulfilling ourselves in relationships or confronting despair and death. August Wilson's characters struggle to show love and affection to one another. The most enduring plays explore what it means to be human beings in special circumstances. These circumstances may be unfamiliar, like the prince dispossessed of his rightful heritage through murder, marriage, and calumny (*Hamlet*); or bizarre, like the family that has literally buried its family skeleton in the back yard (*Buried Child*); or familiar, like the ambitions of a mother for her children (*The Glass Menagerie*).

Drama's most enduring achievements, like the representative plays contained in this book, serve as reflections of ourselves, or what potentially could be ourselves in different times and circumstances. Drama's best moments lead us to discoveries and reflections about our personalities, circumstances, desires, anxieties, hopes, and dreams. Playwrights also move beyond personal concerns to discuss social and political issues that are of a certain time, yet transcend specific historical periods. Playwrights stimulate social awareness and put us in touch with our thoughts and feelings about issues. The aim of great playwrights is to expand our consciousness on old and new social and personal issues, and to endow us with *new perspectives* on our humanity and the human condition.

Plays are written as a process of unfolding and discovery. To read plays successfully is to understand essentially "how" the playwright generates meaning. Scene follows scene in meaningful patterns; dialogue communicates feelings and ideas; characters display motives and emotions; locales give

FIGURE 8.2   Continued.

social and economic contexts. "What" a play means involves the completed action, that is, all that has gone before in organized, meaningful segments that, when taken in their totality, express the writer's vision or conviction about the world. As readers, we share that unfolding—those discoveries—with audiences. We also learn to experience the developing actions, events, and relationships which, in turn, produce a coherent statement about individuals, societies, and the universe. We learn to follow the playwright's ways and means of organizing the dramatic material into a coherent whole and to discover the writer's methods for developing the psychological and physical currents of human endeavor that result in visible (and meaningful) behavior.

The same process is at work in our personal experiences. In our daily lives, we are not instantly aware that some actions have repercussions far beyond our expectations. As we begin a trip, we cannot know the full extent of our experiences. With time, we come to understand the meaning of our experiences, feelings, and actions, as well as the motives and actions of others. In some instances, meanings are elusive—sometimes impossible to pin down. The same is true in understanding the how and the why of the dramatic text. When Tom Wingfield brings the "gentleman caller" to dine with his sister Laura in Tennessee Williams' *The Glass Menagerie*, he is not aware, nor are we as readers and audiences, of the psychological damage he is imposing on Laura's fragile emotional life.

All art condenses, clarifies, and orders the chaos, disorder, and inconsequential happenings of life. The poet William Wordsworth gives shape to girlhood innocence in his "Lucy Gray" poems. Tennessee Williams organizes Tom Wingfield's memo-ries of his chaotic and unhappy life in his mother's home. However, great plays confront life's complexities in such a way that they cannot be reduced to a single meaning. Since there is usually no author's voice in drama, as there is in the novel where the writer can speak directly to the reader, we are left with layers of possible meaning based on the play's events. We can usually agree that Hamlet was given the task of avenging his father's murder, that he hesitated and ultimately achieved his objective at the cost of his life. What remains open to interpretation is the ultimate meaning or significance of the play—"what it was all about." For that reason, we can read and see *Hamlet* any number of times and continue to discover new meanings in this complex text. We want to learn to identify *how* playwrights order, clarify, and distill their imitations of real life in the dramatic text and what higher meanings emerge from these efforts.

Sam Shepard's Pulitzer-Prize-winning *Buried Child* (1978) is an interesting contemporary play with which to begin our process of understanding plays. Along with a post-Vietnam wave of American writers that includes David Mamet, Marsha Norman, Lanford Wilson, August Wilson, and many others, Shepard takes us into the inner workings of modern American family life which are both commonplace and bizarre. He writes about characters searching out their family histories in an effort to explain who they are and how they came to be that way. Similar to *Oedipus the King* and *Hamlet*, the central action of *Buried Child* is the individual's quest for roots and identity. Shepard's means of organizing and unfolding a family's history provide our initial introduction to play analysis. Let us begin this journey into the process of understanding plays with *Buried Child*.

1. *What is the answer to question 1?*

   _____

   _____

2. *What is the answer to question 2?*

   _____

   _____

3. *What is the answer to question 3?*

   _____

   _____

Recite the answers to the questions you asked earlier without referring to notes. Jot down your responses:

_____

_____

_____

_____

_____

Review the entire chapter.

1. *Where were plays first analyzed?*

   _____

   _____

   _____

   _____

2. *What is dramatic space?*

   _____

   _____

   _____

   _____

3. *What is dramatic time?*

   _____

   _____

   _____

   _____

4. *What is a dramaturg?*

_____

_____

_____

_____

_____

Reviewing Class and Textbook Notes

An effective study-skill strategy is *review.* Reviewing your class notes (you may even want to recopy them) and the textbook notes regularly will certainly help you become more successful as a student.

Strategies for note taking were discussed in Chapter 7. Each time you sit down to study, the first thing that you should do is review what you studied last. This is an important critical-thinking skill that will help you see the whole picture. Just as warming up prepares you for exercising, reviewing your notes prepares you for studying. If you study each assignment without reviewing prior lessons first, then you will have difficulty seeing the relationship between the various lessons and assignments.

One way to review class and textbook notes is to write a summary of what you have learned. This activity should be done on loose-leaf paper and added to your class notes in your binder. Writing a summary should only take you 15 to 20 minutes. Use the following questions to help guide you through your summary:

1. What four important facts have I learned in class and/or while reading my textbook?
2. What four associations can I make about today's class notes or reading assignments that relate to previous notes?

Writing a summary can make preparing for exams much easier. This is also an excellent way to remember what you are studying because you are thoroughly learning the material. Thorough learning is the key to remembering information.

Using notes from a class you are currently taking, answer the following questions.

What four important facts have you learned in class and/or while reading your textbook?

1. _____

2. _____

3. _____

4. _____

What four associations can you make about today's class notes or reading assignments that relate to previous notes?

1. _____

2. _____

3. _____

4. _____

Studying Math

Do you dislike numbers? Are you terrified of math? If so, you are not alone. Academic counselors tell us that of the students who seek academic counseling, most express anxiety related to math. Many students will avoid math at all costs. They will put off taking math courses until the last possible semester. Some students will even go as far as choosing degrees that require little or no math. Unfortunately, the fear or anxiety that students suffer from can keep them from learning important mathematical skills that help in all areas of life.

"You can choose to throw stones, to stumble on them, to climb over them, or to build with them."

WILLIAM ARTHUR WARD

The first step in studying math is to overcome the anxiety you may have about math as best you can. Let us begin by identifying what has caused the math anxiety or fear.

List some reasons why you dislike math or suffer from math anxiety:

_____

_____

_____

_____

Math concepts build on top of each other. If you do not understand something, seek help from a fellow student, your instructor, or a tutor to avoid struggling with later concepts.

Your list might include being embarrassed by a peer or teacher, conflict with a teacher, family pressure, a desire to be "perfect," poor teaching methods, perceived lack of a "mathematical mind," self-stereotyping, etc. Your reasons for fearing math are perhaps legitimate, but it is important that you let go of those fears. The negative thoughts that you carry around with you are keeping you from reaching your math potential. Some math instructors feel that the students who don't learn to control their math anxiety may not become academically successful in math.

How you study math is different from how you might study history, for which you may need only to listen and take notes during class and review your notes outside of class. Math requires a great deal more effort. You should not only listen and take notes during class, but you must also practice the math concepts outside of class. Learning and studying math requires a great deal of time, paper and pencil activity, patience, and determination. You need to be committed to daily drill and review. Math concepts build on top of each other. If you do not establish a good foundation, then you will struggle with later concepts. For example, it is very important that you learn and understand the concept of least common multiples (LCM), because finding the LCM of two unlike denominators will allow you to add or subtract fractions.

Identifying Tips for Studying Math Effectively

Listed below you will find several practical suggestions for studying math. If you want to experience success with math, you must be willing to implement as many of these suggestions as possible:

- Purchase a student solutions manual.
- Learn relaxation techniques to control math anxiety.
- Read the directions carefully.
- Ask yourself if your answer makes sense.
- Redo problems to reinforce understanding and to check them.
- Use a scientific/graphing calculator if permitted.
- Ask your instructor about math teaching aids available on your campus such as videos, computer tutors, etc.
- Hire a tutor.
- Create a math study group.
- Copy all examples the instructor puts on the board.
- Above all, practice, practice, practice.

CRITICAL THINKING

Have you ever observed a criminal or civil trial? Maybe you've been a member of a jury or just sat in on a trial to learn more about our judicial system. What is amazing is that while viewing a trial, one can see critical thinking at its best. Lawyers are able to piece together information that is seemingly unrelated and weave a story that the jury decides is either to be believed or not. Critical thinking is a skill that can be developed, but it definitely takes practice.

Have you ever wondered why you are taking a public speaking course if your major is nursing? By looking at all of the requirements for a particular major, one can begin to see how the different parts fit together to enable the student to be better educated and more successful. Yes, oral skills are important in nursing and in any other occupation requiring communication between two or more people. To be able to recognize and understand the connections between courses in your curriculum is to analyze critically and to begin the process of critical thinking. To think critically means to think "with a purpose"—with an "end in mind." Critical thinking is more than just logical thinking. It requires you to remove all emotional biases from your thought process and focus on what is real. Critical thinking also requires you to question, analyze, and solve problems and forces you to think on a higher level.

Why is critical thinking an important skill to develop while in college? Because more often than not, employers indicate that an employee who is able to anticipate situations and then act proactively instead of reactively is the most valuable employee in the organization.

> *"A great many people think they are thinking, when they are merely rearranging their prejudices."*
>
> WILLIAM JAMES

Thinking critically requires that one use emotional restraint when listening. Consider these topics that typically are fairly controversial:

- Should modern science be allowed to clone humans?
- Should airline pilots be allowed to carry guns?
- Should certain drugs be legalized?

When you considered these questions, did you immediately form an opinion? Did an old argument or a bias on your part surface? Were you allowing your prejudices and emotions to cloud your thinking? If you immediately answered yes or no to any of the previous questions, then you probably have allowed your emotions to cloud your thinking and should focus on thinking with a more open mind.

Often, when we read or hear news reports, we are bombarded with information from editors that can be biased or slanted. For this reason, it is important that one gain news from a variety of sources so that an objective opinion may be formed. Realizing that there is a difference between beliefs and facts is the first step in higher order thinking.

Critical thinking is vitally important in manufacturing, technology, and health-related professions. Most likely, your instructors will force you to think objectively about a situation by presenting a real-life scenario or case study for you to review. By sifting through information without emotion, unearthing facts, and then analyzing the information, critical thinking has occurred. Although critical thinking is not an easy skill to develop, it is of vital importance to one's success in college. If you are interested in developing your critical-thinking skills, consider taking a course in philosophy or logic.

ROADWAYS

- Get *organized.*

- Create and use a *notebook* system (a three-ring binder).

- Identify an appropriate study *environment* and study *time.*

- Create and use a study *plan.*

- Use the *SQ3R* studying method.

- Thoroughly *learn* material.

- Use *mnemonic* devices.

- *Summarize* class and textbook notes.

- Use *context clues* and *word analysis* to define unfamiliar words.

- Use the *tips* recommended to study math effectively.

- Use *index cards* for vocabulary, formulas, concepts, etc.

- Above all, study over a *period of time* rather than "cramming."

Now that you have completed the chapter, complete the Milestones checklist again.

How did you do? Do you now feel more comfortable about basic study skills? Do you feel that this chapter has had a positive impact on how you perceive yourself as a student? Do you feel more self-assured and confident about your study skills at this point?

MILESTONES

NOW THAT YOU ARE HERE . . .

Answer each statement by checking "Y" for Yes, "N" for No, or "S" for Sometimes.

1. I am organized.		Ⓨ Ⓝ Ⓢ
2. I use a study plan.		Ⓨ Ⓝ Ⓢ
3. I know how to study math.		Ⓨ Ⓝ Ⓢ
4. I schedule time to study.		Ⓨ Ⓝ Ⓢ
5. I know how to read a textbook.		Ⓨ Ⓝ Ⓢ
6. I always attend class.		Ⓨ Ⓝ Ⓢ
7. I know how to learn vocabulary.		Ⓨ Ⓝ Ⓢ
8. I know how to use the SQ3R study method.		Ⓨ Ⓝ Ⓢ
9. I highlight my notes and textbook.		Ⓨ Ⓝ Ⓢ
10. I have an appropriate place to study.		Ⓨ Ⓝ Ⓢ

Applying What You Know

Learning how to learn is the single most important skill you must master as a student. Knowing how to get organized and applying the strategies presented in this chapter enable you to overcome even the most difficult academic subjects. There are no quick fixes or substitutions for studying. It requires organization and time to achieve academic success.

Now that you have finished this chapter on learning how to study, refer back to the Case Study about Gwen at the beginning of this book. Based on her situation, answer the following questions:

1. How would you help Gwen to identify her best study environment?

_____

_____

_____

_____

2. How would you explain to Gwen how to apply the SQ3R method to her PSY 201 class?

_____

_____

_____

_____

3. What recommendations would you make to Gwen to help her improve her grades in her MAT 101 class?

_____

_____

_____

_____

Observations

CHARTING YOUR COURSE

Learning how to learn is an important step in achieving academic success. The strategies mentioned in this chapter will require commitment, determination, and time. You can reach your educational potential by becoming organized and implementing the study techniques covered in this chapter. We must heed the old saying, "If you give a man food, you feed him once. If you teach him to plant, you nourish him forever." The same is true with learning. If you learn *how* to learn, you can learn forever!

Getting There on Time

Effective study skills can greatly enhance your time-management skills. Have you considered how much time you might save if you routinely used a study plan? After looking at your schedule, how much time *do* you allocate for studying? Is that adequate? Why do you think it might be important to schedule study time?

If you had problems answering any of these questions, go back over this chapter and review some of the tips. Efficient use of time and effective study skills go hand-in-hand.

Exploring Technology

The World Wide Web is quickly becoming the primary research tool for the layperson. People "surf" the Web to shop for merchandise, plan vacations, look up addresses and phone numbers, and search for the answers to all types of questions. Unfortunately, students are also using the Web to research their papers.

Warning! When reviewing private websites for academic papers, do not reference undocumented files. For example, most of "Shotgun's Home of the American Civil War" (www.civilwarhome.com) indicates the information's source; however, there are several files that are commentaries from individuals with no or uncertain *formal* qualifications. Although these files make for interesting reading, *they are inappropriate sources for academic work.* Students should only use credible sources; that is, documented sources or individuals well known in the academic community, such as Civil War historians James McPherson and Albert Castel.

One big advantage individuals have when using the Internet is that they can obtain products not yet available on the market. This is an exercise in Web research.

1. Locate the website for the rock and roll band "My Chemical Romance" and send the Web address to your instructor.

2. In your e-mail, indicate which two songs you can download.

3. Provide your opinion on the songs. Good? Bad? Indifferent? (Don't forget proper e-mail etiquette.)

THE FOLLOWING SEARCH ENGINES MAY BE HELPFUL:

www.my.excite.com

www.lycos.com

www.yahoo.com

www.altavista.com

www.google.com

Web Connections

TRAVELING THE INFORMATION SUPERHIGHWAY

During your journey, you may want to check out some of the following Web addresses to assist with enhancing your studying skills:

www.sdc.uwo.ca/learning/tentt.html

www.gmu.edu/gmu/personal/study.html

www.unc.edu/depts/unc_caps/TenTraps.html

www.ucc.vt.edu/stdysk/stdyhlp.html

As a result of this chapter, and in preparing for my journey, I plan to . . .

Obtaining Your License

9

TEST-TAKING STRATEGIES

**A**nn, a 35-year-old single mother of three, decided to go back to school in order to make a better life for herself and her children. She wanted a better job. But, she didn't have the skills needed to get one.

She had worked as a secretary in a small law office for 10 years, and enjoyed working in the legal system. So, she decided to apply for admission to the paralegal program at the local community college. She enrolled as a night student and decided to take just one course in her first semester. Her advisor encouraged her to take PSY 201, a general requirement for her degree.

The semester seemed to be going fine until her instructor announced the first test date. Ann was terrified of tests. She had never been very good at taking a test. She knew that if she didn't overcome her fear, she'd never be able to earn a degree and reach her goals.

With determination, Ann began studying three weeks prior to the exam. She put all of her notes on large index cards, and she divided the index cards into six different groups. Ann carried the cards with her everywhere she went. She studied and studied and studied.

On the day of the exam, she felt confident that she could pass it. She completed the first part of the exam without much trouble. It wasn't until Ann attempted to answer an essay question that a wave of anxiety swept over her. She remembers feeling very hot, realizing that her hands were sweating, and having a sense of being overwhelmed. Ann's mind had gone blank. She didn't know how to write the essay. She didn't know where to begin. It was a timed test and the time was running short. Ann remembers wanting to give up, crawl into a corner, and cry.

She must have spent 15 minutes trying to get under control. Finally, she decided to write anything that came to her mind. She decided just to do the best she could. Ann was amazed at how easy it became after she took control of the anxiety. Because she had prepared for the exam and thoroughly learned the material, she was able to finish the test with confidence. At the next class meeting, she learned that she had passed the exam. Ann was so relieved and proud. The hard work had paid off and she knew she was going to make it!

"No one can make you feel inferior without your consent."

ELEANOR ROOSEVELT

It is natural to be nervous or anxious about taking tests because we attach great importance to passing or failing tests and to what grade(s) we will receive. Students can increase their ability to succeed and decrease the anxiety by becoming "testwise." Preparing for tests, knowing how to control test fears, and understanding the types of tests makes taking tests a less anxious experience. This chapter will teach you how to take tests. It is important that you understand that the tips and techniques discussed in this chapter should not take the place of studying for a test. The best way to be successful when taking a test is to learn the material thoroughly and to have a positive attitude.

At the end of this chapter, if you complete the exercises, participate in class, read additional assignments issued by your instructor, and keep an open mind, you will be able to complete the following tasks:

- Explain the purpose of tests
- Describe how to control test anxiety
- Use tips for reducing test anxiety
- Apply general test-taking techniques
- Use strategies for answering various types of test questions

You may have been taking tests your entire academic life, but how "testwise" are you? The 10 questions in Milestones are intended to cause you to think about the purpose of tests, about test anxiety, and how to take various types of tests. Take a moment and respond to each statement.

How were your answers on this inventory? Do you feel good about your test-taking ability? If you don't feel confident, this chapter will help you feel more self-assured and confident. Pay close attention to the activities and exercises in this chapter and by the conclusion, you should feel more confident and self-assured when taking a test or exam.

MILESTONES

WHERE ARE YOU NOW?

Answer each statement by checking "Y" for Yes, "N" for No, or "S" for Sometimes.

1.	I am relaxed when taking a test.	Y	N	S
2.	I am always physically and mentally ready to take a test.	Y	N	S
3.	I look at tests as opportunities.	Y	N	S
4.	I read the entire test before answering the questions.	Y	N	S
5.	I know how to answer an essay question.	Y	N	S
6.	I know what qualifiers make a statement true or false.	Y	N	S
7.	I agree that you can never study enough for a test.	Y	N	S
8.	I always set aside time to study for tests.	Y	N	S
9.	I enjoy multiple-choice tests.	Y	N	S
10.	I enjoy fill-in-the-blank tests.	Y	N	S

WHY DO I HAVE TO TAKE A TEST?

Do you enjoy taking tests? Most students don't. Many students dread it and believe that teachers are trying to make their lives miserable through testing. This attitude can defeat you. You should view tests as an opportunity to show how much you know about a skill or subject. Tests should be viewed as a challenge that can help you to learn and grow.

Tests are designed to measure how well you have mastered a skill or concept. In addition, taking a test is another opportunity for you to learn new information. Tests are a fact of life, and they are everywhere. The driver's test, the SAT, employee evaluations, and eye exams, for instance, are types of tests. The list could be endless. Doing your best on a test can mean passing a course, earning a degree, or being promoted at work. Therefore, it is important that you accept test taking as a fact of life. If you prepare appropriately and have confidence, then your chance for experiencing success is greatly enhanced.

List the reasons why you believe your instructors give tests:

1. _____

2. _____

3. _____

4. _____

5. _____

Your list may include the following reasons: to make my life miserable, to motivate me to learn and study, to show me what I don't know or understand, to show the teacher what has to be retaught, to determine my grade in a course, and to learn information.

CONTROLLING TEST ANXIETY

Okay, so test anxiety is a natural response. You may be nervous prior to taking a test because you want to do well on it. Anxiety is created because you fear that you may not do as well as you had hoped. Believe it or not, some anxiety can actually increase your success because you are more aware, attuned, and alert.

However, there are reasons other than the fear of failure as to why you may be anxious during a test.

List the reasons why you think students become anxious during tests:

1. _____

2. _____

3. _____

4. _____

Perhaps your list includes such reasons as studying the wrong material, failing to study, failing to understand the information, getting nervous when taking a test, being unable to concentrate, experiencing distractions in the room, forgetting to bring materials needed during the test, failing to know the day of the test, and being asked questions about information other than what was studied.

Which reasons in your list can be controlled?

1. _____
2. _____
3. _____
4. _____

Test anxiety can cause frustration, but relax; a great deal of it is controllable. Test anxiety can be dramatically reduced when you are in control of the testing situation. By studying and thoroughly learning the material, using test-taking strategies, and entering the test with confidence, you can gain the measure of control that you need. As long as you give 100 percent (your very best), the outcome will be positive. It is important to realize that we all have limitations and academic weaknesses. None of us are good at everything. Identify and focus on your strengths and do not let your weaknesses hold you back.

When do you experience test anxiety?

_____

_____

_____

_____

_____

_____

_____

_____

What could you do to control your anxiety?

_____

_____

_____

_____

_____

_____

"In this age, which believes that there is a shortcut to everything, the greatest lesson to be learned is that the most difficult way is, in the long run, the easiest."

HENRY MILLER

ROADWAYS

- Thoroughly *learn* the material.

- Approach the test with a *positive* attitude.

- Chewing gum or eating hard peppermint candy helps *relax* some students.

- Take a *break* from the test by looking around or leaving the room if permitted.

- Get a good night's *sleep* prior to the test.

- Eat a *healthy* (high protein) meal before the test.

- Arrive 20 minutes *early.*

- Take deep breaths if you find yourself becoming *nervous.*

- Enter the room with all *materials* needed for the test.

- *Reward* yourself for a job well done.

Test anxiety is a fact of life for most students. Learning to cope with this anxiety is a step in the right direction. Understanding the different types of test questions and having strategies for dealing with each type can help you to reduce test anxiety.

PREPARING FOR TESTS

 tudents prepare for tests in many different ways. Below are examples of how three different students (the dreamer, the procrastinator, and the planner) prepare for a test.

The Dreamer

The dreamer is the student who fantasizes or dreams up excuses or scenarios that will keep him from having to take a test. The night before the exam, this student hopes for some type of national disaster such as a snowstorm or flood to close school. Or this student will hope that the instructor will be sick and class will be cancelled. Most of these students will fail the test or just barely squeak by.

The Procrastinator

The procrastinator is the student who puts off studying for the test until the night before. This student will stay up all night cramming as much information as possible into her brain. Some of the procrastinators will manage to make a C on the test, and a few of the procrastinators, those who do their best work under pressure, will manage to do better than a C.

The Planner

The planner is the student who prepares for the exam. This student spends several days, even weeks, preparing for the exam. He reviews reading assignments, notes, and handouts. The planner will create a mock test consisting of questions he feels might be asked on the test. This student tends to be more confident and experiences less test anxiety. He has learned that there is no substitute for studying and planning for a test. The planner is able to do his best on the exam and usually makes the best grades.

Which student best describes your approach? _____

Why? _____

_____

_____

_____

_____

- Create a study *schedule* as soon as a test is scheduled.

- Ask your instructor what specific *information* will be tested.

- Find out *how* you will be tested; for example, by essay or multiple choice.

- Write a list of *questions* you think might be asked on the test.

- Form a study *group* to study with several days prior to the test.

- Make a *list* of questions from notes and reading assignments that still don't make sense and ask the instructor for additional clarification.

- Above all, get a good night's *sleep* the night before the test, and eat a healthy meal before the test.

Effective test taking involves careful preparation. Create a study schedule, study individually and with a group, review, and get a good night's sleep.

TEST-TAKING STRATEGIES

nstructors present information in a variety of ways, and the way they ask questions on tests also varies. When you spend time preparing for a test, your goal is to do well. You can accomplish this by understanding the different kinds of test questions and knowing the best way to answer them. Most students prefer certain types of questions to others. For example, you may prefer multiple-choice questions over essay questions. Regardless of what you prefer, you should be familiar with all kinds of questions and know how to best answer them. The most common kinds of test questions are:

matching questions

true–false questions

multiple-choice questions

short-answer questions

essay questions

In addition to knowing the kinds of tests, it is also helpful to know general test-taking techniques and specific strategies for answering each kind of question. The information in this chapter helps you take tests and answer different kinds of questions. However, relying on the strategies alone will not help you. As previously mentioned (several times), thoroughly learning the material is the best test-taking tool. It reduces anxiety and builds confidence. Being prepared means increasing the odds of doing well on the test.

GENERAL TEST-TAKING TECHNIQUES

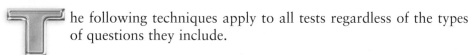

he following techniques apply to all tests regardless of the types of questions they include.

1. Read and follow all directions.
2. Answer the easiest questions first.
3. Watch the time limits.
4. Read the questions carefully.
5. Answer every question if there is no penalty for guessing.
6. Ask for clarification, if permitted.
7. Skim through the entire test before writing a word.
8. Watch for words that may change the meaning of a question such as *not, either/or,* and *always.*
9. Answer the questions neatly.
10. Above all, *think positively!*

The use of these techniques can increase your academic success. The following section offers explanations and simple examples of the various types of test questions.

Strategies for Answering Matching Questions

Matching questions often test your understanding of people, places, things, dates, and vocabulary. The objective when answering matching questions is to match information in two columns. Strategies for answering matching questions are outlined in the following list:

1. First, read through each column.
2. Match the easiest items first.
3. Lightly cross out or check off an item as it is matched.
4. Use the process of elimination to match difficult or unknown information.
5. Leave *no* questions blank if there is no penalty for guessing.

Directions: Match the terms in column A with the characteristics in column B.

A	B
1. Listening	a. Open minded
2. Objective	b. Prejudging
3. Obstacle	c. Automatic

When taking a test, read quickly through all items and estimate how much time you may spend on each section of the test.

Strategies for Answering True–False Questions

In a true–false question, you indicate whether or not a statement is correct. Strategies for answering true–false questions are revealed in the following list:

1. Read the statement carefully.
2. Pay attention to special words that may increase the likelihood that the statement is true. Words such as "some," "few," "many," and "often" are examples.
3. Pay attention to special words that *may* indicate that the statement is false. Words such as "never," "all," "every," and "only" fall into this category.
4. If any part of a statement is false, then the entire statement is considered false.
5. Answer every question *if* there is no penalty for guessing.
6. When in doubt, choose true.
7. Never try to fudge the answer by making the T look like it could be either T or F.

Directions: Write T for true or F for false.

_____ 1. System-imposed time can always be controlled.

_____ 2. Everyone has the same amount of time.

_____ 3. Prioritizing is a technique that identifies what is most important.

Strategies for Answering Multiple-Choice Questions

Multiple-choice questions are commonly found on tests. In fact, most standardized tests use this format. When answering multiple-choice test questions, you must answer a question or complete a statement by selecting the correct answer from two, three, or more possible answer choices. Following are strategies for answering multiple-choice questions:

1. Carefully read the statement and try to answer the question before reading the answer choices.
2. Answers containing words such as "never," "all," "every," "best," "worst," and "only" *usually* can be eliminated as an answer choice.
3. Lightly cross out answers that you feel or know are incorrect.
4. Read all the options before making your decision.
5. If the answers are dates or numbers, you can usually rule out the lowest and highest answer.
6. Answer each question if there is no penalty for guessing.

Directions: *Read each statement and circle the correct answer.*

1. Which is not a step in the listening process?
    a. Receiving   c. Organizing
    b. Reacting   d. Accepting

2. Which is not likely to increase self-esteem?
    a. Embracing the notion: I am responsible for my own life.
    b. Comparing yourself to others.
    c. Controlling your self-talk.
    d. Taking at least one positive risk a week.

3. Which technique should be used when studying a chapter in a textbook?
    a. ROAR   c. SQ3R
    b. DADE   d. L-STAR

Strategies for Answering Short-Answer Questions

Tests that include short-answer or fill-in-the-blank questions ask you to supply the information. Short-answer questions will not provide answer choices; therefore, you must depend on the information you have stored in your long-term memory. Strategies for answering short-answer or fill-in-the-blank questions include the following:

1. Read the question carefully to make certain you understand how to answer it.
2. Be short and to the point.
3. Never leave a blank unless there is a penalty for guessing. Write in something—a few points are better than none.
4. Look for answers or clues to the questions in the test itself.

Directions: Answer each question or statement by filling in the blank or writing a complete sentence.

1. Name four of the five types of mnemonic devices.

_____

_____

_____

_____

2. One of the best ways to study a textbook is to use the SQ3R method. What does SQ3R stand for?

_____

_____

_____

_____

3. A technique used to decode an unfamiliar word by examining parts of the word is known as

_____

Strategies for Answering Essay Questions

An essay question gives you an opportunity to share what you know. Like the short-answer question, the essay question also requires that you supply the entire answer from memory. Answering essay questions can be difficult if you lack certain skills. Being able to write well and to think clearly are two skills that you will surely need. Writing well includes the ability to choose the correct words, to punctuate correctly, and to organize your ideas. If you want to do well answering essay questions, you have to understand what an essay question is asking and to think clearly when organizing your answers. Many essay questions will ask you to explain, to compare, to contrast, or to define an event or idea.

When you are asked *to explain* an event or idea, the instructor will be asking you to give reasons for why an event took place or to offer a description of an idea. An instructor might ask you to explain the events leading up to a particular incident. In this case, you would most likely provide the events in chronological sequence (what happened first, what happened next, and what happened last).

EXAMPLE: *Explain* why you would rather travel on a small, two-lane highway than on a freeway.

There are a number of reasons why I would prefer to travel on a two-lane highway than on a freeway. First, two-lane highways take you to places where freeways are unwelcome. Two-lane roads, for instance, can take you to small towns, through national forests, and to remote areas with beautiful scenery. Second, I prefer traveling on two-lane highways because of the terrible traffic on giant freeways. When traveling on two-lane roads, I don't feel like I'm constantly dodging other cars. Finally, on a two-lane road, I can take my time and enjoy the view. I can, for example, travel at my own pace and stop to look at something that captures my interest.

If an instructor asks you *to compare* an event or idea with another event or idea, you show how the two ideas or events are alike. Similarly, if this same teacher asks you *to contrast* two events or ideas, you show how they are different. An instructor will sometimes ask you to compare and to contrast at the same time. In this case, you simply tell how two events or ideas are alike and how they are different (using a paragraph for similarities and a paragraph for differences is a good idea).

EXAMPLE: *Compare and contrast* a freeway and a two-lane road (sometimes called a country road).

Freeways and two-lane roads are alike in at least two ways. First, they are both pathways designed to take you to some other place. Second, they are alike in the materials used in their construction. Concrete and asphalt, for instance, are used to construct both freeways and two-lane roads.

Although they are similar in at least two ways, freeways and two-lane roads are also different from each other. Freeways take up much more space (because of the numerous lanes of traffic) than do two-lane roads. Unlike two-lane roads, freeways fail to run through many picturesque small towns.

When you are asked *to define* a term, you are being asked to provide information about what something means. A definition should include placing the thing to be defined in a class of similar things and then telling how it is different from all of the other things in the class.

EXAMPLE: *Define* the term "freeway."

A freeway is a type of highway that has many lanes of traffic. The traffic is sometimes going in only one direction; but in most cases, there are numerous lanes of traffic going in two or more directions.

EXPLANATION: The freeway is put in a class (highways). The definition also tells how the freeway is different from other highways (many lanes of traffic).

Strategies for answering essay questions include:

1. When reading the questions, pay particular attention to key words such as "explain," "compare and contrast," or "define." Make sure you are answering the question correctly.
2. Make an outline to organize your thoughts.
3. Be neat.
4. Be careful with grammar, spelling, and punctuation.
5. Mention details (names, dates, events).

6. Write a strong introduction and conclusion.

7. Do not write meaningless information just to fill the page (instructors can't stand that).

DIRECTIONS: Answer the following essay question using complete and coherent sentences. *Explain why it is important to have a good education.*

_____

_____

_____

_____

_____

_____

_____

_____

_____

_____

It is now time to complete the Milestones checklist again.

How did you do on the inventory after reading this chapter? Do you feel that your test-taking skills are where they should be? If not, feel free to go back over some of the tips and suggestions covered in this chapter. After all, being a successful student can often be demonstrated by being a successful test or exam taker. Take some time to master this skill now; it will pay huge dividends in the future.

MILESTONES

NOW THAT YOU ARE HERE . . .

Answer each statement by checking "Y" for Yes, "N" for No, or "S" for Sometimes.

1.	I am relaxed when taking a test.	Y	N	S
2.	I am always physically and mentally ready to take a test.	Y	N	S
3.	I look at tests as opportunities.	Y	N	S
4.	I read the entire test before answering the questions.	Y	N	S
5.	I know how to answer an essay question.	Y	N	S
6.	I know what qualifiers make a statement true or false.	Y	N	S
7.	I agree that you can never study enough for a test.	Y	N	S
8.	I always set aside time to study for tests.	Y	N	S
9.	I enjoy multiple-choice tests.	Y	N	S
10.	I enjoy fill-in-the-blank tests.	Y	N	S

Applying What You Know

It is natural to be nervous or anxious when taking a test. It was the goal of this chapter to provide you with the skills to ease your anxieties and assist you in becoming an effective test taker.

Now that you have finished this chapter on test-taking strategies, refer back to the Case Study about Gwen at the beginning of this book. Based on Gwen's situation, answer the following questions:

1. How would you help Gwen learn how to control her test anxiety?

2. How would you explain to Gwen how to write effective essays on her MUS 105 final exam?

_____

_____

_____

_____

3. You have discovered that Gwen is a procrastinator when it comes to preparing for her tests. Explain how you would help Gwen implement a plan for studying for tests.

_____

_____

_____

_____

Observations

CHARTING YOUR COURSE

Tests do not have to be dreaded. Your instructors are not trying to punish you. Tests are an opportunity for you to show how much you have learned and to impress your instructors with your knowledge. The grades that you earn will reflect the amount of energy you put into studying. Take control by attending class, taking notes, asking questions, completing assignments, and learning material. Striving to always do your best will pay off in the end.

Getting There on Time

Can you see any connection with time management and test taking? What is the best way to manage your time when the test is "timed"? What role does time management play when you are preparing for a test? Do you ever feel that you just don't have enough time to prepare for a test? If so, why? What can you do differently so that you will have enough time to adequately prepare for a test?

Luckily, time management is a learned skill. Test-taking skills are acquired also. In short, you can learn to be successful in school by using time-management tips discussed elsewhere in this book and you can be a successful exam or test taker by following some of the simple guidelines listed in this chapter.

Exploring Technology

Have you seen the automobile crash test results on popular news programs? Just like you, even the cars we drive are subjected to *tests!!* The results are used in the development of safer automobiles. Safety features for the automobile have come a long way since the first Model T. Although early cars had practically no safety features incorporated into the design, today's automobile manufacturers take pride in the safety of their vehicles. In fact, the models with the highest ratings use that fact as a marketing tool.

Stop and think for a minute of all the safety devices installed in your car; the list is quite impressive. Here is a good, although incomplete, list: seat belts (lap and shoulder), air bags (front, side, and head), safety glass, headrest, bumpers, side impact beams, "crash crumple" zones, daytime running lights, proximity warnings, back-up horn, and of course "ABS" antilock brakes.

This is a practical assignment to help you learn more about your car:

1. What did "ABS" originally mean?
2. What makes "ABS" brakes better than traditional brakes? In other words, what is the major benefit?
3. Briefly describe how "ABS" brakes work.

Note: Do not "cut & paste" this assignment. You are to learn the material and provide a succinct answer *in your own words!*

HELPFUL REFERENCES:

- automobile manual
- automobile shop (e.g., Auto Zone, NAPA)
- friendly neighborhood mechanic

THE FOLLOWING WEBSITES MAY BE HELPFUL:

www.autoshop-online.com/auto101/braketext.html

www.autoshop-online.com/auto101/abs.html

www.autoshop-online.com/auto101.html

www.mattsauto.com/b.htm

Web Connections

TRAVELING THE INFORMATION SUPERHIGHWAY

During your journey, you may want to check out some of the following Web addresses to enhance your test-taking skills:

www.ohiou.edu/aac/tip/EXAMS.html

www.testtakingtips.com

http://caps.unc.edu/TestTake.html

As a result of this chapter, and in preparing for my journey, I plan to . . .

Extending Your Warranty

10

Jane is a 26-year-old student and mother of two young children. She married right out of high school and had her first child at age 19. To help her husband make ends meet, she began working part-time that same year. With the arrival of their second child, her part-time job evolved into a full-time job. Her young husband did not continue his education after high school and is working a low-paying, laborious job in the local manufacturing company. Jane's mother tries to help with childcare responsibilities; nevertheless, Jane has to depend more and more on a daycare center for her children.

As Jane approached her 26th birthday, she decided to fulfill her lifelong dream of becoming a dental hygienist. Jane was not academically prepared for the rigors of the hygienest program and was required to take several prerequisite courses her first year. Life for Jane has become very complicated this first year in college. She has very little time for her children, her husband, or herself. She has cut many corners, including some that affect the basics of good health. She has cut back on her work hours, but could not give up work altogether. She gets up early in the morning and goes to bed late at night. She eats almost exclusively at fast-food restaurants. With no time for exercise; no time for adequate rest; no time for well-balanced meals; and no time for family, friends, or her church, Jane is beginning to reach a point of total exhaustion.

Jane has resorted to coffee and soft drinks to get the stimulating effects of the caffeine to wake her up in the morning and to keep her awake late at night to study. Many times, breakfast is just a couple of cups of coffee or a cola on the way to school or work. Jane has also begun smoking as a quick fix or way to relax for a few minutes between classes or enroute from class to work.

After two successful semesters in the dental hygienest program at the local community college, Jane is mentally, physically, and spiritually drained. One day during a class clinical, Jane passed out and had to be hospitalized. Jane has ignored the importance of the harmony of her mind, body, and spirit, and now she will have to repeat a semester. She also has had to take time to recuperate from her rundown condition.

"Look to your health; and if you have it, praise God, and value it next to a good conscience; for health is the second blessing that we mortals are capable of; a blessing that money cannot buy."

IZAAK WALTON

In his classic book *Think and Grow Rich* (1937), Napoleon Hill encouraged us to develop strong character: body, mind, and spirit. Today, the YMCA movement around the world emphasizes the importance of developing your mind, body, and spirit in a harmonious way to maintain a true sense of health and well-being. Articles in many national publications explore topics such as the importance of exercise and overall fitness; the benefits of vegetarianism; the importance of a well-balanced approach to our health; and others.

The management of your health is just as important as the management of your time. It requires some thought and planning to be successful. In Chapter 4, we discussed goal setting and the techniques for establishing goals and measurable objectives. Health and wellness go hand in hand and require a certain amount of planning, implementation, and follow-up. This chapter is designed to help you understand the importance of health and wellness and to learn to manage your own health to ensure a well-balanced approach to wellness. After reading this chapter and completing the exercises, you should be able to:

- Understand the concept of wellness
- Understand the importance of balancing mind, body, and spirit
- Identify your strengths and weaknesses relative to health and wellness
- Understand how to build on these strengths and improve on the weaknesses
- Understand the eight components of the NEWSTART® program
- Understand how to develop and implement a wellness program
- Understand how to integrate your wellness program into your daily life
- Develop and maintain a well-balanced mental, physical, and spiritual life

Using the Milestones checklist, take a few moments and determine where you stand in relation to making health and wellness decisions.

If you have more "No" and "Sometimes" answers to these statements, do not be too concerned at this point. This chapter is designed to address each of the components of an effective wellness program and provide you with valuable lessons and tools that will enable you to become better balanced mentally, physically, and spiritually.

MILESTONES

WHERE ARE YOU NOW?

Answer each statement by checking "Y" for Yes, "N" for No, or "S" for Sometimes.

		Y	N	S
1.	I know how to develop a wellness plan.	Ⓨ	Ⓝ	Ⓢ
2.	Eating well-balanced meals is important to me.	Ⓨ	Ⓝ	Ⓢ
3.	I get adequate rest each day.	Ⓨ	Ⓝ	Ⓢ
4.	I drink six to eight glasses of water each day.	Ⓨ	Ⓝ	Ⓢ
5.	I understand the importance of adequate sunshine.	Ⓨ	Ⓝ	Ⓢ
6.	Exercise on a regular basis is important to me.	Ⓨ	Ⓝ	Ⓢ
7.	Moderation and temperance in food and drink is important to me.	Ⓨ	Ⓝ	Ⓢ
8.	Getting adequate fresh air is important to me.	Ⓨ	Ⓝ	Ⓢ
9.	Belief in a supreme being is important to me.	Ⓨ	Ⓝ	Ⓢ
10.	I understand that being healthy helps me to become a better student.	Ⓨ	Ⓝ	Ⓢ

WELLNESS STRATEGIES

What is health and wellness anyway? Health is defined in the *American Heritage Dictionary* as "the overall condition of an organism at a given time; soundness, especially of body or mind; freedom from disease; and a condition of optimal well-being." Wellness, as defined in *Webster's Eleventh New Collegiate Dictionary,* refers us back to *healthy,* defined as "enjoying health and vigor of body, mind, or spirit." Do we have to take a scientific approach, balancing calorie intake and output exactly? Not necessarily. However, we all should take a serious approach to developing a wellness plan that provides each of us a sense of well-being.

Health and wellness strategies are numerous and have become a tremendous commercial success in this country. In this chapter, we look at the basics of good health and provide a road map to your sense of well-being. Wellness is just as important to your success as a student as any other component of a student success program.

IDENTIFYING HEALTH AND WELLNESS STRENGTHS AND WEAKNESSES

Are you healthy? How do you know if you are healthy? Do you see a physician every year? Do you eat right? Do you get enough sleep, water, fresh air, sunshine, etc.? These and other questions have been integrated into an assessment exercise (Exercise 10.1) designed to identify your strengths and weaknesses in terms of health and wellness. This assessment takes about 25 minutes and can be completed in class or as a take-home assignment.

Exercise 10.1 is similar to Exercise 2.3 completed in Chapter 2. It is a three-step exercise. The first step is to read each question and assign a score of 1 to 5 (with 5 being the highest) to each. The next step is to add these numbers to compute an overall score. A score of 100 to 125 is an outstanding score that indicates that you are on your way to a healthy and productive life with good health habits. In the final step, transfer or record the individual question scores from page 219 to the corresponding question numbers on page 220. For example, the score for question 1 is transferred to 1 under the Health Status column.

"Nobody can be in good health if he does not have all of the time fresh air, sunshine, and good water."

FLYING HAWK

Question 2 from the first page is transferred to 2 under the Exercise and Rest column. A score of 20 or higher on any one of the five areas indicates strength in that area. A score of 15 or higher is another strong area that could be improved. Scores of 14 or less indicate a weak area that needs improvement. Once your strengths and weaknesses have been identified, how do you go about improving in those areas? As in the time-management assessment in Chapter 2, the first and simplest approach is to go back to the original 25 questions. These 25 questions are based on the principles and practices of good health and wellness. For example, question 1 and every fifth question thereafter deals with your understanding of the basic principles of good health. Question 2 and every fifth question thereafter deals with exercise and rest and its impact on physical fitness. After identifying your strengths and weaknesses, determining possible solutions and ways to build on your strengths and improve on your weaknesses, the next step is to develop a lifelong plan that you can use on a daily basis to ensure a healthy and productive life.

Answer the following questions by writing in a score of 1 to 5, with 5 being the highest score.

_____ 1. Do you know what your blood pressure is?

_____ 2. Do you exercise at least three to five times a week for 30 minutes?

_____ 3. Most people need 6 to 8 glasses of water each day; do you get your share?

_____ 4. Do you eat and drink in moderation?

_____ 5. Do you have a positive spiritual life?

_____ 6. Do you know what your HDL and LDL cholesterol levels are?

_____ 7. Most adults need 7 to 8 hours of sleep each night; are you getting adequate sleep?

_____ 8. Are you getting enough vitamin D–producing sunlight each week?

_____ 9. Are you a nonsmoker?

_____ 10. Do you pray or meditate on a daily basis?

_____ 11. Do you know your ideal body weight?

_____ 12. Do you take a technology break (e-mail, cell phones, beepers, etc.) each day?

_____ 13. Are you getting enough fresh air each day?

_____ 14. Are you a nondrinker?

_____ 15. Do you support others through prayer or meditation?

_____ 16. Do you have a family doctor and do you get an annual physical?

_____ 17. Do you practice positive self-talk?

_____ 18. Do you have one indoor plant for each room of your house and workplace?

_____ 19. Did you know that caffeine addiction has been linked to health problems?

_____ 20. Do you trust in a divine power?

_____ 21. Do you know what causes diabetes, cancer, and heart disease?

_____ 22. Weight lifting is good for all adults; do you include it in your exercise program?

_____ 23. During the summer, do you take steps to prevent sunburn?

_____ 24. Are you aware of the problems of prescription and over-the-counter drug abuse?

_____ 25. Are you growing spiritually?

_____ TOTAL SCORE

HEALTH STATUS	EXERCISE & REST	WATER, AIR, & SUNLIGHT	TEMPERATE, DRUG-FREE	SPIRITUAL WELL-BEING
1._____	2._____	3._____	4._____	5._____
6._____	7._____	8._____	9._____	10._____
11._____	12._____	13._____	14._____	15._____
16._____	17._____	18._____	19._____	20._____
21._____	22._____	23._____	24._____	25._____

TOTAL SCORES

_____	_____	_____	_____	_____

Exercise, fresh air, nutrition, and rest are all important components of overall wellness.

A score of 100 to 125 is an outstanding score that indicates very effective health and wellness habits and skills. Scores below 75 indicate that there may be one or more areas that need improvement. But which areas are strong and which are weak?

This section provides you with an indication of your strong areas where you have effective health and wellness skills or habits and your weak areas that will need some improvement. As mentioned earlier in this chapter, transfer the scores from the first page to the corresponding question numbers on this page.

A score of 20 or higher on any one of the five areas indicates strength in that area. A score of 15 or higher is another strong area that can be improved upon. Scores of less than 14 indicate a weak area that needs improvement. As mentioned earlier, once your strong and weak areas have been identified, you can return to the 25 questions to look for solutions or ways to improve upon any area of strength or weakness. For example, question 2 and every fifth question thereafter deals with exercise and rest and its impact on health and well-being. If you scored low in exercise and rest, questions 2, 7, 12, 17, and 22 provide effective practices of good health that, when implemented, will improve overall wellness.

COMPONENTS OF A HEALTHY LIFESTYLE

n 1978, the Weimar Institute of Weimar, California, established the NEW-START® Lifestyle Program. The eight components of the NEWSTART® program are:

1. Nutritious food
2. Exercise
3. Water
4. Sunlight
5. Temperance
6. Air
7. Rest
8. Trust

You should recognize these eight components as the basis for the Health and Wellness Assessment described in the previous paragraph. In the following sections, we touch on each of these areas, providing information and an understanding of the concept, as well as an approach that can fit into your wellness plan.

Nutritious Food

Food is the building block for any health and wellness program. There are literally hundreds of diet programs on the commercial market today, all promising a well-balanced, nutritious diet. Where do you start to ensure that your diet is nutritious and enjoyable? A good place to start is the new USDA MyPyramid (Figure 10.1) at www.mypyramid.gov/index.html. For vegetarians or someone interested in a vegetarian diet, there is also a vegetarian food guide (Figure 10.2). Your meals should be planned following one of these guides. Is it easy to follow these guidelines? *Muscle & Fitness* magazine reported in the June 2000 issue that the Agricultural Research Service of the USDA found, in two continuing surveys of 15,000 individuals of all ages across the United States, that Americans are consuming less than the minimum servings recommended for the fruit, dairy, and meat groups. They also found that grain and vegetable consumption is also at the lower end of the recommended ranges and that calories from fats and sugars exceed guideline recommendations. Is it any wonder that the United States leads the world in a number of lifestyle diseases such as obesity, diabetes, high blood pressure, and heart attacks?

As a student with many different responsibilities (college, work, family), it is more difficult to plan your meals for each day. Nevertheless, with the food pyramid as a guide and a meal planner, this difficult task can be simplified.

Exercise 10.2 instructs you to create your own healthy eating pyramid. Exercise 10.3 offers a Daily Meal Planner. Use this form to develop your daily meals and as an exercise for understanding and implementing MyPyramid. Once you have completed your first draft of the Daily Meal Planner, compare it with MyPyramid to see if you

"If we could give every individual the right amount of nourishment and exercise, not too little and not too much, we would have found the safest way to health."

HIPPOCRATES

FIGURE 10.1 USDA's MyPyramid.

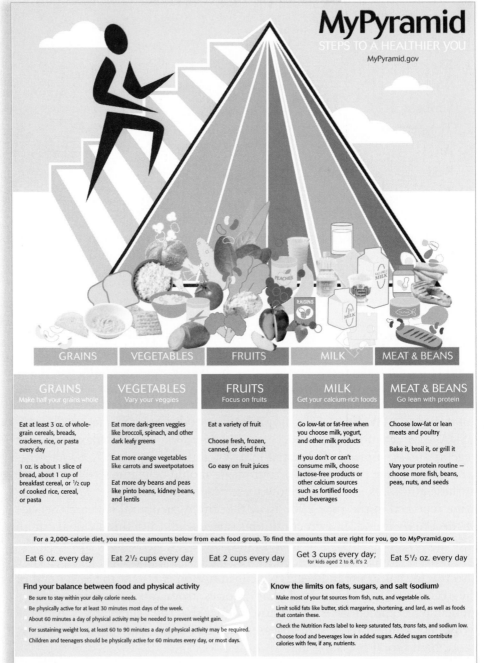

FIGURE 10.2

My Vegetarian Food Pyramid.

Variety ⊛ Quality ⊛ Safety ⊛ Exercise ⊛ Moderation ⊛ Low Fat ⊛ Low Sodium ⊛ Low Cholesterol

GRAINS Go for Whole	VEGETABLES Vary the Veggies	FRUITS Focus on Fruit	DAIRY/EQU Go Low Fat	FATS Favor Healthy Fats	BEANS & NUTS Power with Plant Proteins	DESSERTS De-emphasize the Desserts
6 ounces or 170 grams daily*	2½ cups or 600 ml daily*	2 cups or 480 ml daily*	3 cups or 720 ml daily*	1-2 ounces or 30-60 grams daily*	5½ ounces or 165 grams daily*	

Source: Copyright © GC Health Ministries. Layout/design by Elizabeth Petit. Adapted from USA Dietary Guidelines and mypyramid.gov. Used with permission.

*Based on 2,000 calories per day. For a detailed chart offering specific food and portion suggestions, contact GC Health Ministries, 301.680.6717, 12501 Old Columbia Pike, Silver Springs, MD 20904.

met your daily intake of the various recommended foods and number of servings.

Several studies have identified food for longevity and the perfect foods. Use these studies when planning your meals each day and take advantage of the most nutritious foods that have been identified. For example, an article in *Muscle & Fitness* magazine (February 1999) listed and discussed the best foods to eat for peak fitness and health. Listed in no particular order were: soy protein powder, soymilk, and tofu; whole-grain, enriched cereals; low-fat milk and yogurt; eggs; legumes; fish high in omega-3 fats; tomatoes and tomato sauce; citrus fruit and juices; broccoli; and not surprisingly, water. A similar article in *USA Weekend* (July 1999) created a list of 10 foods for longevity. Again in no particular order, they listed: tomatoes, olive oil, red grapes, nuts, whole grains, salmon and other fatty fish, blueberries, garlic, spinach, and green and ordinary black tea.

 **EXERCISE 10.2　Create Your Own Healthy Eating Pyramid**

What are you doing to develop healthy habits and maintain your physical and mental well-being? Here is your challenge: Use the USDA's "MyPyramid: Steps to a Healthier You" to create your own personalized plan to healthy eating and physical activity. Begin by going to the USDA's website www.MyPyramid.gov/index.html. Click on "Tour MyPyramid" for an animated tour of the pyramid. After viewing this presentation, go back to the top of the page to "MyPyramid Plan" and create your own personal plan. Key in your age, sex, and physical activity level; then click submit. Your plan will appear. For example, my personal plan indicates that I need 2,400 calories per day. You may use the "Meal Tracking Worksheet" on the web page or the "Daily Meal Planner" form found in Exercise 10.3 on the following page to track your daily food intake. Track your plan by clicking on "MyPyramid Tracker" and then choose "Assess Your Food Intake" or "Assess Your Physical Activity." Once you have your plan, share it with your instructor for his or her input and comments. After you have made any needed changes, track your plan for food intake and physical activity for one week and share the results with your instructor.

 **EXERCISE 10.3　Planning Daily Meals**

Understanding and Using MyPyramid
Using the chart below, list the foods that you plan to eat at each meal, record the amount in cups or ounces for each meal, total the five serving columns, and compare your plan with the recommended number of servings on the MyPyramid. How did you do? Remember, this is only a guide; your results may vary each day. Nevertheless, what is important is well-balanced meals each day. Note that this is a 2,000 calorie per day plan. Your plan may vary.

DAILY MEAL PLANNER

(Based upon the MyPyramid 2,000 calorie diet)

NUMBER OF SERVINGS:	Grains	Vegetables	Fruits	Dairy	Meat & Beans
BREAKFAST *(Breaking a fast, hearty meal)*					
LUNCH *(Lighter meal)*					
DINNER *(Eat early and light)*					
TOTAL CUPS OR OZ.:					
	Eat 6 oz	Eat 2 ½ cups	Eat 2 cups	Eat 3 cups	Eat 5 ½ oz.

Exercise

What is involved in an exercise program? How do you get started? How much exercise do you need each day? There are really three components to an effective exercise program: stretching, weight resistance training, and cardiovascular training. To begin any exercise program, you must warm up the major muscle groups of your body. Stretching is the best way to warm up your muscles and get into the mode of exercising. Your legs, arms, upper body, and back are all areas that should be stretched and warmed up before exercising. Weight resistance or weight lifting training provides strength and muscle tone. Studies have shown that adults of any age, even adults in their 70s and 80s, can gain strength through proper weight resistance training. The body functions better if you maintain adequate muscle mass. This type of training does not have to involve

All forms of exercise and activity are beneficial. Make some form of exercise and activity a part of your daily routine.

heavy weights and pain. You do not have to have "pain to gain" with weight resistance training. After age 30, an average adult loses about 1 percent of his or her muscle mass each year and gains additional fat without a proper exercise program. If you are counting calories, keep in mind that muscle burns more calories than fat. To prevent heart disease and obesity, cardiovascular exercise is essential.

Where do you start? Naturally, you should always talk to your doctor before starting any exercise program. See what is available at your college. Many times, college organizations schedule exercise or wellness programs for the students. Health screenings, weight loss programs, yoga, intramural sports programs, and various other wellness programs are offered by churches and community groups. If you are able to pay a monthly fee, the best bet is a YMCA, a hospital-based wellness center, or a private health club. Most of these facilities have discounts for students and employ professional trainers.

If you want to start a program of your own that you can do anytime and anywhere, consider jogging or walking. If it has been a long time since you exercised or you have never had a regular exercise program, walking is a good way to start. Walking can be done almost any time of the day and requires no equipment or fees. If the weather is bad or it is too hot or cold, almost all shopping malls have walking tracks inside the mall property. Malls usually open early in the morning (before the stores open) for regular walkers. Brisk walking with light weights in each hand, three to five times a week for 30 to 60 minutes, is an excellent way to stay in shape. Walking also provides an opportunity to do some constructive thinking or go over your class assignments and tests, or rehearse a speech. Sometimes, you can combine other activities with your exercise routine. For example, several times a week, you can catch up on your reading at the same time you ride a stationary bicycle.

To acquire and maintain good health, exercise must be a part of your daily routine. It helps you feel good. It lowers blood pressure. It lowers LDL cholesterol, the bad cholesterol, and often raises HDL, the good cholesterol. It lifts depression, relieves anxiety and stress. Make exercising a fun and natural part of your life. Find an exercise partner. Exercising with someone who can walk with you in the morning, at lunch, or in the late afternoon is a way to stay on track and keep committed to your program and your partner.

Water

Water plays an important role in every body function. Your body cannot function without it. It makes up almost 70 percent of your body. Water eliminates body heat through sweat; carries oxygen, carbohydrates, and fats to muscles; flushes waste products from your body; lubricates your joints; curbs your appetite; and assists in the digestion process.

How much water does the average person have to drink to stay healthy? Most Americans drink too little water to maintain healthy body functions. We need to take in the same amount of water we lose each day through the skin, lungs, urine, and feces. That is about 10 to 12 cups of water each day. Food provides two to four cups of water. That means that most people need about 8 additional cups of water each day in addition to any other beverages consumed. One simple axiom is drink enough water to keep your urine pale.

Soft drinks, tea, coffee, and alcoholic drinks do more harm than good when it comes to adequate water intake. These beverages add empty calories, increase the secretion of acid in the stomach, and contain phosphoric acid that can deplete calcium supplies. If you are thirsty, you have already lost 1 percent of your body's water. Your best choice of drinks to quench that thirst is water.

How can you get enough water into your body each day? The best thing to do when you first wake up in the morning is to drink two glasses of water. Remember that your body has had no food or water for eight hours. The two glasses of water will cleanse your system, begin to hydrate your body, and get you started on that eight-cup quota for the day. Drink a glass of water early and mid-morning. Drink a glass 30 minutes before lunch—it will get you halfway there and will diminish that hungry feeling that usually leads to overeating at lunch. Drink another glass an hour and a half after lunch, another 30 minutes before dinner, and a final glass one and a half hours after dinner. You also should drink some water before and after exercising. Following this routine is a great way to ensure that you are getting plenty of water.

Is it easy to remember to drink water and to stay on a routine? One suggestion to help keep you on track is to carry a bottle of water wherever you go. During your first break of the day, if you have a chance to purchase a soft drink, drink your bottle of water instead. After drinking a bottle of water you will feel more refreshed and will also feel a shot of energy. Remember that water is nature's perfect beverage.

Sunlight

Is the fourth component of NEWSTART® a friend or foe? Sunlight is both a friend and an enemy to the body. We know that excessive exposure to sunlight can cause sunburn, wrinkles, and eventually, skin cancer. However, adequate sunlight provides the body with that much-needed vitamin D that enables the body to pick up calcium from the intestines for use in building healthy bones. Vitamin D also prevents rickets and aids in the prevention of osteoporosis. Sunlight can also help your body's immune system, alleviate arthritic joint pain, and lower blood cholesterol levels.

If sunlight is both beneficial and detrimental, how much sunlight do you need to stay healthy? A few minutes of sunshine on your face and hands each day or as little as 15 minutes three times a week is all the sunlight you need to produce the vitamin D your body requires. Modest tanning can be protective; however, more is not always better. Always use sunscreen if you are going to be exposed to direct sunlight for more than 15 minutes. For fair-skinned people, it may be less.

Just remember that you should never sunburn. Sunlight is critical to overall wellness. It is a great germ killer, it makes us feel better, and it allows the body to produce vitamin D. A good way to get your needed sunlight each day is to go outside during your work or lunch break for a few minutes.

If there is little sunlight for long periods of time in your area of the country, make sure that you eat foods fortified with vitamin D or take a vitamin supplement daily.

Temperance

I am sure you have heard the phrases, "Everything in moderation" and "Live a balanced life." What do these phrases really mean and what impact do they have on our health? It is no secret that Americans eat and drink too much. We indulge in the finer things of life. Too much of a good thing can be a bad thing when our health is concerned. Surveys tell us that the majority of older Americans, those that live into their 80s and 90s, do not smoke or consume alcoholic drinks.

One of the problems that Jane (in our story at the beginning of this chapter) experienced was a dependence on coffee and soft drinks to get by each day. She was depending on a drug, caffeine, to help keep her alert when she really needed rest. There are studies that show people becoming ill because they consumed too much of a particular vegetable. They felt that more of a good thing was better when it actually was bad and led to toxicity. There have been a number of cases in which patients' skin turned an orange color because they consumed too much carrot juice. Too many vitamins can also cause a toxic situation.

The key is balance and the avoidance of unnecessary stimulants. USDA's MyPyramid, discussed earlier, provides the guidelines for a balanced meal plan. NEWSTART® is a program designed to create a balanced, healthy lifestyle. Once you have developed your own wellness program, make up your mind to stick with it for at least 30 days. At the end of the 30-day period, review your progress and see how you feel. That good feeling of well-being will be enough to keep you on track.

Air

Air? What has air got to do with wellness? Air is defined by the *American Heritage Dictionary* as "a colorless, odorless, tasteless gaseous mixture, mainly nitrogen (approximately 78 percent) and oxygen (approximately 21 percent), and other gases." It has also been defined as the breath of life. Oxygen is essential for well-oxygenated cells and contributes to our overall well-being. Oxygen is vital for each cell in your body. Anything that prevents an adequate supply of oxygen in the body is detrimental and reduces the mind's ability for clear thinking and studying.

"Plants are the lungs of the world!"

DEWITT S. WILLIAMS

In today's society of self-contained buildings, central heating, and air conditioning, pollutants and contaminants abound. Because buildings are so airtight or sealed with insulation, contamination can be five times higher in indoor air than outdoor air. Many of these buildings, as well as our homes, are sometimes called "sick buildings." These pollutants collect in our furniture, carpets, office equipment (particularly computers), toys, and clothes that are dry cleaned. Symptoms include headaches, irritation of the throat and eyes, and other sinus problems. Air pollution is also a problem in many big cities.

What can we do to ensure a good source of fresh air and oxygen for our bodies and minds? One of the first things we can do is exercise on a regular basis, following a program that includes deep breathing. In addition, several times during the day, take several deep-breathing breaks. It will energize and refresh you.

What about the quality of the air we breathe? To address this question, we should use a little common sense. Most daily weather reports provide an air quality update. Pay attention to this valuable information and any tips. For example, many days are categorized as bad air days in certain large cities. Reporters warn citizens to say indoors as much as possible on those days and not to exercise outdoors. Can we clean the air and generate more oxygen in our workplace and homes? The answer to this question is a resounding Yes! Houseplants are powerful natural air cleaners. Plants have been shown to remove nearly 87 percent of indoor air pollutants within a 24-hour period. Houseplants can suppress spores and molds and add moisture to the atmosphere. A simple rule for houseplants is one plant for every 100 square feet of floor space or one plant for every 10 ft. by 10 ft. of living space. This simple rule applies for your work area as well. To ensure fresh, oxygenated air, make sure you have at least one houseplant for each room of your house and one for your office or workspace.

Rest

In the story at the beginning of this chapter, inadequate rest (primarily sleep) was Jane's biggest health problem. It is a problem for many of us in today's fast-paced world. Surveys of high school students have shown that A- and B-grade students usually get seven and a half hours or more of sleep each night. Once they fall below this average, their grades begin to decline.

Well, what is sleep and how much of it do we need? Sleep is a time when your body rests and restores its energy. It is also an active state that is critical to good health. Young children need 10 to 12 hours of sleep each night, whereas adults need 7 to 8 hours. It varies a great deal among adults, but the 7 to 8 hours is a good benchmark.

> *"Early to bed and early to rise, makes a man healthy, wealthy, and wise."*
>
> BENJAMIN FRANKLIN

Our ability to sleep for long periods of time and to get into the deep restful stages of sleep decreases with age; nevertheless, we still need the same amount of sleep. Our bodies have a biological clock that is programmed for two natural periods of sleepiness each day. We cannot store sleep; therefore, we will experience these two periods of sleepiness each day. The first period is from about midnight to 7:00 A.M. and the other is between 1:00 P.M. and 3:00 P.M. Unless you live in a country like Mexico where it is customary to take a nap or siesta each day in the early afternoon, there is not much that you can do about the second period except to be aware and plan your day accordingly. However, the first period, we can address. To get that good night's sleep, try the following suggestions. Try to go to bed at the same time every night and get up at the same time every morning. During the day, get exposure to natural outdoor light. Make sure that your bedroom is a cool, dark, quiet place. Eat your evening meal at least four hours before you go to sleep. Your stomach at rest will be more conducive to a good night's sleep. Finally, use a daily planner to maintain a regular schedule of going to bed, getting up, eating, and exercising. The body responds better to regularity and good habits of wellness. These habits, like all habits, are created through repetition.

Trust

In recent years, several research studies have shown that hospitalized patients who believed in a divine power and had a circle of friends praying for them had a shorter time in recovery. In their book *The Stress Solution*, Lyle Miller, Alma Smith, and Larry Rothstein (1994) say, "Having trust in a higher power decreases feelings of isolation and abandonment and gives life a sense of meaning and purpose. Developing a source of guidance in your life will help put stressful events in perspective."

> "A cheerful heart does good like medicine, but a broken spirit makes one sick."
>
> PROVERBS 17:22

Trust is an important part of a balanced wellness plan. American prisoners of war who survived in the North Vietnam prison camps testified that it was their strong faith that kept them alive. All of us can learn from men and women of strong faith. Dr. Dale Matthews, after reviewing over 200 studies on the connection between faith in a supreme being and health, concluded that the weekly observance of one's faith is good medicine. It had a very positive effect on an individual's ability to deal with drug abuse, alcoholism, depression, cancer, high blood pressure, and heart disease. The ultimate wellness plan is one that is not just designed for mental and physical health, but spiritual health as well. It includes spiritual growth that brings quality, fulfillment, and hope for the present and the future.

A WELLNESS PLAN: PUTTING IT ALL TOGETHER

Putting it all together is not as difficult as it might first appear. You must begin with a goal. Earlier, we shared with you John Lee's goal of living a long and productive life free of preventable diseases. By referring back to Chapter 4 and using a goal-setting sheet, decide what your wellness goal will be. For example, Dr. Lee *values* (What do you value most in life?) living a long and productive life. He is *going* (Where are you going in life?) to live it free of preventable diseases. He will *accomplish* (How are you going to get there?) his goal by following his wellness plan that includes *objectives* (What specific steps are you taking to achieve your goal?) addressing each of the NEWSTART® elements.

> "Physical fitness isn't enough. You need balance in your life, spiritual balance."
>
> DONNA RICHARDSON

If you have not had an annual or general physical in the last 12 to 18 months, see your doctor before you start finalizing your wellness program. If you are under a doctor's care, it is even more important to see him or her before you start. It is also important to your health to find a doctor who uses nutrition to prevent and treat such illnesses as obesity, diabetes, and hypertension, along with medication if necessary. Educate yourself as well. Do your own research on health and wellness. Refer to the websites listed at the end of this chapter as a start. A well-educated patient with a well-educated doctor is a great combination.

Now that you have completed this chapter on Health and Wellness, take a few minutes to complete the Milestones checklist again.

Did any of your "No" and "Sometimes" answers become "Yes" answers as result of completing the exercises in this chapter? Hopefully, you will begin using the strategies presented to develop your health and wellness plan. Your wellness plan can be an excellent tool that you can use the rest of your life.

MILESTONES

NOW THAT YOU ARE HERE . . .

Answer each statement by checking "Y" for Yes, "N" for No, or "S" for Sometimes.

1. I know how to develop a wellness plan. (Y) (N) (S)

2. Eating well-balanced meals is important to me. (Y) (N) (S)

3. I get adequate rest each day. (Y) (N) (S)

4. I drink six to eight glasses of water each day. (Y) (N) (S)

5. I understand the importance of adequate sunshine. (Y) (N) (S)

6. Exercise on a regular basis is important to me. (Y) (N) (S)

7. Moderation and temperance in food and drink is important to me. (Y) (N) (S)

8. Getting adequate fresh air is important to me. (Y) (N) (S)

9. Belief in a supreme being is important to me. (Y) (N) (S)

10. I understand that being healthy helps me to become a better student. (Y) (N) (S)

- Have your *health* status, blood pressure, cholesterol levels, height, and weight checked regularly.

- *Exercise* three to five times a week for 30 to 60 minutes.

- Drink eight glasses of *water* each day.

- Get 15 minutes of *sunlight* three times a week.

- Eat and drink in *moderation.*

- Get eight hours of *sleep* each night.

- Have one indoor *plant* in each room of your home and workspace.

- Practice positive *self-talk* each day.

Applying What You Know

Health and wellness are topics that are in the news every day. Our physical well-being is well within our reach, more so today than in any other time in history. We have the research and benefits of technology that can assist us in living long and healthy lives. Now that you have finished this chapter on Health and Wellness, refer back to the Case Study about Gwen at the beginning of this book. Based on Gwen's situation, answer the following questions:

1. How will Gwen's situation affect her health and wellness if she does not take appropriate action?

2. What health and wellness strategies or techniques should Gwen follow?

3. How can Gwen use the eight components of the NEWSTART® program to assist her in reaching her goals?

Observations

CHARTING YOUR COURSE

Your health and well-being, like many things in life, are up to you. It is a matter of choices. It has often been said that the body was designed to support the brain and that the body was the base of the mental and spiritual processes of the person. If you are healthy and physically feel good, it is much easier to be mentally and spiritually positive. In this chapter, we have laid out a logical approach to wellness. Following the NEWSTART® program is an excellent way to ensure good health and well-being. Students who follow this or similar programs are more likely to be more successful and maintain a healthy lifestyle throughout their lives. A life free of preventable diseases is more than a goal. It is a way of life.

Getting There on Time

1. How can you use your planner to implement a physical fitness program?

_____

_____

_____

_____

2. How can you use your planner to implement a meal scheduling program?

_____

_____

_____

_____

3. What are the benefits of integrating your wellness plan into your daily schedule and planner?

_____

_____

_____

_____

Exploring Technology

Earlier in this chapter, the term *vegetarian* was mentioned. What is a vegetarian? What do they eat? To answer these questions and to challenge your ability to navigate the Internet, go to the following website and play the vegetarian game: www.vrg.org. Click on Vegetarian Game in the left menu and click on Play to play the game. Once you have completed the game, you can click on Score for an immediate score and analysis. How did you do? There are several tests and you can play it as many times as you wish.

Web Connections

TRAVELING THE INFORMATION SUPERHIGHWAY

Numerous websites deal with health, wellness, and fitness. Check out the following Web addresses to assist you on your journey to a healthy and productive life.

www.mypyramid.gov/index.html

www.weimar.org

www.health.com/health/fitness

www.americanyogaassociation.org

www.vrg.org

www.gssiweb.com

www.somethingbetternaturalfoods.com

www.thevegetariansite.com/health.htm

www.nadadventist.org/hm

www.lomalindamarket.com

www.RevivalSoy.com

www.nal.usda.gov/fnic/etext/000058.html

www.lungusa.org

www.nih.gov

As a result of this chapter, and in preparing for my journey, I plan to . . .

Reaching Your Destination

11

*G*race was 56 when she first entered college. Her life had been anything but "normal." She had two grown children, had gone through a divorce, lost a home to a fire, and, one week before classes began, moved to a new home from 1,500 miles away. Needless to say, Grace was dealing with a great deal of stress in her life, but she was determined to become a nurse. This had been her lifelong dream.

She did not go to college after high school but got married and settled down to raise her family. When her children were older, she studied for the real estate exam and became an agent in Texas, where they were living at the time. For several years, Grace did very well. One year she made more than $100,000 selling real estate. However, as the market changed and real estate became a tougher market in Texas, she lost her job and eventually moved "back home" near her family.

Grace could have continued in real estate, but her heart was not in it. She had always wanted to have a career in nursing. She enrolled in the nursing program at a local technical college and was devastated to find two major roadblocks to her dream. First, her SAT scores and her admissions test indicated that she was not academically prepared to enter the nursing program, and second, there was a three-year waiting list to get into the two-year program of nursing.

After much thought and consideration, Grace decided to enroll in the transitional studies program at the college and begin traveling the road to her dream. She put her name on the waiting list for the nursing program and began to take courses that would upgrade her basic skills in math, reading, and vocabulary. Over the course of the next two years, Grace hired tutors, went to study sessions, stayed up into the late hours of the night, and finally, she passed all of the tests to admit her into the Associate Degree Nursing Program.

The phone rang one day and the nursing department told Grace that there was an opening in the department. She was admitted almost one year earlier than she expected. Her first course was very demanding. The subject matter dealt with calculating drug doses for patients. In order to continue in the program, students *had* to pass the first test on

"*It is easy to live for others. Everybody does. I call on you to live for yourselves.*"

RALPH WALDO EMERSON

mathematical calculations. If you failed the first test, you were not only removed from the class, but from the entire nursing program.

Grace failed the first test! She was asked to leave the nursing program.

Not to be beaten, Grace enrolled in a developmental math course and studied harder, stayed up longer, hired more tutors, and finally passed the course. She then enrolled in another math course and continued to build her math skills for the nursing curriculum. One year later, Grace was invited to rejoin the nursing program. She enrolled in the same drug dosage calculation class. She passed the first test. She passed the second test . . . she passed the course.

Two years after readmission, Grace walked down the aisle of the local civic center to be "pinned" as a nurse. Five years after she began her journey to fulfilling her dream, she was living that dream. There were countless times when her life and experiences would have led most of us to quit, but Grace was determined to have a career in nursing. She knew in her heart what she wanted to be "when she grew up."

fter reading this chapter and completing the exercises, you will be able to:

- Understand the value of your "career daydreaming"
- Identify the seven steps to career decision making
- Recognize how valuable a mentor can be
- Develop a personal success plan

WHAT DO YOU WANT TO BE WHEN YOU GROW UP?

ave you been asked that question before? Do you know the answer? You probably have given some thought to the question; maybe you have even imagined yourself doing different things. The process of career selection can be lengthy, but it is by far one of the most important things you can do for yourself. The key phrase here is "for yourself." *You* are in charge here—no one else can make this decision for you. Also, this is a personal journey, one on which it is okay to "ask for directions," but one that you control. You control the speed and,

MILESTONES

Answer each statement by checking "Y" for Yes, "N" for No, or "S" for Sometimes.

1. I have a good idea of what I want to be when I graduate. (Y) (N) (S)

2. I know how to find a mentor. (Y) (N) (S)

3. I think about my career daily. (Y) (N) (S)

4. I would consider seeking advice from an advisor or counselor. (Y) (N) (S)

5. I use the *Dictionary of Occupational Titles*. (Y) (N) (S)

6. I daydream about my career. (Y) (N) (S)

7. I know how to research a career. (Y) (N) (S)

8. I understand how shadowing works. (Y) (N) (S)

9. I understand how personality inventories work. (Y) (N) (S)

10. I can use a computer to help research a career. (Y) (N) (S)

ultimately, the direction your career takes you. You can change your "route" at any time. As a matter of fact, the world of technology and information is changing so rapidly that almost every person will change careers at least once in their lives. This was not true of your parents. It is estimated that today, three out of every *four* workers will need retraining for the new jobs of this century! The decisions that you make about your career choices and the roads that you take to get there are *yours* and belong to no one else.

In the Milestones checklist, take a few moments and determine where you stand in relation to making career decisions.

After completing the questions in Milestones, if you would like to turn more of your "No" and "Sometimes" answers into "Yes" answers, consider some of the following activities to help you with your career decision making:

- Research your career
- Decide on a major
- Shadow someone currently working in the field in which you are interested

If you do not have a good idea of what you are interested in for your life's work, don't worry. If you read this chapter carefully and complete the exercises, your career decision-making skills will be enhanced.

DAYREAMING

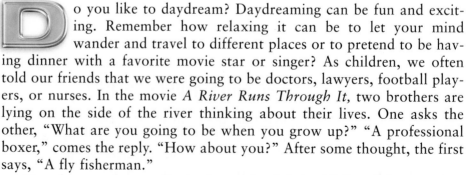

o you like to daydream? Daydreaming can be fun and exciting. Remember how relaxing it can be to let your mind wander and travel to different places or to pretend to be having dinner with a favorite movie star or singer? As children, we often told our friends that we were going to be doctors, lawyers, football players, or nurses. In the movie *A River Runs Through It,* two brothers are lying on the side of the river thinking about their lives. One asks the other, "What are you going to be when you grow up?" "A professional boxer," comes the reply. "How about you?" After some thought, the first says, "A fly fisherman."

Very few people actually do the work of their childhood dreams (e.g., boxing, fishing, dancing, acting, and being a fireman). Those dreams may come true for people who do not change their minds, but most of us eventually modify our aspirations. This is natural. However, there are those who only want to do one thing from childhood—and they *do it.*

Take a moment, clear your mind. Allow yourself to think about your first-grade classroom. Remember your teacher? Do you remember talking to your friends about what you would "be" when you "grew up"? List the different occupations you may have mentioned as a child. Enjoy the journey!

> "I went into the woods because I wished to live deliberately, to front only the essential facts of life, and see if I could not learn what it had to teach, and not, when I came to die, discover that I had not lived."
>
> HENRY DAVID THOREAU

1. _____

2. _____

3. _____

4. _____

5. _____

Now, think about what you have just written. Why did you, even as a child, select the occupations you listed? Take a minute and write down why you wanted to "be" these things.

For #1 _____

_____

For #2 _____

_____

For #3 _____

_____

For #4 _____

_____

For #5 _____

_____

Now, think for just a moment about the occupations you listed. What are your "daydreams" like now? What occupations do you see yourself doing now? If money were not a concern, if time in school or location or family did not play a part in your decision and you could do one thing for the rest of your life, *what would you do for the rest of your life?* Think about that question.

If money was not a part of the picture and you could do anything for the rest of your life, what would it be? List a few of those occupations in the space below. You may only have one; and that's fine.

1. _____

2. _____

3. _____

4. _____

5. _____

Now, we need to take a strong look at your answer(s) and determine if you want to do something or to *be* something.

DO YOU WANT TO DO SOMETHING OR BE SOMETHING?

If you were to ask most people on the street the simple question, "What do you do for a living?" they would respond, "I'm a welder," or "I'm an engineer," or "I'm a teacher." Most people answer the question without ever thinking about what is really being asked.

This is one of the first questions that you will need to examine when deciding on a career. Do I want to "do" something or do I want to "be" something? Just because a person is called a welder, an engineer, or a teacher, the title alone does not necessarily confer an identity. The art of "being" is a mind-set that is developed on your own. There are many people who teach for a living, but there are very few "teachers." There are people who do social work, but few are actually "social workers." To "be" something, you have to make a philosophical decision regarding your future. The questions you have to ask are, "How do I want to spend my time?" and "What is my purpose in life?" As an individual, you can "do" almost anything. You can *do* the work of medicine, you can *do* the work of upholding the law, you can *do* the work of instruction, but in order to "*be*" a doctor, lawyer, or teacher, you have to want to "*become*" the epitome of those professions. "Doing" the work is not enough to bring fulfillment to your life; doing is the easy part. "Being" the person who heals, protects justice, or teaches will bring you joy.

There is an old story about a stranger who was walking down the road one day when he came upon three men cutting stone. He stopped to ask the first man what he was doing. "I'm cutting these rocks in half. Can't you see that?" The stranger approached the second man cutting stone and asked that gentleman what he was doing. "I'm shaping these stones into blocks. Can't you see?" Finally, the stranger came upon the third stonecutter and stopped to ask him what he was doing. Replied the last stonecutter, "I'm building a cathedral. Can't you see?" Where it takes only physical strength to "do" something, it takes vision to "be" something. So, what do you want to "be"? Have you decided? If not, there's help for the undeclared.

> *"Not all who wander are lost."*
>
> J. R. R. TOLKIEN

HELP ME! I'M UNDECLARED!

No, it isn't a fatal disease. Being "undeclared" is not a disgrace or a weakness. It is a temporary state of mind and the best way to deal with it is to stop and think. A person should never declare a major simply because he or she is ashamed to be undeclared. Also, you should never allow yourself to be pressured into declaring a major. There are certain measures that you can take to work toward declaring a major and being satisfied with your decision.

Seven Steps to Career Decision Making

STEP ONE: DREAM! As was asked earlier, if money was not a problem or concern, what would you do for the rest of your life? If you could do anything in the world, what would you do, where would you do it? These are the types of questions that you should ask yourself as you try to select a major and career. Let your mind wander and let the sky be the limit. Write down your dreams. These dreams may be closer to reality than you know. In the words of Don Quixote, "Let us dream, my soul, let us dream."

STEP TWO: TALK TO YOUR ADVISOR. Academic advisors are there to help you. Do not, however, be surprised if some of their doors are closed. First, always make an appointment to see an advisor. They teach, conduct research, perform community service, and sometimes advise a large number of students. Always call in advance. However, when you have an appointment, make that advisor work for you. Take your college catalog with you and ask probing questions. Your advisor will not make a career decision for you, but if you ask the proper questions, the advisor can be of monumental importance to you and your career decisions.

Use some of your college electives to delve into new areas of interest. You may find that an elective changes your career direction.

You should also use students in your program as advisors. They will prove to be invaluable to you as you work your way through the daily workings of the college. Upperclassmen can assist you with making decisions regarding your classes, electives, and college work-study programs. They can even help you join and become an active member of a pre-professional program.

STEP THREE: USE COLLEGE ELECTIVES. Most accreditation agencies working with your college require that you be allowed at least one free elective in your degree program. Some programs allow many more. Use your electives wisely! Taking courses just to get the hours can be a waste of time. The wisest students use their electives to delve into new areas of interest or take a block of courses in another area that might enhance their career decisions. Perhaps you are interested in business; you may want to use your first elective to take an introductory business course. Maybe you should use your first elective to take an art course, a music course, or even one in psychology. Be creative, be courageous, be wild, but don't play it safe. Take a chance. It can be the best thing that ever happened to you. One of these electives might be the key to choosing your career.

STEP FOUR: GO TO THE CAREER CENTER. Even the smallest colleges have some type of career center or a career counselor. *Use them!* Most of the time, career centers on campus are free. If you go into the community for the same types of services, you could pay anywhere from $200 to $2,000. The professionals in the career center can show you information on a variety of careers and work fields. They can perform certain interest and personality inventories that can help you make career decisions.

STEP FIVE: READ! . . . READ! . . . READ! Nothing will help you more than reading about careers and majors. Ask your advisor or counselor to help you locate as much information on your areas of interest as possible. Gather information from colleges, agencies, associations, and places of employment. Then *read it!*

STEP SIX: SHADOWING. No, this is not what vampires do when the full moon is out. This is a term used to describe the process of "following someone around on the job." Perhaps you have an interest in the field of medicine but you don't know exactly what a general practitioner does all day. It might be possible for you to ask your doctor if you could spend the day "shadowing" his or her activities. You might call an engineering office and ask if you can sit with several of their engineers for a day over spring break. This is the *very best* way to get firsthand, honest information regarding a profession in which you might be interested. You might ask questions such as: Why do you do this for a living? What training do you have? How long did you go to school in order to get this job? What is your salary range? Is there room for growth? What is your greatest achievement on this job? What was your weakest moment?

STEP SEVEN: JOIN PRE-PROFESSIONAL ORGANIZATIONS. One of the most important decisions you will make as a college student is getting involved in organizations and clubs on campus that offer educational opportunities, social interaction, and hands-on experience in your chosen field. Pre-professional organizations can open doors that will assist you in making a career decision, growing in your field, meeting professionals already working in your field, and eventually getting a job.

Another important aspect of studying and researching a career is finding a mentor with whom you can work and shadow.

What Is a Mentor?

Webster's Eleventh New Collegiate Dictionary defines mentor as "a trusted counselor or guide; a tutor or guide."

The thoughts expressed by Jimmie on the following page truly define what a mentor can mean to a student. Mentors have been around for ages. Scholars had young students study under their guidance who, in turn, became scholars themselves. Mentors can be anyone that you admire professionally, personally, intellectually, or socially.

When trying to imagine what a mentor is, it might be helpful to explore what a mentor is *not*. In this case, a mentor is not an idol or god to be revered. This person should be someone with whom you feel comfortable and in whom you can place trust. When you become successful, you will be a professional peer to this individual if your career follows the same course. A mentor does not necessarily have to be a lot older than you. People can be mentors at any age; likewise, you are never too old to have a mentor. It is important that you eventually let the mentor know that you perceive them as such. By doing so, you let them know that you value who they are and what they have achieved.

Think for just a moment about mentors in your life. As you do, list any mentors you may have and explain why you respect this person:

1. _____

   Why do you admire this person? _____

   _____

   _____

2. _____

   Why do you admire this person? _____

   _____

   _____

3. _____

   Why do you admire this person? _____

   _____

   _____

> **JIMMIE'S STORY**
>
> "I remember my first mentor, a gentleman who served as provost at the college I attended. Dr. Thomas was everything I wanted to be—successful, self-assured, intelligent, and fun loving. He had achieved much in his career, traveled widely, yet never lost the "common touch." He could relate to almost anyone on any level and was an excellent judge of character. I soon realized that not only was he my professional mentor but also my mental and emotional mentor as well. I depended on his advice and his friendship. I find myself wishing that he was still alive today to offer advice about my career and about my life in general."

Make the decision right now that you will let the people you listed know that you admire them—you will be surprised at the reaction it may elicit. You may very well be making the first professional contacts of your career, ones that can help you find jobs as your career progresses.

Now, reflect back on all of the responses you have listed. Are you being influenced by another person or by an idea about a career? How much *original* thought have you given to career selection? Many people end up majoring in a certain discipline because a friend is majoring in that field or because a parent or grandparent majored in that field. Remember, one of the most important decisions you will *ever* make in your life is choosing a career. The decision should be your own. If you are still having some trouble thinking about a career or narrowing your focus, you might consider seeking the advice and assistance of a career counselor.

What Is a Career Counselor?

A career counselor could be viewed as a "career travel agent" of sorts. This person can help you understand the variety of options that you might have and can help you "map" your way. Career counselors can help you learn more about yourself and help you clarify goals for the future. Career counselors can be located in schools, colleges, and the private sector. They will assist you with the processes outlined previously, but you must remember that ultimately, *you* are in charge. You may want to ask your counselor to administer the Myers-Briggs Type Indicator® instrument or the Campbell Interest and Skill Survey (CISS) to assist you with this process. These instruments give you an idea of who you are and for what type of work you are best suited. If your counselor or college cannot provide this kind of assistance to you, look for private companies in your area that can.

ONCE YOU KNOW WHERE YOU ARE GOING, HOW DO YOU GET THERE?

The next step in this process is *research*. This is where *you* come in. Deciding to do the research will yield remarkable results. This process is lengthy and, if done correctly, can take *lots* of time, especially if you want to examine several careers.

Here are some "things" you need to do:

First, spend some time listing the careers from the career interests inventories or personality inventories you have completed at your school's career center. If you have not completed an inventory, look back at your mentor list and your "dream" list. Develop a list of careers that you wish to explore.

After you have identified a career in which you are interested, the research begins. Look at the *Dictionary of Occupational Titles (DOT)*. This is usually available in the reference section of your library. Look up the careers that you have selected. *Read every bit of information you can on these careers. Take notes.* While looking at the *DOT,* you should answer the questions found next in "Roadways to Career Decision Making."

- Will I *work* with people, things, or ideas?

This is a most important question. Do you enjoy working with people, or do you enjoy working with machinery? If someone is a "people person" but works with machines all day, he is probably not going to be very happy. The same is true of those who do not enjoy working directly with people but do it anyway. Make your career fit your personality!

- How much *Training* am I going to need to do this job?

For some students, the answer to this question will determine what they do for the rest of their lives. Some people are not interested in going to college, or if they do go, they only want a two-year degree or a certificate. Others do not mind going to college for several years. This decision is up to you. However, it is important to note that according to *U.S. News & World Report,* students who attend college and graduate tend to earn more than those students who do not.

- How much *money* will I make in this profession?

Recently, a friend of mine was offered a job making $90,000 per year . . . for *nine* months' work. She did not take the job because she told me that money did not motivate her. She said, "My family is here (where I live now), my friends are here, my church is here, and I love the weather. I'm not going to take it . . . I wouldn't be happy." For some people, money *will* be a driving force. For others, money will matter less. This decision is up to you.

- Do I know *anyone* who already works in this profession?

It is always good to talk to people who already work in the profession that you are interested in. Go to that person and ask questions about money, raises, promotions, work atmosphere, climate, and overall satisfaction. This information may help you make some hard decisions about your career.

- Will I work *indoors* or outdoors?

For many people, this question is the driving force behind their career decisions. Nothing could be worse than a person who loves the outdoors to be trapped behind a desk for 8 to 10 hours a day. On the other hand, if someone does not enjoy the outdoors, she would be miserable working construction or in the areas of wildlife or forestry.

- Will the work I do be *mental* or physical?

Again, this depends on you as an individual. Some people love to work with heavy objects and use their bodies. Others love to think and work with their minds daily. Usually, you are going to find jobs that require that you do a little of both. You should always use your mind, but some jobs require that you use it more often and in different ways.

- Where will I *live* while doing this job?

Some people do not care if they have to move far away to do their work. Others prefer to stay in a familiar area. Some people love colder climates while others would rather live near the beach. Your attitude toward this issue could determine your career as well. You will have a hard time being an ocean diver or deep-sea fisher if you live in Utah.

- Will I *Travel* with this job?

Some people feel that one of the most exciting things in the world is constant travel. They live mostly in hotels and love every minute of every new destination. Others do not enjoy this lifestyle at all. They prefer to have a job that does not require them to travel at all. Again, you must evaluate your own preference.

- Do I want to do this for the rest of my *life?*

Think about your career choices. Do you see yourself doing this job for the rest of your life? That is a long time, hopefully. Would you be happy to look back on your life and say, "This is what I did for a living; this is how I made my mark on the world"?

These are important issues and questions that you must answer when researching and considering a career. Take time to answer these questions about your life's work.

DEVELOP A PERSONAL SUCCESS PLAN

Now that you have all of your directions, write them down in a place where you will be able to refer to them often; for example, file them behind your planner in your binder. Some career consultants suggest following the format described in the box below as a personal success plan.

Finally, you should realize that there are numerous places to find information regarding careers, majors, professions, and the world of work. Listed below are just a few of the places you should look when examining careers:

College counseling centers

Dictionary of Occupational Titles (DOT)

Guide for Occupational Exploration

What Color Is Your Parachute? by Richard Bolles

The Three Boxes of Life by Richard Bolles

The United States Armed Forces

The Holland Self-Directed Search

The Myers-Briggs Type Indicator®

Computer databases such as SIGI, SIGI Plus, or DISCOVER

MY PERSONAL SUCCESS PLAN: CAREER RESEARCH

Use the following questions as a guide for developing your own personal success plan. For each career in which you are interested, complete the following activity: Write a paragraph for each of these questions, keeping all of your answers in one place, such as your three-ring binder. This section in your binder then will become your own Personal Success Plan Research diary. By referring to this diary, you can compare careers and the process will hopefully allow you to make more informed decisions about the world of work. Also include in your binder a copy of your current resume. Techniques for creating a resume will be discussed later in this chapter.

> ### SUCCESS PLAN OUTLINE
>
> Write down your goals (refer to Chapter 4)
>
> Make an appointment to see an advisor (counselor)
>
> Visit your school career center
>
> Research your interests at the library
>
> Read about your interests
>
> Take classes that interest you as electives
>
> Find someone to shadow
>
> Tell others about your dreams
>
> Review your goals

CAREER TO BE RESEARCHED:

Why am I interested in this career?

Will I work with people or things?

How much training is required?

How much money am I likely to make?

Who do I know already working in this field?

What did this person say about this profession?

Will I work indoors or outdoors?

Will the work be mental or physical?

Where will I live while doing this work?

Will this work involve much travel?

What is the best thing I found out about this career?

What is the worst thing I found out about this career?

Whom did I interview about this career?

What sources did I use for my research on this career?

ROAD PLAN DECIDED? WHERE DO I GO FROM HERE?

Let's say that you've taken all of the advice provided so far and that you're ready to meet the "real world" head on. You've decided what career is best for you, you've selected a college and major to get you to your final destination, and you're suddenly faced with the stark reality of *finding a job!* Where do you turn? First, turn to your college placement office. This resource can be invaluable in helping you with writing your resume and putting together a logical, coherent, and effective cover letter. The staff members of your college placement office are professionals who understand what you're going through and can help you land a job that will enhance your career and provide you with invaluable experience.

RESUME WRITING

Before you begin your job search process, however, you must first learn to write a professional and effective resume. A resume tells prospective employers who you are, what you know. It gets your "foot in the door" so you can get an interview and a chance to demonstrate your potential value as an employee. Think of a resume as a sales plan—then, when you get your "foot in the door" (through an interview), you have a chance to really shine and "close the sale."

Effective resume writers all say basically the same thing—be brief, positive, action-oriented, honest, precise, and use some basics of presentation and style. *Above all else, make sure that your resume is flawless, typographically and grammatically!*

By being brief, we mean you should list all relevant job experience (in order of current or most recent job to earliest) and the corresponding dates of employment. It is important that you highlight (possibly with bullets) some of the relevant experiences you had with each job—this is where you need to be especially brief. Don't go on and on about mundane tasks that you had with the job—highlight the items you were "responsible" for rather than the items you were required to "do." Prospective employers look to hire individuals who did an excellent job at mundane or routine tasks and so were given more responsibility. They look for potential employees who can accept responsibility and "get the job done." Highlight any experiences you might have had that reflect this kind of work experience. Be action-oriented in your choice of verbs. Instead of "I did XXX," say, "I was responsible for assuring that XXX was completed." This is where your career counselor can be *most* helpful, by turning your passive verbs into active verbs, which will get employers' attention. Above all else, keep the discussions simple. Potential employers do not want to read extensive biographies!

It is not too much to assume that you will be honest and truthful as you write your resume. Do not attempt to exaggerate your qualifications. Honesty really is the best policy here. There have been documented cases where employees lied on their resume or applications and when the employer found out, the employee was fired immediately and legal proceedings were initiated. Always remember this when writing your resume: Would you want your doctor to have lied on her resume just to get the job that she has? The same policy applies with *any* job, not just positions within the health-care industry. In short, *do not lie* on your resume.

Regarding presentation, there are some basic and simple rules. *Always* have your resume neatly typed and on the best quality paper you can afford. A tip here is to share costs with friends and buy quality paper (25 percent rag bond) and envelopes on which to print your resume. Generally, subdued, neutral colors are best: tan, gray, or white. Avoid colors such as pink, yellow, green, or blue. You want your resume to stand out among a sea of other resumes—you don't want it to scream! With the advent of word processing, spell checking, and grammar checking, there is *absolutely no reason* for a resume to contain any errors. If your resume does have errors, it will stand out for all of the wrong reasons. Have a friend or relative (someone you trust) proofread your resume and cover letter before you mail it. It is better to delay mailing by one day than to have a resume with an obvious error.

To assist you in answering some basic questions about resume writing, a sample resume is included as a guide (see Figure 11.1). Generally speaking, it is a good idea to keep your resumes to one page or, at most, two pages.

When writing your resume, be truthful and accurate. Customize your resume and highlight experience and education that are relevant to the position you seek.

PREPARING FOR THE INTERVIEW

Once you have been called for an interview, it is time for you to aggressively approach learning more about the company. It is perfectly appropriate, and actually expected, that you will dig into many aspects of the company to find out more about the operation. An excellent first stop is your local or college library. Another first stop could even be the Internet. Many manufacturing, retail, and service industries now have websites that tell you a lot about the company. You should also tap into your network of friends and relatives. Perhaps you know someone who works with the company, or you "know someone who knows someone." Use this resource, but be careful that you only take factual information from these sources. The last thing you want to do is to have your opinion of the company wrongfully discolored by what another person thinks. For example, if an employee is disgruntled or dissatisfied, he or she generally will tell you all of the negative aspects of the company. On the other hand, if the employee is happy, you will learn many positive things about the industry that you can later use in your interview.

FIGURE 11.1 | Sample resume.

Jane Doe

138 Brentwood Ave.   (333) 555-4568
Any City, USA 12345   doej@internetprovider.com

OBJECTIVE   Meaningful employment in the career service field

QUALIFICATIONS   - Strong written and oral communication ability
                     - Excellent computer skills
                     - Outstanding interpersonal skills
                     - Part-time experience in career services field

EDUCATION   Bachelor of Science, Business Administration (5/05)
                     XYZ University, Anytown, USA

                     - Concentration in Personnel and Human Relations
                     - 3.05 GPA
                     - Full-time Trustee Scholarship

                     Associate of Applied Technology (5/03)
                     USA Community College, Anytown, USA

                     - Phi Theta Kappa National Honor Society Member
                     - 3.895 GPA

RELEVANT   University Career Center, Anytown, USA
EXPERIENCE   As a part-time college employee, I was responsible for:

                     - Designing and implementing Web pages for the center and for
                       individual students.
                     - Helping to conduct resume critiques, workshops, and seminars.
                     - Helping students to complete online research and prepare for
                       college-based interviews.

OTHER   Peace Corps Volunteer (2000–02)
EXPERIENCE   Served in Shanghai, China, for one year, helping to teach English as a
                     second language and working with fish-farming enterprises.

REFERENCES   Available upon request.

As you prepare for an interview, it is appropriate to discuss dress and hygiene. Basic daily hygiene and conservative, understated dress is appropriate for any interview. You should follow this simple list of "Do's and Don'ts" as you prepare for an interview:

DO:

- Spend an appropriate amount of time on grooming. A bath or shower, fresh haircut, clean nails, and freshly brushed teeth are appropriate.

- For men, if you are not clean-shaven, make sure that your beard or facial hair is neatly trimmed and clean.

- Dress in a manner appropriate to the position for which you are interviewing. It is always a good idea to be a little "overdressed" for the position. Men who are unsure whether or not to wear a tie should wear one. Likewise, women who are unsure whether or not to wear slacks should not wear them.

- Always wear shoes that will "hold a shine" and make sure that they are shined.

- Some jewelry (watch, ring, necklace for women) is appropriate.

- Always, and as soon as possible, write a thank-you note to the person, expressing gratitude for his or her time and the opportunity to learn more about the company.

- *Be on time.*

DON'T:

- Wear gaudy or revealing clothing.
- Wear excessive cologne, makeup, or jewelry (individual statements are fine but not for a job interview—leave nose-rings and lip-rings at home).
- Wear any clothing that will distract the interviewer from you, your qualifications, or your abilities.
- Chew gum during an interview.
- Use tobacco products during an interview.
- Bring spouses, children, or significant others to the interview.
- Show up late.

Though many of the items on these lists may seem elementary, some job hunters may not know that these items are either expected or considered taboo. A good rule of thumb is that when you are in doubt, err on the side of the conservative. You will not be viewed as a prude but as a professional.

Complete the Milestones checklist. As a result of this chapter, do you feel that you now know more? Are you better equipped to research a

MILESTONES

NOW THAT YOU ARE HERE . . .

Answer each statement by checking "Y" for Yes, "N" for No, or "S" for Sometimes.

1.	I have a good idea of what I want to be when I graduate.	Ⓨ Ⓝ Ⓢ
2.	I know how to find a mentor.	Ⓨ Ⓝ Ⓢ
3.	I think about my career daily.	Ⓨ Ⓝ Ⓢ
4.	I would consider seeking advice from an advisor or counselor.	Ⓨ Ⓝ Ⓢ
5.	I use the *Dictionary of Occupational Titles.*	Ⓨ Ⓝ Ⓢ
6.	I daydream about my career.	Ⓨ Ⓝ Ⓢ
7.	I know how to research a career.	Ⓨ Ⓝ Ⓢ
8.	I understand how shadowing works.	Ⓨ Ⓝ Ⓢ
9.	I understand how personality inventories work.	Ⓨ Ⓝ Ⓢ
10.	I can use a computer to help research a career.	Ⓨ Ⓝ Ⓢ

particular career and know what is involved on a daily basis? Have you made a decision about the particular major you will pursue and how that major relates to the world of work? Did you shadow a person who currently works in the field in which you are interested? Do you have a current resume, and do you feel comfortable going on a job interview? If your answer to any of these questions is "No," revisiting some of the activities in this chapter might help. In addition, making an appointment with your campus career counselor will be invaluable to you. These decisions are some of the most important decisions you will ever make, so do not take this process lightly. The time you spend now researching, reading, investigating, questioning, and learning is minimal compared to the time you will spend earning the appropriate degree, diploma, and certificate for your chosen career. Don't skimp on this chapter or this concept. Invest in yourself in order to realize your full potential.

Applying What You Know

Now that you have completed this chapter, refer back to the Case Study about Gwen at the beginning of this book. Based on her situation, answer the following questions:

1. Gwen actively researched a career in the medical field based on a broad category identified with a variety of assessments. How have your career goals been shaped by research you have completed?

_____

_____

_____

_____

2. Given what you know about the value of "dreaming" and setting goals, where do you see yourself in five years? Ten years?

_____

_____

_____

_____

3. How might you apply what you have learned in the "Seven Steps to Career Decision Making" section to your own situation?

_____

_____

_____

_____

Observations

CHARTING YOUR COURSE

You are in charge here. Whatever you become, whatever you make of yourself, is ultimately a choice that *you* make. Your decisions may be with you for the rest of your life. A career is more than a job. A career is a state of mind that leads to your "life's work." As you begin your personal journey, remember this quote:

> "People are always blaming their circumstances for what they are. I don't believe in circumstances. The people who get on in this world are the people who get up and look for the circumstances they want, and, if they can't find them, they make them."
>
> —*George Bernard Shaw*

Getting There on Time

1. How will your career choice affect your personal time?

   _____

   _____

2. How much time outside of your education will be expected for you to be successful in your career?

   _____

   _____

3. Describe the importance of time as it relates to getting a job.

   _____

   _____

4. How long will it take you to achieve your career goal?

   _____

   _____

Exploring Technology

This activity is designed to help you research your career. You will begin the exploration by visiting the America's Job Bank website at www.americasjobbank.com. This informative site will provide you with answers about wages, employment trends, fastest growing occupations by education levels, and so on. While navigating through the site, answer the following questions:

- What is the fastest growing career?
- How much education or training is needed?
- Is your future occupation listed as one of the top 25 fastest growing occupations?
- What kind of wages can you expect from your chosen career?

Web Connections

TRAVELING THE INFORMATION SUPERHIGHWAY

During your journey, you may want to check out some of the following Web addresses to assist you with your career planning and research:

www.americasjobbank.com

www.acinet.org/acinet

www.ttrc.doleta.gov/network

http://stats.bls.gov/ocohome.htm

www.bumblebeetech.com/CareerLinks.html

As a result of this chapter, and in preparing for my journey, I plan to . . .

Financing Your Roadtrip

12

MONEY MANAGEMENT

Jim is a single parent with two young children. At 28 years of age, he is in his eighth year working at a local manufacturer. His employer has guaranteed him a promotion once he has obtained a college degree. Jim is attending college as a full-time evening student, going to classes every Monday, Tuesday, Wednesday, and Thursday night. Financially, Jim has followed a "pay as you go" plan to the extent possible. He has also developed a realistic annual financial plan and a monthly budget that will provide for the needs of his family for the next two years. To finance his plan, he has the support of his employer, who provided tuition reimbursement for all classes in which he earns a grade of C or better up to a maximum of $1,000 each year, and some support from his parents. Jim will have little time for himself over the next two years; however, he knows that with some of his tuition expenses covered by his employer and with a very rewarding promotion upon graduation, his time spent in college will be well worth the sacrifice. He also knows the value of money management and financial planning.

Susan, on the other hand, comes from a low-income family. Her father left the family when she was 16. Now at 18, Susan is facing her biggest challenge: going to college as a full-time student, working part-time to help finance college expenses, being on her own for the first time in her life, and developing a financial plan that would sustain her for the next four years. With the help of her college advisor and the director of financial aid, Susan has been awarded a Pell Grant and was able to develop her annual financial plan with a monthly budget.

Both Jim and Susan have been able to finance their college expenses. Naturally, it was not as easy as it appears. Each had to develop a plan. Jim has two children to care for and was required to work full-time. In Susan's case, she was able to obtain a grant; nevertheless, she still needed a part-time job to meet all of her financial obligations. Financial planning and a realistic monthly budget based on their financial needs were the common elements that held Jim's and Susan's plans together. They are both committed to a multi-year financial program that will assist them in attaining their academic goals. They know that it will be difficult to stay within their monthly budgets, but sticking to their plans will bear financial and emotional fruit upon graduation.

"The better you manage your money, the more money comes your way. Conversely, if you don't manage your money properly, the funds that you do have will not be enough."

DWIGHT NICHOLS

fter reading this chapter and completing the exercises, you will be able to:

- Understand the principle of budgeting your money
- Develop an annual financial plan
- Develop a monthly budget
- Reduce your monthly expenses
- Understand the importance of adequate health, auto, life, and homeowner's/renter's insurance
- Understand the principles of financial aid
- Understand the concept of debt-free living and how to achieve it

Using the Milestones checklist, take a few moments and determine where you stand in relation to money management.

You should not be too concerned if you have more "No" and "Sometimes" answers to these questions. Few students have more "Yes" answers. Money management is not easy for anyone. It is like time management in that you have to set goals, develop a plan of action, execute your plan, and track your results. If you follow the principles and complete the exercises presented, you should have all "Yes" answers when you complete this assessment at the end of this chapter.

WHERE ARE YOU NOW?

Answer each statement by checking "Y" for Yes, "N" for No, or "S" for Sometimes.

1. I understand the importance of budgeting my money.	(Y) (N) (S)
2. I have an annual financial plan.	(Y) (N) (S)
3. I have a monthly budget.	(Y) (N) (S)
4. I understand the principle of reducing expenses.	(Y) (N) (S)
5. I know the importance of insurance.	(Y) (N) (S)
6. I have or plan to have adequate insurance.	(Y) (N) (S)
7. I have researched all sources of financial aid.	(Y) (N) (S)
8. I have applied for financial aid.	(Y) (N) (S)
9. I understand the principle of becoming debt-free.	(Y) (N) (S)
10. I am or have a plan to become debt-free.	(Y) (N) (S)

PRINCIPLES OF BUDGETING YOUR MONEY

The heart of any money management program is budgeting. Everyone needs to budget his or her income and expenses. The executive with a $200,000 salary needs an effective budget. The single-parent college student needs an effective budget. The 18-year-old college student on her own for the first time needs an effective budget.

But what *is* a budget? What is involved in the budgeting process? What are incomes and expenses? It is important to understand the principles of budgeting your money before you try to create and maintain an effective budget. The *New World Dictionary* defines a budget as "a plan or schedule adjusting expenses during a certain period to the estimated or fixed income for that period." It also states that a budget is "the cost or estimated cost of living, operating, etc." Simply stated, a college student budget is part of a planning process in which (a) all sources of income are determined for a certain period of time; (b) all sources of expenses or costs are determined for that same period of time; (c) total income is compared with total expenses; and (d) decisions are made to create a balanced budget. If expenses exceed income, then income must be increased, expenses will have to be decreased, or a combination of both measures. Determining the income, expenses, time period, and method of balancing the budget is what we call the budgeting process. Naturally, income and expenses will vary from student to student; however, there are many income and expense items that are common to most students.

Let's first look at sources of income for students. Student income is derived from many sources, for example, full-time and part-time salaries, gifts from parents or friends, government and private grants, student loans, scholarships, work-study programs, savings accounts, etc. Expenses can be divided into two areas: *wants* and *needs*. As a college student, it is very important to concentrate on *needs* until your income stream is more consistent and reliable. Expenses that are considered *needs* include tuition, books, college fees, food, clothing, housing, transportation, and insurance. *Want*-based expenses are CDs, video games, certain fashionable clothing, sports cars, and all sources of expenses associated with parties and entertainment.

We will now discuss and demonstrate several principles of budgeting your money. The first and most important for college students is to develop an *annual financial plan*. With recent changes in the timing of the distribution of government grants to students, it is more important than ever to develop an annual financial plan. Once this annual plan is in place, a monthly budget must be developed and followed if you are to ensure financial stability. *Reducing expenses* is always a challenge and can be a positive habit for future financial decisions as well. The cost of adequate insurance varies from student to student. Financial aid, while not directly under your control, is an important component of any student's annual financial plan. Last but not the least of these principles is debt-free living. *Debt-free living* is really a principle for life that can be started during your college years.

Developing an Annual Financial Plan

A key principle of money management is to write out your financial goals, which will vary depending upon the various stages of your life. For example, as a college student, one of your financial goals might be to finance your college education without taking out a student loan. This worthy goal can be developed and tracked by following the goal-setting process described in Chapter 4 as well as following the principles of time management and the use of a time planner explained in Chapter 2.

"A prudent person foresees the difficulties ahead and prepares for them; the simpleton goes blindly on and suffers the consequences."

PROVERBS 22:3

The principles of developing an annual financial plan are explained and demonstrated in the following example. First, you need to determine the period covered by this annual plan. For example, you can use the calendar year, January 1 to December 31, or the academic calendar, September to August. In this example, we are using January 1 to December 31. Next you need to determine how much income you will receive from any work you do for pay during this period. In this example (see Figure 12.1), our student, Jim of the story you read earlier, has a full-time annual salary of $25,200 and a part-time job with an annual income of $5,000. Jim has been very studious over the years and has earned an annual scholarship of $1,000 for maintaining a grade point average (GPA) of 3.0 on a 4.0 scale. Jim may not seem too typical; however, we are using his example to show one of many profiles of student income and expenses. Jim's employer provides a maximum $1,000 grant annually for

Jim's annual financial plan.   FIGURE 12.1

Dates: Jan. 1st to Dec. 31st   Year:

INCOME		BUDGET	ACTUAL
Full-time Salary	$	25,200	$
Part-time Salary		5,000	
Scholarship		1,000	
Grant		1,000	
Student Loan		2,000	
Gifts		2,400	
Other:	0		
Other:	0		
Other:	0		
TOTAL		$ 36,600	$

EXPENSES		BUDGET	ACTUAL
College Expenses:		$ 7,700	$
Tuition	$ 6,000		
Fees	500		
Books	1,200		
Other	0		
Other	0		
Housing		6,000	
Food		6,000	
Taxes		2,000	
Utilities		1,200	
Telephone		900	
Clothing		1,000	
Medical		500	
Dental		100	
Auto/transportation		2,400	
Auto/gas		1,800	
Childcare		1,200	
Insurance:			
Car	$ 1,200		
Tenant	200		
Health	1,200		
Life	600		
Church/Charity		1,200	
Entertainment		0	
Other		0	
Savings		1,200	
TOTAL		$ 36,400	$

	BUDGET	ACTUAL
ANNUAL INCOME	$ 36,600	$
ANNUAL EXPENSES	$ 36,400	$
SURPLUS/DEFICIT + or −	$ +200	$

any full-time employee who attends the local college. In addition, Jim has a student loan that provides $2,000 annually. Parents and relatives are a likely source of income for many students. In this case, even though Jim is out on his own as a single parent with two children, his parents have committed to paying part of his tuition and books required each semester, a gift of $2,400 each year. Jim's total income for this plan is $36,600.

Expenses are determined in much the same way—by adding all anticipated expenses for a one-year period. For example, college expenses for the year total $7,700: $6,000 for tuition, $500 for fees, and $1,200 for books. Jim rents an apartment for $500 per month, or $6,000 a year. Food is another $6,000. Jim's taxes will be about $2,000. He will have an earned income credit from the IRS on account of his children, as well as an education credit, both of which will keep his federal taxes low; however, he will still have to pay property taxes on his car, etc. Other expenses include utilities, $1,200; telephone, $900; clothing, $1,000; medical, $500; dental, $100; automobile expenses, $2,400; gas, $1,800; childcare, $1,200; insurance, $3,200; and his church and charitable gifts, $1,200. Jim's annual income and expenses were shown in Figure 12.1.

Several important points need to be made about Jim's situation. Jim's taxes are low because of deductions for his children and federal tax credits; however, his costs to clothe, feed, and otherwise care for his family are considerable. His medical and dental expenses are relatively low because he has a full-time job that provides a health plan. His car insurance is very high because of his age. Unlike other younger, childless college students, he cannot take advantage of his father's auto or health insurance programs. Jim attends college at night and uses his college's childcare program, paying a small fee for his children to attend. Finally, Jim has budgeted no money for entertainment for the year. He does not have the time or the income to provide entertainment for himself or his children. He knows this situation during his college years will not last forever, and he has planned well for his future through effective goal setting and money management. Younger, childless college student budgets will differ from Jim's because such budgets are unlikely to include $3,200 a year for various kinds of insurance for a family.

Once this plan is in place, a monthly budget must be developed each month to ensure that the plan is followed.

Monthly Budget

Because bill-paying cycles are usually monthly, a monthly budget makes sense for efficiency and effective tracking of expenses and income. There are two approaches to developing a monthly and annual budget simultaneously. You can determine your annual financial plan and divide this plan by 12, for the 12 months of the year, to estimate your monthly budget, or you can develop a monthly budget and multiply it by 12 to get an annual financial plan. In our example, we developed an annual financial plan for Jim. Now, to estimate Jim's monthly budget, we can divide the annual financial plan by 12 and record our answers on the monthly budget sheet shown in Figure 12.2.

As we established, Jim's annual full-time salary is $25,200, or $2,100 per month (i.e., $25,200 ÷ 12 = $2,100). Each income item is thus divided by 12 and recorded on the monthly budget sheet. The expense items that were determined for the annual financial plan are also divided by 12, providing the figures

Sample monthly budget.	**FIGURE 12.2**

MONTH OF: January

INCOME		BUDGET	ACTUAL
Full-time Salary	$	2,100	$
Part-time Salary		417	
Scholarship		83	
Grant		83	
Student Loan		167	
Gifts		200	
Other:			
Other:			
Other:			
TOTAL		$ 3,050	$

EXPENSES	BUDGET	ACTUAL
College expenses:	$ 643	$
Tuition		
Fees		
Books		
Other		
Other		
Housing	500	
Food	500	
Taxes	167	
Utilities	100	
Telephones	75	
Clothing	83	
Medical	42	
Dental	8	
Auto/transportation	200	
Auto/gas	150	
Childcare	100	
Insurance:	266	
Car		
Tenant		
Medical		
Life		
Church/Charity	100	
Entertainment		
Other		
Other		
Savings	100	
TOTAL	$ 3,034	$
MONTHLY INCOME	$ 3,050	$
MONTHLY EXPENSES	$ 3,034	$
SURPLUS/DEFICIT + or –	$ +16	$

It may seem like there is no time to keep track of your finances or to plan, but budgeting can save you time and money in the end.

recorded as expenses in our example. Monthly expenses for tuition would be $7,700 \div 12 = \$643$ per month, housing $500 per month, etc.

Because we divided the annual financial plan by 12, each month has the same budget. One of the keys to money management is to receive income equal to your monthly budget income and spend no more than your monthly budgeted expenses. Unless there is a significant change in income or expenses, you live by the same monthly budget 12 times per year. If you do have a significant change in income or expenses, you need to adjust your monthly budget to reflect that change.

Some of the bills or expenses come every month; for example, the cost of housing, insurance, food, telephone, and childcare are essentially the same every month. However, other expenses that we initially determined on an annual basis may come semiannually or quarterly. For example, auto insurance policies have premiums that are usually due annually or every six months. However, for a small fee you can pay them monthly. College tuition at many colleges is paid once each semester. In Jim's case, he pays tuition three times a year, at the start of fall semester, spring semester, and summer session, respectively. To allow for this inconsistency in his budgeting process, Jim has set up a passbook savings account to hold money to be used as tuition becomes due. For example, Jim's loan is $2,000 a year. He deposits this money in his savings account and withdraws the tuition payment for each semester when it comes due. A passbook account or a money market account is an excellent way to create an interest-bearing holding account for a portion of your income held in reserve.

The *key* here is to create a realistic monthly budget that is derived from your annual financial plan and use it to balance your expenses with your income. Once you are satisfied with your monthly budget, you can make 11 copies and use one for each month. At the end of each month, you record your actual expenses in the ACTUAL column of your monthly budget sheet and compare your budgeted income and expenses with your true income and expenditures. If you overspend in any area, you need to reduce spending in that or other categories in the following month. For example, if you budget $75 for the telephone each month but spend $125 in a given month, you will have to reduce your telephone expenses by $50 the next month. If you do not make these types of adjustments as they happen, your annual financial plan will fail because your expenses exceed your income. Debt-free living is jeopardized when monthly expenses exceed monthly income, a pitfall we want to help you avoid.

Use Exercise 12.1 to set up your monthly budget. At the end of the year, income and expenses for your annual financial plan can be determined by adding the individual items from the monthly budgets, recording them in the actual column of your annual financial plan (Exercise 12.2), and totaling the column. At this point, you can see how you did with your money management plan. Did you exceed your budget or were you right on track? Exercise 12.2, an annual financial plan form, can be used for your current as well as future plans.

MONTH OF:

INCOME	BUDGET	ACTUAL
Full-time Salary	$	$
Part-time Salary		
Scholarship		
Grant		
Student Loan		
Gifts		
Other:		
Other:		
Other:		
TOTAL	$	$

EXPENSES	BUDGET	ACTUAL
College expenses:	$	$
Tuition		
Fees		
Books		
Other		
Other		
Housing		
Food		
Taxes		
Utilities		
Telephones		
Clothing		
Medical		
Dental		
Auto/transportation		
Auto/gas		
Childcare		
Insurance:		
Car		
Tenant		
Medical		
Life		
Church/Charity		
Entertainment		
Other		
Other		
Savings		
TOTAL	$	$
MONTHLY INCOME	$	$
MONTHLY EXPENSES	$	$
SURPLUS/DEFICIT + or −	$	$

Dates: _____ Year: _____

INCOME	BUDGET	ACTUAL
Full-time Salary	$	$
Part-time Salary		
Scholarship		
Grant		
Student Loan		
Gifts		
Other:		
Other:		
Other:		
TOTAL	$	$

EXPENSES	BUDGET	ACTUAL
College Expenses:	$	$
Tuition		
Fees		
Books		
Other		
Other		
Housing		
Food		
Taxes		
Utilities		
Telephone		
Clothing		
Medical		
Dental		
Auto/transportation		
Auto/gas		
Childcare		
Insurance:		
Car		
Tenant		
Health		
Life		
Church/Charity		
Entertainment		
Other		
Savings		
TOTAL	$	$
ANNUAL INCOME	$	$
ANNUAL EXPENSES	$	$
SURPLUS/DEFICIT + or −	$	$

REDUCING EXPENSES: NEEDS VS. WANTS

There are numerous ways to reduce expenses. One way is to develop your annual financial plan based on "needs" rather than "wants," and to stick to your plan. If your income increases, make adjustments to the plan. However, do not increase expenses arbitrarily simply because you want something. As a college student, your income will be affected by many variables and will usually be much lower than that of a college graduate working full-time. Therefore, you really need to hold the line on items that are "wants."

Another *key* is to view every expense as an opportunity to seek a way to reduce, replace, or even eliminate that expense. Insurance presents an excellent example. All insurance can be negotiated; that is, you can shop around with many different companies and compare premiums. Payment options on insurance are another opportunity to save money. For example, if you pay insurance premiums on an annual basis, you can usually eliminate certain fees and reduce your overall premium. Auto insurance presents one of the best opportunities to save money. College students buying their own auto insurance can choose to take the minimum liability coverage and the highest collision deductibles possible, particularly if they own a car that is seven or more years old. As with all our advice, however, individual circumstances may vary.

Other commonsense tips are to buy clothing on sale or at a thrift shop where decent clothes can be bought at reasonable prices. Use the coupons in the newspaper for food items and other necessaries. Buy used college textbooks or buy them online. Use college childcare and other facilities that are less expensive and more convenient for students. Constantly look for bargains and ways to reduce your expenses.

ADEQUATE INSURANCE

College students probably need three or four types of insurance to be financially secure. Health insurance, renter's or tenant's insurance (assuming the student does not yet own a home), and auto insurance (if she or he has a car) are absolutely necessary. A fourth type to consider is life insurance.

Today, when you go to a hospital or a doctor's office for any services, the first thing the receptionist asks for is your health insurance card. Without this card, you may not be admitted or accepted as a patient. For students who are not over 23 years old and are still considered dependents of, say, their parents, health insurance normally will come under the parents' policy. However, it will likely be required that you maintain a full load of courses (i.e., 12 semester credit hours each semester) to be eligible for coverage under your parents' policy. Once you are on your own (i.e., you are self-supporting or are over the age of 23), you can no longer depend on your parents' health insurance program. If you need health insurance, first check with your parents' agent or a trusted friend of the family who works in the insurance business. Always shop around for insurance to get the best price and coverage for your particular needs.

Renter's or tenant's insurance is designed to cover the cost of property lost in a fire or by theft. Again, your status as a student will partly determine what coverage you need and the cost of this class of insurance. Students listed as dependents on someone else's tax forms can usually obtain tenant's insurance through that person's homeowner's policy. Self-supporting students may have to purchase a separate policy at a higher rate.

Auto insurance is very expensive for anyone 25 years of age or younger. It is important to present yourself as a low-risk client. For example, successful completion of driver's education training and a record clear of speeding tickets and other traffic violations will greatly reduce the overall premium for students.

Your status and position in life has a big impact on the need for life insurance. Jim, a single parent with two children living at home (whom we read about earlier), definitely needs life insurance coverage. Jim is the only "breadwinner" for his young family. From where would the revenue come to support his family in the event of his death? A single, 18-year-old student may not need life insurance if he or she is covered in a parent's policy by what is called a rider. As a full-time employee, Jim's benefits include a small, term life insurance policy of $10,000. Furthermore, Jim has the option of buying additional term life insurance through a group policy offered by his employer. An important principle to remember about life insurance (or any insurance) is to shop around for the best coverage at the lowest rate.

FINANCIAL AID

As a college student, your income may be relatively low; nevertheless, your expenses will likely be high. There are basically two things you can do to compensate for this. You can either reduce your expenses, which we discussed in some detail earlier, or you can increase your income. How do you go about increasing your income as a college student? What are the sources of financial aid? These and other questions about financial aid are discussed in the following paragraphs.

Traditionally, parents, relatives, family friends, and the like have been a primary source of income. However, for older and nontraditional students, this source may not be available. Employers provide a financial opportunity for many students through full- or part-time employment. Employers may be willing to provide tuition assistance or tuition reimbursement programs for both full- and part-time employees. Some employers provide sponsorships, grants, scholarships, paid internships, and other education financing programs for students. For example, many manufacturing companies recruit high school students and graduates to enter sponsorship programs. These programs provide tuition, books, fees, and part-time jobs (usually 15 hours a week) for students who are willing to commit to successful completion of a particular program, often in a technical field. Sometimes full-time employment is offered to those who complete the program within a specific time frame.

The federal government, through Title IV Financial Aid programs, has been providing various forms of financial aid for students for many years, available at most colleges and universities. Pell Grants are entitlements that are awarded annually for up to $4,050 currently, and the amount is subject to change each year. The Federal Supplemental Education Opportunity Grant is awarded to undergraduate students with exceptional financial need. The Federal College Work-Study program is a work program that is usually controlled on campus by the financial aid office and provides jobs on campus to qualified students. The Stafford Loan program provides loans for educational expenses with a specific pay-back (or "remittance") period after graduation. The Perkins Loan program is a need-based program. In recent years, state governments have also begun providing grants, scholarships, loans, and other types of financial aid. Some states now offer scholarships to students who maintained a B grade point average in high school. These scholarships continue for each year that the student maintains a B average in college.

The armed forces (including the National Guard) have in recent years begun offering various college funding programs. The G. I. Bill has been in place since the end of World War II.

Scholarships from individual donors and private foundations are numerous and available to students at most colleges. Thousands of dollars in scholarship funds go unclaimed each year, often because no or too few qualified students apply. Don't overlook an excellent possible source of funding—do your research!

Nontraditional students are likely to require sources of income such as employment and financial aid, rather than depending solely on family resources.

It is impossible to list here all sources of financial aid available or to explain fully the implementation of these programs. The most important lesson is to research all sources of financial aid. Start in high school, if possible, by contacting the college's financial aid office. Apply for all grants and scholarships for which you think you may be eligible. If you are working, talk to your employer regarding tuition assistance programs and scholarships. If not employed, talk to your college's placement office about part-time jobs, paid internships, or cooperative education programs.

Before you commit to a college major course of study, talk to the department head in each area that you are considering about paid internships, sponsorships, and other employer support programs. For example, many hospitals have sponsored nursing and allied health students by paying for tuition, books, and fees and promising a specific number of years of employment upon graduation.

"The rich rule over the poor, and the borrower is a servant to the lender."

PROVERBS 22.7

DEBT-FREE LIVING

ebt-free living is not merely a concept or a principle, but a way of life. To become debt-free and to stay debt-free requires a great deal of planning and execution.

The credit card has become the greatest contributor to the "American Dream," which for many consists of new cars, new furniture, clothes, etc. Unfortunately, the credit card has also spurred tremendous growth in personal debt and bankruptcy.

To be successful in handling debt, particularly that accumulated on credit cards, you must develop an action plan, execute the plan, and track your results. Some basic principles apply as well. For example, if you need a credit card, shop around as always to find the best credit card program for the least cost. Have one or two credit cards at the most. Promise yourself and your family that you will never make major purchases using credit cards. Take time to understand the difference between the various types of cards that banks and other financial institutions offer.

There are basically three types of cards available. The most common and most troublesome is the charge card. A charge card carries a fee each year and monthly interest charges. You can make purchases up to a certain maximum limit (say, $2,000), and extend your payments over several months or years by making a minimum payment each month. The problem with this type of program is that many people charge up to the maximum limit and make payments over several years with a very high annual interest rate. The interest rates are sometimes stated at 1 percent or 2 percent a month. That does not sound like much, but when computed on an annual basis, it can come out to 12 to 24 percent per year.

The true credit card is a card for which you receive a monthly statement that requires immediate payment, or perhaps a 30-day grace period. As long as you pay the monthly charges within the specified time period, there is no interest charge.

The best card for controlling spending and debt is the debit card. This type of card looks just like a credit card, but it functions more like a check written on a checking account. When you use a debit card, you are actually debiting or charging against your checking account. If you have money available in the checking account, the debit card works. If you do not have a positive balance in your checking account and use your debit card, you are creating debt and defeating the purpose of having a debit card. Some debit cards do allow a line of credit or overdraft protection, but beware, the services often carry hefty fees or interest.

Here is a very simple yet effective debt-free living plan. Step one is to write out your financial goals (you can use the goal-setting sheets discussed in Chapter 4). Once you have your goals set, develop specific objectives for each goal. Your objectives can be quantified by developing an annual financial plan. Execution of this plan is accomplished by using monthly budgets that can be recorded on the monthly budget sheets. Finally, use your to-do list to record daily and monthly tasks associated with your financial objectives and to track your progress toward debt-free living.

Some basic principles of debt-free living are as follows:

- Develop and use your monthly budget.
- Live on a cash basis, particularly as a college student.
- If you do not have the money in the bank, do not spend it or charge it.
- If you need a card, obtain a debit card and never use the overdraft.

- If you need a credit card, make sure that you can pay off any charges made when the bill comes.
- Always pay off the balance on your credit card each month.
- Never use credit cards for major purchases, such as furniture or a season's worth of clothes.

Always save a little of your income each month. As a college student, 10 percent of your total income is an excellent target for monthly savings. Routine savings as a college student will become a habit for life.

There is at least one, and maybe there are two, exceptions to these principles regarding debt. It is very difficult to save enough money to purchase a car or to buy a house with cash. However, you should never finance the full selling price of a car. Always make sure that you have saved enough to make a 20 to 25 percent down payment for your car. When you drive your car off the lot, it will depreciate about 20 percent. Thus, if you finance the entire purchase price, your loan balance will exceed the market value of your car. This predicament can also be true for buying a house. This condition is called surety. Surety results from making a purchase or creating a debt without having reliable means to repay it. Surety has contributed to the debt problem more than any other factor among American consumers. If you have existing debt, large credit card balances, etc., you need to establish a debt-reduction plan as soon as possible. If you are in over your head, you may need to contact a debt counselor for additional guidance. Beware: Effective October 2005, major reforms in the U. S. bankruptcy system took place, making it more difficult for an individual to wipe out debt by declaring bankruptcy.

Credit and Credit Reports

Credit is defined by the Federal Reserve Bank of Dallas as "the granting of money or something else of value in exchange for a promise of future repayment." We have already discussed credit cards, as well as the consequences of too much credit. However, did you know that once you secure and use your first credit card or create a charge account of any kind, a credit report is created on you that will impact all future credit activities? Did you know that this "credit report" will be used by all of your future lenders to determine your credit worthiness? Have you ever looked at your credit report?

Car dealers, mortgage companies, and other creditors expect borrowers to have established "good credit." Usually, it takes about two years of consistently paying bills on time to establish good credit. However, it takes only a few late payments, or a default on an account, to become a "risk" for a lender and develop a "bad credit" report. How do you go about getting a copy of your credit report?

It is important to know and understand your credit report. There are three major credit bureaus, Equifax, Experian, and Trans Union Corporation. You are eligible for a free credit report once a year. Additional credit reports can be obtained for a fee. If you have been denied credit, you can get

MILESTONES

NOW THAT YOU ARE HERE . . .

Answer each statement by checking "Y" for
Yes, "N" for No, or "S" for Sometimes.

1. I understand the importance of Ⓨ Ⓝ Ⓢ
   budgeting my money.

2. I have an annual financial plan. · Ⓨ Ⓝ Ⓢ

3. I have a monthly budget. Ⓨ Ⓝ Ⓢ

4. I understand the principle of reducing Ⓨ Ⓝ Ⓢ
   expenses.

5. I know the importance of insurance. Ⓨ Ⓝ Ⓢ

6. I have or plan to have adequate Ⓨ Ⓝ Ⓢ
   insurance.

7. I have researched all sources of Ⓨ Ⓝ Ⓢ
   financial aid.

8. I have applied for financial aid. Ⓨ Ⓝ Ⓢ

9. I understand the principle of becoming Ⓨ Ⓝ Ⓢ
   debt-free.

10. I am or have a plan to become Ⓨ Ⓝ Ⓢ
    debt-free.

a credit report free within 30 days of the denial. Their addresses, phone numbers, and websites are as follows:

Equifax
EISC
PO Box 105873
Atlanta, GA 30348
1 (800) 685-1111
www.equifax.com

CBA
Information Services
PO Box 677
Cherry Hill, NJ 08003
1 (888) 397-3742
www.experian.com

Trans Union Corporation
Consumer Relations Center
PO Box 390
Springfield, PA 19064
1 (800) 916-8800
www.transunion.com

At this point, you have had the opportunity to learn the principles of money management, develop an annual financial plan, develop monthly budgets, and research financial aid. Complete the Milestones checklist and see how you're doing.

You should have all "Yes" answers at this point. If not, go back over the chapter and put into practice the principles we discussed. By following these principles, using the forms provided, and following the tips listed in the next section, you can be well on your way to a balanced budget, the basis for a plan that will lead you to financial success now and in the future.

ROADWAYS

TO MONEY MANAGEMENT

Following the tips below can help you stay on track with your financial plans and your budget.

- Write down your financial *goals* for college.

  Use the goal-setting sheet presented in Chapter 4 to determine your financial goals while you are in college. In addition, use the annual financial plan sheet that has been illustrated in this chapter to write out your college financial plan for each year that you will attend.

- Learn to use a monthly *budget* and stick with it.

  Once you have developed a monthly budget and followed it for several months it will become a habit. The basic principle here is to "live within your means." You must adjust your lifestyle to that of a college student. You may not have the discretionary income for "wants" during your college years.

- Don't be a *spendthrift.*

  Buy used books, get used clothes at discount shops, use coupons when shopping for food, eat out less, and always be on the lookout for bargains.

- Beware of *credit* cards.

  Credit cards can be a great asset when used properly. However, too many people have gotten into the credit card trap and have created debt that will take them years to repay. Many of these debtors started their credit card spiral in college with an interest-free offer from a credit card company.

- Seek and use student *discounts.*

  Many merchants in college towns offer discounts on purchases. Check with your student affairs office for a student discount card or coupons from participating merchants.

- Use a *savings* account as a holding account.

  Set up a savings account at a local bank. Many have free accounts for college students that you can use to hold or protect money that you will need for tuition, books, or fees.

- Apply for financial *aid.*

  There are numerous financial aid programs available. Some scholarships are never awarded because no one applied. Visit your financial aid office and explore all sources of financial aid.

- Keep good *records.*

  Use your planner to record and track your budget and other financial records.

- Save a little *each* month.

  Try to save as much as 10 percent of your total income each month. Saving money is very difficult in college; however, if you can start this habit as a college student, it will be a very positive habit that can continue for the rest of your life. An 18-year-old college student who saves $100 a month and invests his or her savings could be a multimillionaire upon retirement.

- Never put yourself in a *surety* situation.

  This simple but difficult-to-execute principle was discussed earlier, but it is worth mentioning again. If you borrow or use a credit card to the point that you have no sure way of paying it off, you have not only created a surety situation for yourself but have taken the first step on the way to bankruptcy.

Applying What You Know

Financial planning is agony for most people. We all love to spend money and buy things but we seldom love to pay the bills at the end of the month. This chapter has provided valuable tools to help you with this difficult task. Now that you have finished this chapter on Money Management, refer back to the Case Study about Gwen at the beginning of this book. Based on her situation, answer the following questions:

1. What money-management strategies or techniques should Gwen employ?

2. How should Gwen utilize the Annual Financial Plan and Monthly Budget to help her address her financial challenges?

3. If faced with problems similar to Gwen's (reduced work hours, reduced take home pay, and less time available to work), what would you do?

Observations

CHARTING YOUR COURSE

Money management is a difficult subject to study and more difficult to enact. As a college student, it is even more difficult because your income is likely to be low and your expenses are usually very high. You have many wants but need to concentrate on your needs. Also, you have little time or energy to worry about budgeting. That is why developing a financial plan is so important! If you develop a solid financial plan using the principles and forms presented in this chapter and in Chapters 2 and 4, you will have a simple-yet-effective plan that will assist you in every financial decision you have to make during your college career. You will also have in place financial and budgetary habits that will sustain you throughout your life and will lead you to debt-free living.

DETOUR Getting There on Time

Now that you understand the principles associated with budgeting your money and developing financial plans or budgets, the question must be asked, how are you going to track your budgeting process quickly and efficiently? Half the battle is understanding budgeting; however, to be successful you must address the other half of the battle: accurately tracking your income and expenses in an expeditious manner.

We discussed earlier in this text that most people view their working lives in terms of weeks. But in effective money management, the financial cycle encompasses an entire month. The budget forms presented in this chapter can be used to develop and execute your monthly budgets. Another excellent tool for tracking and maintaining your budget sheets is your planner. Once budgets are developed, file and reference them in your planner. Then, at the end of each month, you can review your current month's planned and actual budget, make adjustments, and develop next month's budget. Record this activity in the note section of each monthly schedule as Budget Review and Development and transfer it to the last day of the month of your daily schedule in your planner. We used the month of September in our time management examples in Chapter 2. You might have noticed the note section of the monthly schedule for August. Here you can enter "Review August's budget and develop September's budget." We recorded this note as a reminder to execute your budget process each month. In addition, on the to-do list for August 30th, "Review August's budget and develop September's budget" can be recorded as a top priority for that day.

Exploring Technology

"Good credit" is very important in today's society. It is extremely difficult to secure a loan or a credit card or buy a car without good credit. Use one of the credit bureaus mentioned earlier and request your credit report. If you have not established credit previously, ask one of your parents or a friend if you can request their credit report. It is easy and will save you a great deal of time if you go to the credit company's website. What did you discover? Do you have a good credit rating? If not or you find an error in the report, work with the credit bureau that you contacted and the creditor that has indicated a problem with your credit to resolve the issue. Clearing up any errors or issues with your creditors will prevent future negative reports.

Web Connections

TRAVELING THE INFORMATION SUPERHIGHWAY

During your journey, you may want to check out some of the following Web addresses to assist you with your money management:

www.collegeview.com/

www.collegeboard.com/paying

www.equifax.com

www.experian.com

www.transunion.com

www.usnews.com

www.bankofamerica.com/studentbanking/

As a result of this chapter, and in preparing for my journey, I plan to . . .

The People You Meet Along the Way

13

DIVERSITY

John transferred from a small, southern community college to a major metropolitan university located in the Northeast. He had been an average student, graduating from a relatively small, rural high school. He had attended elementary, middle, and high school for 12 years with many of the same people. He had excelled at sports and had difficulty deciding on a major. He chose to enroll at the local community college to get some basic courses out of the way and to establish a career path. There he decided that engineering was to be his career. John had blossomed while enrolled in the community college and had taken his course work very seriously. As a consequence, his grades were high enough to earn him a scholarship so that he could attend a prestigious school. His transfer was effortless, and when he visited the university he noticed a lot of different people milling around the campus, but he did not pay too much attention to any one person.

On the first day of class in engineering school, he faced an unexpected number of professors from foreign countries. He had a male professor from Pakistan, a male professor from Korea, a female professor from Germany, and a female African American professor from Chicago. None of the professors fit the mold of what he knew, they were as different from his Anglo-Saxon, Protestant upbringing as could be. John encountered a variety of issues, from understanding language barriers to facing cultural differences, that he did not understand or appreciate. In short, the transfer for John threw him into "culture shock." At least John had an open mind and did not prejudge people. With that attitude, and an extra concerted effort to fully understand his professors, he was able to appreciate each of them for the diversity they brought to his education. As a successful engineer, John now affirms that having professors from many different countries and cultures was one of the best learning experiences of his college career. He was able to gain skills in dealing with differences and appreciating differences that serve him well in his professional life today.

"Diversity is the one true thing we all have in common. Celebrate it every day."

ANONYMOUS

THE IMPORTANCE OF DIVERSITY

This chapter is designed to make you more aware of diversity issues and to assist you in learning to appreciate differences among people. Diversity and diversity training are often confused with affirmative action. At the conclusion of this chapter, you should be able to:

- Understand what diversity is
- Learn how we can appreciate others and their differences
- Understand why diversity is important and should be embraced
- Have an informed discussion of discrimination (both intentional and unintentional)
- Understand what affirmative action is and what it is not
- Understand culture and how culture is defined
- Understand how to foster a diversity mind-set

Before you begin this chapter, take a few moments to complete the Milestones checklist. The statements are designed to determine what you already know about diversity and differences.

If you want to turn more of your answers into positive responses, then carefully consider what is included in this chapter and take part in the activities that are contained herein.

MILESTONES

WHERE ARE YOU NOW?

Answer each statement by checking "Y" for Yes, "N" for No, or "S" for Sometimes.

1. I have friends who are of a different race.		Ⓨ Ⓝ Ⓢ
2. I have friends who are of different religions.		Ⓨ Ⓝ Ⓢ
3. I understand that diversity is important in my friendships.		Ⓨ Ⓝ Ⓢ
4. I understand that diversity is important in the workplace.		Ⓨ Ⓝ Ⓢ
5. I have felt the effects of discrimination.		Ⓨ Ⓝ Ⓢ
6. I have been in a minority.		Ⓨ Ⓝ Ⓢ
7. I know the difference between intentional and unintentional discrimination.		Ⓨ Ⓝ Ⓢ
8. I understand what culture is.		Ⓨ Ⓝ Ⓢ
9. I understand what tolerance is.		Ⓨ Ⓝ Ⓢ
10. I understand the value of open communication.		Ⓨ Ⓝ Ⓢ

UNDERSTANDING DIVERSITY

Are you a fan of vegetable soup? On a chilly autumn day, a bowl of hot, steamy vegetable soup can do more than satisfy your hunger—it can give you a sense of comfort. We usually find comfort in things that we know well—an old pair of sneakers, a favorite shirt, or a pair of jeans. Soup, and some other foods as well, can evoke those same feelings of comfort. Have you ever considered how different all of the vegetables are that are key ingredients? Tomatoes are a far different consistency from corn or beans. In fact, if you look at those three vegetables, there is more that is different about them than is similar, yet when combined, with a pinch of salt and pepper, these vegetables take on an entirely different flavor and "taste." Collectively, they are the basis for good, homemade, comforting vegetable soup.

"Diversity is the acknowledgment of humanity within ourselves."

D. THORESON

Primary and Secondary Dimensions of Diversity

Why all of this talk about soup and vegetables? Because in life, just as in "soup," we all have individual characteristics that when combined make up a wonderful mix. These differences are characterized by diversity. Diversity comprises several *primary dimensions*—factors that can be seen and potentially can lead to discrimination. The primary dimensions of diversity are:

1. Age
2. Ethnicity
3. Gender
4. Physical ability
5. Race
6. Sexual orientation

You are likely to encounter individuals from all parts of the world in your college classes. Take the opportunity to learn from them and benefit from the diversity that surrounds you.

When we observe people with physical characteristics other than what we are familiar with, we have the potential to discriminate based on those characteristics. You are probably thinking to yourself that you would never discriminate against anyone based on any of the above listed characteristics. In fact, in our society, discrimination based on many of these characteristics is not only frowned upon socially, it is illegal. Sometimes, however, we use more subtle dimensions of diversity to discriminate against one another. These more subtle characteristics, or *secondary dimensions of diversity*, include:

1. Educational background
2. Geographic location
3. Income
4. Marital status
5. Military experience
6. Parental status
7. Religious beliefs
8. Work experience

These differences can cause us to act and react in a particular situation based on beliefs and assumptions we have about these characteristics. For example, some people may assume that someone from the South with a distinct southern accent is less intelligent, less well read, less traveled, or less cultured than others. That may or may not be the case. As with each of these dimensions, we cannot judge others until we know each person individually. When we begin to assign traits to certain categories of people, we begin to "stereotype" individuals. We often misjudge people and don't give them a chance to let us know who they really are.

Think of a time when you might not have had an open mind and mis-judged someone whom you later learned to like and respect. What were your first impressions of that person?

_____

_____

_____

Were your impressions based on what you observed or based on what someone else told you about this person?

_____

_____

_____

Often, we are not even aware of some of the biases that we have when we meet someone. We automatically begin thinking of reasons why we don't like the person and are not aware of the basis of our prejudices. Prejudice exists in modern society regardless of what one would like to believe. This has never been more apparent than with the use of "profiling." Many times, law enforcement determines what the "profile" of a particular criminal might be based on the characteristics of former criminals. This may be a helpful method for law enforcement to use, but it can cause true agony. Profiling is simply assuming that a certain set of characteristics exists in a particular situation based on past experience. Clearly, an entire culture cannot be judged by the actions of a few. To be truly educated is to know that there are many ways of viewing problems or situations. When you realize the various ways you can view the world, the world becomes a much more interesting place in which to live and work.

> *"You are not educated as long as you have prejudices against anyone for any reason other than his or her character."*
>
> —MARTIN LUTHER KING, JR.

Exploring Diversity

EXERCISE **13.1**

Find at least one person in your class or school who is of a different religious faith than you. Spend some time talking about his or her faith and what the faith means.

Do you feel comfortable? _____

Do you feel uncomfortable? _____

Why do you feel the way you do? _____

_____

_____

Is this an easy exercise or one that you find difficult?

Why?

CULTURE

According to the *Merriam-Webster* online dictionary, culture is defined as "the customary beliefs, social forms, and material traits of a racial, religious, or social group." It is further defined as "the set of shared attitudes, values, goals, and practices that characterizes a company or corporation." Often, we define culture as involving people, places, and things. Culture plays an important role in any diversity situation. Culture allows us to be ourselves, based on our shared past and our beliefs, and to call on problem-solving techniques that have proven to work for us in the past. A person's culture can help to predict how he or she may react to certain situations. Some Asian cultures, for example, stress honor and loyalty. Should an individual act in a way that is not within the cultural expectations, harmony is interrupted and confusion may occur. In the Japanese business culture, for example, if you are presenting your business card to another individual, you should do so using both hands to demonstrate that the "gift" has some level of importance. By the same token, if you are handed a business card, you should not immediately place the card in your suit pocket. You should spend a moment to acknowledge the card and then read the contents before putting it away. It is a sign of disrespect in both situations for you to dismiss the card—either as the giver or the receiver.

Working with and getting along with others is not always easy. This is especially true when we factor in the many cultural differences that exist in any group. Our families, the various roles we play in our families, and the hierarchies within our families all contribute to our belief system. In addition, our language, how we use language, and the communication breakdowns that are bound to occur can affect our ability to get along with one another. These factors, along with our religious differences and our ethnicity, all present challenges when trying to deal with one another.

The appreciation of various cultures enables us to see the world as a mosaic and challenges us to think of diversity as something that is to be valued. Harmonious cultural diversity goes beyond merely understanding someone else's belief system and the way he or she has been raised—it allows us to celebrate and embrace the "differences" that are inevitable.

"We are a nation of communities . . . a brilliant diversity spread like stars, like a thousand points of light in a broad and peaceful sky."

—GEORGE H. W. BUSH (WRITTEN BY PEGGY NOONAN)

DISCRIMINATION

Would you ever purposely exclude someone based on the color of his or her skin, hair, or eye color? Probably not. We have all been taught, through school and various other formalized situations, that discrimination has no place in our society. The United States has enacted legislation to prevent discrimination in certain situations, including the Civil Rights Act, the Americans with Disabilities Act, and affirmation action. Yet, although we would not discriminate against anyone knowingly, we may be biased in the way we deal with people. When we think of an individual who is blind and mute, would we assume that individual is unable to learn? If that were the case, then the late Helen Keller would never have been given a chance to learn or to teach others. Often, our uninformed and misguided thoughts and prejudices cause us to incorrectly judge other people. If we exclude certain classes of people from our social and business settings, if we stereotype people based on an incorrect set of assumptions, or if we assume that certain groups of people, based on their language are "less than . . . ," then we are discriminating against others. Learning to be aware of our own biases and then learning to eliminate them from our actions leads to greater inclusion and acceptance. Think of a birthday party. We decide to have a party and invite a number of friends. People receive invitations and are considered "invitees." Usually they do the proper thing and RSVP by the date indicated. Unfortunately, with every social situation, there are people who are not invited. In this scenario, there are the "invited" and the "un-invited." Think on this—how often do we "un-invite" others with our actions and our words? No, this is not intended to be a discussion about who our friends are or how they get invited to parties, but rather an awareness that regardless of our situation, we are always "inviting" or "un-inviting" others based on our actions. Learning to embrace a more "inviting" philosophy should make us more aware of discriminatory acts and enable us to include more people into our circle of friends and acquaintances.

Exploring Discrimination

EXERCISE **13.2**

Think of a time when you were not invited to a party or social event.

How did it make you feel to know that others were invited and that you were not?

_____

_____

_____

_____

_____

Why do you think you were "eliminated" from the guest list? Were you discriminated against? If so, why?

_____

_____

_____

_____

Can you think of situations in which you unintentionally discriminated against someone?

_____

_____

_____

_____

AFFIRMATIVE ACTION

Often, when people talk about diversity, culture, and discrimination, the notion of affirmative action finds its way into the conversation. Just what *is* affirmative action? It is a deliberate process designed to remedy the effects of past discrimination, eliminate present discrimination, and prevent future discrimination. It is a mandated law (Executive Order 11246), and quite a number of public and private debates abound regarding affirmative action and how the law should be defined. California is the best-known state to deal with the affirmative action issue, specifically in regard to scholarships and admission to universities. An affirmative action plan will likely be in place in many places a student might eventually work. The plan should be specific about what is to be accomplished and should be designed to correct statistical differences caused by discrimination. Ultimately, affirmative action should be used as a "tool" to reach the goal of fair employment.

Myths and misconceptions about affirmative action include:

- It is another name for a quota system.
- African Americans are the only previously oppressed group that benefits from affirmative action.
- Affirmative action programs are not really needed, not in this day and time.
- Minorities are stealing jobs and opportunities from qualified majority applicants.

In reality, affirmative action plans are designed to:

- prohibit the use of quotas.
- prohibit employers from hiring unqualified people.
- involve proper training of employees and an awareness of fairness issues in the workplace.
- demonstrate a "good faith" effort on the part of the employer to ensure that barriers to employment, education, etc., are removed.

Affirmative action programs demonstrate a good faith effort on the part of employers to ensure that barriers to fair employment are removed.

Another popular, and often-misunderstood, term in the world of work is "equal opportunity." Equal opportunity is applicable to *all* citizens and not just groups that have been discriminated against historically. Likewise, it is not applicable only to minorities and to females and it is certainly not a social program. Equal opportunity means just what it says—an equal consideration for *all* for a particular job. Equal opportunity is essential for fair employment and is required by both federal and state law. On the other hand, equal opportunity is not a guarantee of a job. Both affirmative action and equal opportunity combine to make sure that in the world of work and education every citizen, regardless of race, creed, sexual orientation, etc., is given equal and fair treatment. In short, affirmative action and equal opportunity are good for the entire nation, and as such the preservation of these two programs has enjoyed national support.

In conclusion, we all enjoy working and learning in an environment that respects us for who we are. We must all become more aware of one another and know that diversity exists among all groups of people. One of the most important life skills that a student can develop is to be tolerant of other individuals and their ideas. Having open and honest communication with our coworkers, fellow students, and friends is vital. The Golden Rule is still appropriate today: We should treat people just as we would like to be treated and learn to enjoy and appreciate the mosaic of life around us.

THE NEXT STEP

Now that you have completed this chapter, revisit the Milestones checklist.

How did you do on this inventory after reading this chapter?

If you would like to be more successful and learn from your environment, then it is vital that you understand cultural diversity and discrimination and

MILESTONES

be aware of your own actions toward others. Developing and maintaining an organizational structure that values diversity is the goal of many businesses, and as a graduate of this college you will be expected to possess the skills and abilities to work harmoniously with other people.

NOW THAT YOU ARE HERE . . .

Answer each statement by checking "Y" for Yes, "N" for No, or "S" for Sometimes.

1. I have friends who are of a different race. Ⓨ Ⓝ Ⓢ

2. I have friends who are of different religions. Ⓨ Ⓝ Ⓢ

3. I understand that diversity is important in my friendships. Ⓨ Ⓝ Ⓢ

4. I understand that diversity is important in the workplace. Ⓨ Ⓝ Ⓢ

5. I have felt the effects of discrimination. Ⓨ Ⓝ Ⓢ

6. I have been in a minority. Ⓨ Ⓝ Ⓢ

7. I know the difference between intentional and unintentional discrimination. Ⓨ Ⓝ Ⓢ

8. I understand what culture is. Ⓨ Ⓝ Ⓢ

9. I understand what tolerance is. Ⓨ Ⓝ Ⓢ

10. I understand the value of open communication. Ⓨ Ⓝ Ⓢ

Applying What You Know

Now that you have completed this chapter, answer the following questions:

1. Describe the differences between primary and secondary dimensions of diversity:

2. How does the culture that you were raised in affect your actions and beliefs today?

3. Explain the difference between discrimination and affirmative action.

Observations

CHARTING YOUR COURSE

Why do we value diversity? Just as one of the opening paragraphs suggested: When we enjoy a tasty dish such as vegetable soup, we begin to realize the harmony of flavors and colors that come together to give us comfort. This analogy can be applied to the real world as we begin to appreciate, and celebrate, the differences that we possess. A valuable employee will be one who can work with a variety of people in harmony and free of conflict—in short, one who knows how to get along with others!

Web Connections

www.doi.gov/bureau-indian-affairs.html
http://info.lanic.utexas.edu/
www.wku.edu/~yuanh/China/
www.freemaninstitute.com/AfAmSites.htm
www.euroamerican.org/
www.personal.umich.edu/~kdown/multi.html

As a result of this chapter, and in preparing for my journey, I plan to . . .

"COLLEGEEZE"—THE LANGUAGE OF SUCCESS

I can remember going to my first day of college and walking into the auditorium for orientation. I was excited and afraid, but I knew the information that I would get in the orientation session would ease my fears. I was wrong! When I left that auditorium, I felt as if I had gone to another country and had understood nothing of what had been said.

We were to register for 15 semester credit hours, use appropriate prefixes, choose one elective outside the curriculum or discipline, and take our registration forms to be keyed. We were not to co-op our first semester, nor were we to audit, because we could ruin our GPA and not be on the dean's list. If we did that, we would have to go to the provost or the registrar!

Now, I certainly did not know what my GPA was, but I knew that I did not want it ruined. Would it be painful? And who was this registrar? Rumor had it that it hid under the main building and would eat freshmen who were on Pell Grants.

It wasn't that bad, but I did not know the terminology or the lifestyle of college students or where to go to find the answers. It took me over a year to come to grips with the new language of college. This chapter is intended to assist you in learning the basic terminology of college life to empower you to do your best when you arrive on campus.

The very first difference that you will notice is the amount of freedom and time that you have compared to high school. You decide, with the assistance of your advisor, what your schedule will entail. If you want to come to school at 8:00 A.M., you will be able to do so. If you prefer that your classes begin at 10:00, that can be arranged also. Although there are attendance policies at all colleges, it will be up to you to attend classes. If you do not attend, that is your business. No teacher will call your parents and tell them that you are not in class. No attendance report will be sent to your parents' address. In fact, the Family Education Rights Act of 1976 prohibits this from happening. This freedom will be the best of times and the worst of times. You will have hours during the day you might not be in class. You could use this time to study, work on college cocurricular activities, or catch a nap. That decision is up to you. One of your first challenges in college will be to utilize Chapter 2 in this book on Time Management. There will be many exciting and wonderful events and people, but your studies *must* come first.

Another great difference between high school and college will be the attitude and behavior of your instructors. In high school, it is assumed that there is a line between the student and the instructor and that line is seldom

> *"The knowledge of words is the gate of scholarship."*
>
> JOHN WILSON

crossed. In college, you can visit with your professors, go to their offices, or go to lunch with them, and it is not uncommon for the professor to have a group of students come to his or her home. The relationship is based on a more open set of standards.

It might be quite possible, however, that as a freshman or sophomore, you will have graduate assistants teach your classes. This means that a student, one who is in graduate school seeking a master's or doctorate degree, also teaches classes to undergraduate students. The graduate assistant, or teacher's assistant (TA), works under the direction of a full professor, but seldom, if ever, will you see the professor. This usually occurs only in larger institutions where master's and doctorate degrees are awarded.

Another interesting aspect of college is the number of cocurricular activities available. You could become involved with a sorority or fraternity; work on the college newspaper, the yearbook, or the literary magazine; or join an organization directed toward a social cause. You might also want to join the student organizations of professional scholars such as the Student Psychological Association of America or Student Speech, Language, and Hearing Association. These organizations allow you to be involved in activities related to your field of study. You will also find activities that are related to specific matters, such as religious organizations. You are encouraged to find an organization in which you can grow and learn. Cocurricular activities are a wonderful way to meet new people and broaden your horizons.

Research has proven that students who join organizations on campus are more likely to complete their degrees. You must remember, however, that your academic performance *must* come first. In fact, some organizations have a grade requirement just to be a member.

QUESTIONS ABOUT TERMS

You may have questions regarding some of the terms used thus far in this book. The following section is intended to give you a glossary of terms so that you will have a working knowledge of the "language of college" when you arrive on campus.

Academic freedom This is a term used by professors in institutions of higher education. Academic freedom allows them to conduct research and then teach that research, regardless of its controversial issues. The professor has the freedom to teach certain aspects of materials that might not have been allowed in high school.

Accreditation Most high schools and colleges in the United States are accredited by a regional agency. This agency is responsible for ensuring that a minimum set of standards is met at all institutions that are members of the accreditation agency. The Southern Association of Colleges and Schools is one of the accreditation agencies.

Adding This term is usually used during registration periods or during the first week of classes. When a student adds a class, it means that she is adding another class to her schedule.

Administration The administration of a college is usually made up of nonteaching personnel who handle all of the administrative aspects of the college. The administration is headed by the president and vice presidents. The structure of the administration at each college varies.

Advising To make sure that you know what classes to take and in which order, you will be assigned an advisor when you arrive on campus. This advisor will usually be with you during your entire degree. He is responsible for guiding you through your academic work at the college. Your advisor is most often a faculty member in your discipline or major.

Alumna, alumni, alumnus These terms are used to describe students who hold degrees from a college. The term *alumna* refers to women, *alumnus* refers to women and men. The term *alumni* is the plural term.

Articulation An articulation agreement is a signed document between two or more institutions guaranteeing that the courses taken at one college will transfer to another college. If Oak College has an articulation agreement with Maple College, it means that the course work taken at Oak will be accepted toward a degree at Maple.

Associate degree Several types of degrees can be earned in college. The associate degree is a two-year degree that usually prepares the student to enter the workforce with a specific skill or trade.

The associate degree is also offered to students as the first two years of their bachelor or four-year degree. Not all colleges offer the associate degree.

Attendance Each college has an attendance policy such as "a student can miss no more than 10 percent of the total class hours or they will receive an 'F' for the course." This policy is followed strictly by some professors and on a more lenient basis by others. You should *always* know the attendance policy of *each* professor with whom you are studying.

Auditing Most colleges offer a choice of enrolling in a course or auditing a course. If you enroll in a course, you pay the entire fee, attend classes, take exams, and receive credit. If you audit a course, the fee is usually less, you do not have to take exams, and you *do not* receive credit. Course auditing is usually done by people who are having trouble in a subject or by those who want to gain more knowledge about a particular subject. Some colleges charge full price for auditing a course.

Baccalaureate The baccalaureate degree, more commonly called the bachelor's degree, is a four-year degree in a specific field. Although this degree can be completed in as few as three years or as many as six years, traditionally, the amount of academic work required is four years. This degree prepares students for careers such as teachers, social workers, engineers, fine arts professions, and journalism. Graduate work is also available in these fields.

Board of trustees The board of trustees is the governing body of the college. The board is appointed by government officials (usually the governor) of each state. The board hires the president and must approve any curriculum changes in degree programs. The board also sets policy for the college.

Catalog The college catalog is a book issued to you at the beginning of your college career. This book is one of the most important tools that you will use in developing your schedule and completing your degree. This catalog is a legal, binding document stating what your degree requirements are for the duration of your studies. You will need to obtain and *keep* the catalog for the year in which you entered college.

Certificate A certificate program is a series of courses, usually one year in length, designed to educate and train an individual in a certain area such as welding, automotive repair, medical transcription, tool and die, early childhood, physical therapy assistant, or fashion merchandising. Although these programs are certified and detailed, they are not degrees. Often, associate and bachelor degrees are offered in these areas as well.

CLEP The College Level Examination Program is designed to allow students to "test" out of a course. CLEP exams are nationally normed and are often more extensive than a course in the same area. If you CLEP a course, it means that you do not have to take the course because you passed the CLEP exam. Some colleges have limits on the number of hours that can be earned by CLEP.

Cognate A cognate is a course (or set of courses) taken outside your major. Some colleges call this a minor. For instance, if you are majoring in English, you may wish to take a cognate in history or drama. Cognates are usually in a field close to the major. It is unlikely that a student will major in English and take a cognate in pharmacy.

Communications College curricula often state that a student must have nine hours of credit in communications. This most commonly refers to English and speech (oral communication) courses. The mixture of these courses is usually English 101 and 102 and Speech 101. This varies from college to college.

Continuing education Almost every college in the nation offers continuing education or community education courses. These courses are not offered for college credit, but continuing education units are awarded in many cases. These courses are usually designed to meet the needs of specific businesses and industries or to provide courses of interest to the community. Continuing education courses range from small engine repair to flower arranging, from stained glass making to small business management.

Counseling Most colleges have a counseling center on campus. Do not confuse counseling with advising. Trained counselors are at the college to assist you with problems that might arise in your personal life, with your study skills, or with your career aspirations. Academic advisors are responsible for your academic progress. Some colleges do combine the two, but in many instances, the counselor and the advisor are two different people with two different job descriptions.

Course title Every course offered at a college has a course title. You may see something in your schedule of classes that reads: ENG 101, SPC 205, or HIS 210. Your college catalog will define what this means. ENG 101 usually stands for English 101, SPC could be the heading for speech, HIS could mean history, and so forth. Headings and course titles vary from college to college.

Credit This is the granting of money or the use of money usually for the purchase of various products with the promise to repay in the future.

Credit hour A credit hour is the amount of credit offered for each class that you take. Most typical classes are worth three credit hours. Science courses, foreign languages, and some math courses are worth four credit hours because labs are required for the class. If a class carries three credit hours, this usually means that the class meets for three hours per week. This formula will vary greatly during the summer or a mid-session.

Curriculum The curriculum is the area of study in which you are engaged. It is a set of classes that you must take in order for a degree to be awarded.

Dean The word dean is not a name, but a title. A dean is usually the head of a division or area of study. Some colleges might have a Dean of Arts and Sciences, a Dean of Business, and a Dean of Mathematics. The dean is the leader of a division. She is the policy maker and usually the business manager and final decision maker of an area of study. Deans usually report to vice presidents.

Dean's list The dean's list is a listing of students who have achieved at least a 3.5 (B+) on a 4.0 scale (these numbers are defined under GPA). This achievement may vary from college to college, but generally speaking, the dean's list comprises students in the top 5 percent.

Degree When a student completes an approved course of study, he is awarded a degree. The title of the degree depends on the college, the number of credit hours in the program, and the field of study. A two-year degree is called an associate's degree and a four-year degree is called a bachelor's degree. These usually take two and four years, respectively, to earn. If a student attends graduate school, he may receive a master's degree (approximately two to three years) and a doctorate degree (anywhere from three to 10 years). Some colleges even offer post-doctorate degrees.

Diploma A diploma is awarded when an approved course of study is completed. The diploma course work is not as detailed or comprehensive as an associate degree and usually consists of only 8–12 courses specific to a certain field.

Dorms A dorm is a residential facility on campus where students live. Dorms can be single sex or coeducational. If a student lives in another state, she may opt to live "on campus." The college usually staffs each dorm with a full-time supervisor and a director of student housing. Each dorm usually elects a student representative to be on the student council.

Dropping When a student decides that he does not enjoy a class or will not be able to pass the class because of grades or absenteeism, he may elect to drop the class. This means that the class will no longer appear on his schedule or be calculated in his GPA. Rules and regulations on dropping vary from college to college. All rules should be explained in the catalog.

Elective An elective is a course that a student chooses to take outside of her major field of study. It could be an area of interest or an area that complements the chosen major. For example, an English major might choose an elective in the field of theatre or history because these fields complement each other. However, a student majoring in English might also elect to take a course in medical terminology because he or she is interested in that area.

Emeritus, emerita, emeriti This Latin term is assigned to retired personnel of the college who have performed exemplary duties during their professional careers. For example, a college president who obtained new buildings, added curriculum programs, and increased the endowment might be named President Emerita upon her retirement. *Emeriti* is plural.

Evening college The evening college program is designed to allow students who have full-time jobs to obtain a college degree by enrolling in classes that meet in the evening. Some colleges offer the entire degree program in the evening, others only offer some courses in the evening.

Faculty The faculty of a college is the body of professionals who teach, do research, and perform community service. Faculty members have prepared for many years to fulfill the responsibilities conferred by that title. Many have attended school for more than 25 years to obtain the knowledge and skill necessary to train students in specific fields.

Fees Fees refer to the amount of money charged by colleges for specific items and services. Some fees may be tuition, meal plans, books, health, and activity fees. Fees vary from college to college and are usually printed in the catalog.

Financial aid If a student is awarded money from the college, the state, the federal government, private sources, or places of employment, this is referred to as financial aid. Financial aid can be awarded on the basis of need or the basis of merit. Any grant, loan, or scholarship is formally called financial aid.

Fine arts Many people tend to think of fine arts as drawing or painting, but in actuality, fine arts encompasses a variety of artistic forms. Theatre, dance, architecture, drawing, painting, sculpture, and music are considered members of the fine arts. Some colleges also include literature in this category.

Foreign languages Almost every college offers at least one course in a foreign language. Many colleges offer degrees in this area. For schools in America, foreign languages include Spanish, French, Russian, Latin, German, Portuguese, Swahili, Arabic, Japanese, Chinese, and Korean.

Freshman This is a term used by high schools and colleges. The term *freshman* refers to a student in his first year of college. Traditionally, a freshman is someone who has not yet completed 30 semester hours of college level work.

GPA or grade point average The grade point average is the numerical grading system used by almost every college in the nation. GPAs determine whether a student is eligible for continued enrollment, financial aid, or honors. Most colleges operate under a 4.0 system. This means that all As earned are worth 4 quality points, Bs worth 3 points, Cs worth 2 points, Ds worth 1 point, and Fs worth 0 points. To calculate a GPA, you multiply the number of quality points by the number of credit hours carried by the course and then divide the total points by the total number of hours carried. EXAMPLE:

If a student is taking English 101, Speech 101, History 201, and Psychology 101, these courses usually carry 3 credit hours each. If a student made all As, she would have a GPA of 4.0. If the student made all Bs, she would have a 3.0. However, if she had a variety of grades, the calculation is as follows:

COURSE	GRADE	CREDIT	Q. POINTS	TOTAL POINTS
ENG 101	A	3 hours	× 4	= 12 points
SPC 101	C	3 hours	× 2	= 6 points
HIS 201	B	3 hours	× 3	= 9 points
PSY 101	D	3 hours	× 1	= 3 points

The total of 30 points divided by 12 hours results in a GPA of 2.5 (or C+ average).

Grant A grant is usually money that goes toward tuition and books and does not have to be repaid. Grants are most often awarded by the state and federal governments.

Health Health is the overall condition of the student at a given time. It is soundness of the body and mind. It is the freedom from disease and a condition of optimal well-being.

Higher education This term is used to describe any level of education beyond high school. All colleges are called institutions of higher education.

Honors Academic honors are based on a student's GPA. Each college usually has many academic honors including the dean's list, the president's list, and departmental honors. The three highest honors awarded, however, are Summa Cum Laude, Magna Cum Laude, and Cum Laude. These are awarded at graduation to students who have maintained a GPA of 3.5 or better. The GPA requirement for these honors varies from college to college. Usually they are awarded as follows:

3.5 to 3.7	Cum Laude
3.7 to 3.9	Magna Cum Laude
4.0	Summa Cum Laude

Honors college The honors college is usually a degree or a set of classes offered for students who performed exceptionally in high school.

Humanities The humanities are sometimes as misunderstood as the fine arts. Courses in the humanities include history, philosophy, religion, and cultural studies, and some colleges also include literature, government, and foreign languages. The college catalog will define what your college has designated as humanities.

ID cards Identification cards are essential for any college student. Some colleges issue them free, some charge a small fee. The ID card allows the student to use the college library, participate in activities, and use physical fitness facilities, and may allow the student to attend college events for free. They are also useful in the community. Movie theatres, museums, zoos, and other cultural events usually charge less if a student has an ID and many events will be free. The card also allows the student to use most area library facilities with special privileges.

Independent study Many colleges offer courses by way of independent study, meaning that there are no formal classes and no classroom teacher. The student works independently to complete the course under the general guidelines of a department and with the assistance of an instructor. Many colleges require that a student maintain a certain minimum GPA before enrolling in independent study classes.

Junior This term refers to a student who is enrolled in her third year of college or a student who has completed at least 60 credit hours of study.

Lecture The word *lecture* refers to the "lesson" given by an instructor in a class. The term usually refers to the style in which material is presented. Some instructors have group discussions, peer tutoring, or multimedia presentations. The lecture format means that the professor presents most of the information.

Liberal arts Liberal arts suggests that a student has gone through a series of courses that go beyond training for a certain vocation or occupation. For instance, a student at a liberal arts college might be majoring in biology, but he will have to take courses in fine arts, history, social sciences, math, and "hard" sciences also. The liberal arts curriculum ensures that the student has been exposed to a variety of information and cultural experiences.

Load A load refers to the amount of credit or the number of classes that a student is taking. The normal "load" for a student is between 15 and 18 hours or five to six classes. For most colleges, 12 hours is considered a full-time load, but a student can take up to 21 hours for the same amount of tuition.

Major A major is the intended field of study for a student and refers to the amount of work completed in one field. In other words, the majority of the courses have been in one field such as English, engineering, medicine, nursing, art, history, or political science. A student is usually required to declare a major by the end of the sophomore (or second) year.

Mentor A mentor is someone students can call on to help them through troubled times, assist them in decision making, and give advice. Mentors can be teachers, staff members, outstanding classmates, or upperclassmen. Mentors seldom volunteer to be a mentor; they usually fall into the role of mentoring because they are easy to talk with, knowledgeable about the college and the community, and willing to lend a helping hand. You may, however, be assigned a mentor when arriving on campus.

Minor A student's minor consists of the courses that she takes that usually complement the major. The minor is usually six to eight courses in a specific field. If a student is majoring in engineering, she might minor in math or electronics, something that would assist her in the workforce.

Natural sciences Natural and physical sciences refers to a select group of courses from biology, chemistry, physical science, physics, anatomy, zoology, botany, geology, genetics, microbiology, physiology, and astronomy.

Orientation Every student is requested, and many are required, to attend an orientation session. This is one of the most important steps that a student can take when beginning college. Important information, such as the material covered in this book, will be presented. Details concerning individual colleges and their rules and regulations are also discussed.

Planner or time-management system A planner is a systematic approach to time management using a commercially produced system that usually includes a yearly calendar, a monthly calendar, a daily schedule, and a "to-do" list.

Prefix A prefix is the code used by the office of the registrar to designate a certain area of study. A prefix for English is usually ENG, religion is REL, theatre is THE, history is HIS, and so forth. Prefix lettering varies from college to college.

Pre-professional programs Pre-professional programs usually include majors that *require* advanced study to the master's or doctorate level to be able to practice in the field. Such programs include, but are not limited to, law, medicine, dentistry, psychiatry, nursing, veterinary medicine, and theology.

Prerequisite A prerequisite is a course that must be taken *before* another course. For example, most colleges require that English 101 and 102 (Composition I and II) be completed before *any* literature class is taken. Therefore, English 101 and 102 are prerequisites to literature. These are always spelled out in the college catalog.

President A college president is the visionary leader of an institution. He or she is usually hired by the Board of Trustees of a college. Primary responsibilities include financial planning, fund-raising, community relations, and the academic integrity of the curriculum. Every employee at the college answers to the president.

Probation This term is used when a student has not performed well in his academic studies. Many times, a student who has below a 2.0 GPA in any given semester or quarter is placed on academic probation for one semester. If that student continues to perform below 2.0, suspension may be in order. The rules for probation and suspension *must* be displayed in the college catalog.

Professor Many people believe that all teachers on the college level are professors. This is *not* true. A full professor is someone who has been in the profession for a long time and someone who usually holds a doctorate degree. There is a system of promotion for college teachers that goes as follows:

Adjunct instructor

Instructor

Lecturer

Assistant professor

Associate professor

Full professor (Professor)

Provost The provost is the primary policy maker at the college with regard to academic standards. He usually reports directly to the president. Many colleges do not have a provost, but will have a Vice President for Academic Affairs or a Dean of Instruction.

Readmit When a student has "dropped out" for a semester or two, he will usually have to be readmitted to the college. This term does *not* apply to a student who elects not to attend the summer sessions. Usually, there is no application fee for a readmitted student. He does not lose his previously earned academic credit unless that credit carries a time limit. For example, some courses in psychology carry a 5- or 10-year limit, meaning that if a degree is not awarded within that time, the course must be retaken.

Registrar The registrar has one of the most difficult jobs on any college campus. She is responsible for all student academic records. The registrar is also responsible for entering all grades, all drops and adds, printing the schedule, and verifying all candidates for graduation.

Residency requirement Many colleges have a residency requirement, meaning that a certain number of hours must be earned at the "home" institution. For many two-year colleges, at least 50 percent of the credit used for graduation must be earned at the home college. For four-year colleges, many require that the last 30 hours be earned at the home college. All residency requirements are spelled out in the college catalog.

Room and board If a student is going to live on campus, many times the fee charged for this service is called "room and board." This typically means a place to stay and food to eat. Many students may opt to buy a meal plan along with their dorm room. These issues are usually discussed during orientation.

Scholar A scholar is usually someone who has performed in a superior manner in a certain field of study.

Section code At many larger colleges, many sections of the same course are offered. The section code tells the computer and the registrar the hour and instructor assigned to a particular class. When you see a schedule, it may look something like this:

English 101	01	MWF	8:00–8:50	Smith
English 101	02	MWF	8:00–8:50	Jones
English 101	03	T TH	8:00–9:15	McGee

The number 01, 02, or 03 refers to the section of English in which the student wishes to enroll.

Senior The term *senior* is used for students in their last year of study for on undergraduate degree. The student must have completed at least 90 credit hours to be a senior.

Social sciences Social Sciences are courses that involve the study or interface with society and people. Social science courses may include: psychology, sociology, anthropology, political science, geography, economics, and international studies.

Sophomore The term *sophomore* refers to students who are in their second year of study. A student must have completed at least 30 credit hours to be a sophomore.

Staff Personnel in the college setting are usually divided into three categories: administration, staff, and faculty. The staff is responsible for the day-to-day workings of the college. Usually people in admissions, financial aid, the bookstore, housing, student activities, and personnel hold staff titles. The people heading these departments are usually in administration.

Student loan Unlike a grant, a student loan *must* be repaid. The loans are usually at a much lower rate of interest than a bank loan. For most student loans, the payment schedule does not begin until six months after graduation. This allows the graduate to find a job and become secure in her chosen profession. If a student decides to return to school, she can get the loan postponed, with additional interest, until a graduate degree is completed.

Syllabus In high school, you may have been given a class outline, but in college, you are given a syllabus. This is a legal, binding contract between the student and the professor. This document contains the attendance policy, the grading scale, the required text, the professor's office hours and phone number(s), and important relevant information regarding the course. Most professors also include the class operational calendar as a part of the syllabus. This is one of the most important documents that you will be issued in a class. You should take it to class with you daily and keep it at least until the semester is over.

Tenure   You may hear someone call a college teacher a tenured professor. This usually means that the instructor has been with the college for many years and has performed in a manner that ensures him lifelong employment.

TOEFL   TOEFL is an acronym for the Test of English as a Foreign Language. This test allows foreign students to use English as their foreign language requirement.

Transcript   A transcript is a formal record of all work attempted or completed at a college. If a student attends more than one college, she will have a transcript for *each* college. Many colleges have a policy that all classes, completed or not, remain on the transcript. Some colleges allow Ds and Fs to be removed if the student repeats the course with a better grade. Many colleges, however, leave the old grade *and* continue to count the D or F in the GPA. Rules regarding transcripts vary from college to college. Many employers now require that a prospective employee furnish a transcript from college.

Transfer   This term may refer to course work or a student. If a student enrolls in one college and then wants to go to another, she is classified as a transfer student. The course work completed is called transfer work. Many colleges have rules regarding the number of credit hours that may be transferred from one college to another. Most colleges will not accept credit from another college if the grade on the course is below a C.

Transient   A transient student is someone who is attending another college to take one or two courses. If a student comes home for the summer and wants to enroll in a college near his home *and* maintain himself as a student at his chosen college, he is a transient student.

Transitional studies   Many colleges have an open admission policy, meaning that the door is open to any student. In these cases, the college usually runs a Transitional Studies Program to assist the students in reaching their educational goal. A student who has not performed well in English, math, or reading, may be required to attend a Transitional Studies class to upgrade basic skills in certain areas.

Veteran affairs   Many colleges have an Office of Veteran Affairs to assist those students who have served in the military. Many times, a college will accept the credit earned by a veteran while in the service and most of the time, the veteran's financial package is different because of the GI Bill.

Vice president   Many colleges have several vice presidents who serve under the president. They are senior level administrators who assist with the daily operations of the college. Most colleges have vice presidents of academic affairs, financial affairs, and student affairs.

Volumes   This term is used by most libraries in the nation. A volume is a book or a piece of non-print material used to assist the student in his studies. You may see that a college library has 70,000 volumes. This means that the library has 70,000 books and other pieces of media. Many colleges have volumes that range in the millions.

Wellness   This is the enjoyment of good health and vigor of body, mind, and spirit. A student needs to develop a wellness plan to reach good health and vigor.

Wellness plan   A wellness plan is a plan based upon a student's goal for lifelong good health. It should be designed with the eight components of the NEWSTART® approach or another similar program.

Who's Who   This is a shortened title for the national *Who's Who in American Colleges and Universities.* Students are nominated by the college because of their academic standing and their achievements in cocurricular activities and community service.

CONCLUSION

ollege will be one of the, if not *the*, most exciting and rewarding times of your life. If you ask anyone who has attended college, "When were you happiest?" most would reply, "During my college years." Sometimes, however, college can be a cruel and harsh place for the most prepared student, let alone an unprepared student. College requires commitment and dedication. It requires that you surrender yourself to the notion of change and growth. It demands that you reevaluate all that you know and hold to be true. College should not be the end of your formal education, but the beginning of your pursuit of lifelong knowledge.

BIBLIOGRAPHY

Adler, R., Rosenfeld, L., & Towne, N. (1989). *Interplay, The Process of Interpersonal Communication,* 4th ed. New York: Holt, Rinehart and Winston.

Barranger, M. (1994). *Understanding Plays,* 2nd ed. Boston: Allyn & Bacon.

Bennett, William. (1993). *The Book of Virtues.* New York: Simon & Schuster.

Bits and Pieces. Vol. N, no. 2. Fairfield, NJ: The Economic Press.

Carper, Jean. (July 2–4, 1999). "10 Foods for Longevity," *USA WEEKEND.*

Chappell, Cloris. (1938). *If I Were Young.* Nashville, TN: Abingdon Press.

Clark, Kristine. (February 1999). "Perfect 10: The Best Foods to Eat for Peak Fitness and Health," *Muscle & Fitness.*

Corliss, R. (July 15, 2002). "Should We All Be Vegetarians?" *Time.*

Douglass, M. E., & Douglass, D. N. (1993). *Manage Your Time, Your Work, Yourself.* New York: American Management Association.

Ellis, D., Lankowitz, S., Stupka, E., & Toft, D. (1990). *Career Planning.* Rapid City, IA: College Survival.

"Food Facts: What We Eat in America." (June 2000). *Muscle & Fitness.*

Gardner, J., & Jeweler, J. (1995). *Your College Experience.* Belmont, CA: Wadsworth.

Hill, Napoleon. (1937; reissued in 1992). *Think and Grow Rich.* New York: Fawcett Crest.

Lakein, Allen. (1973). *How to Get Control of Your Time and Your Life.* New York: Signet.

Miller, L., Smith, A., & Rothstein, L. (1994). *The Stress Solution.* New York: Pocket Books.

Pauk, W. (1997). *How to Study in College.* New York: Houghton Mifflin.

INDEX